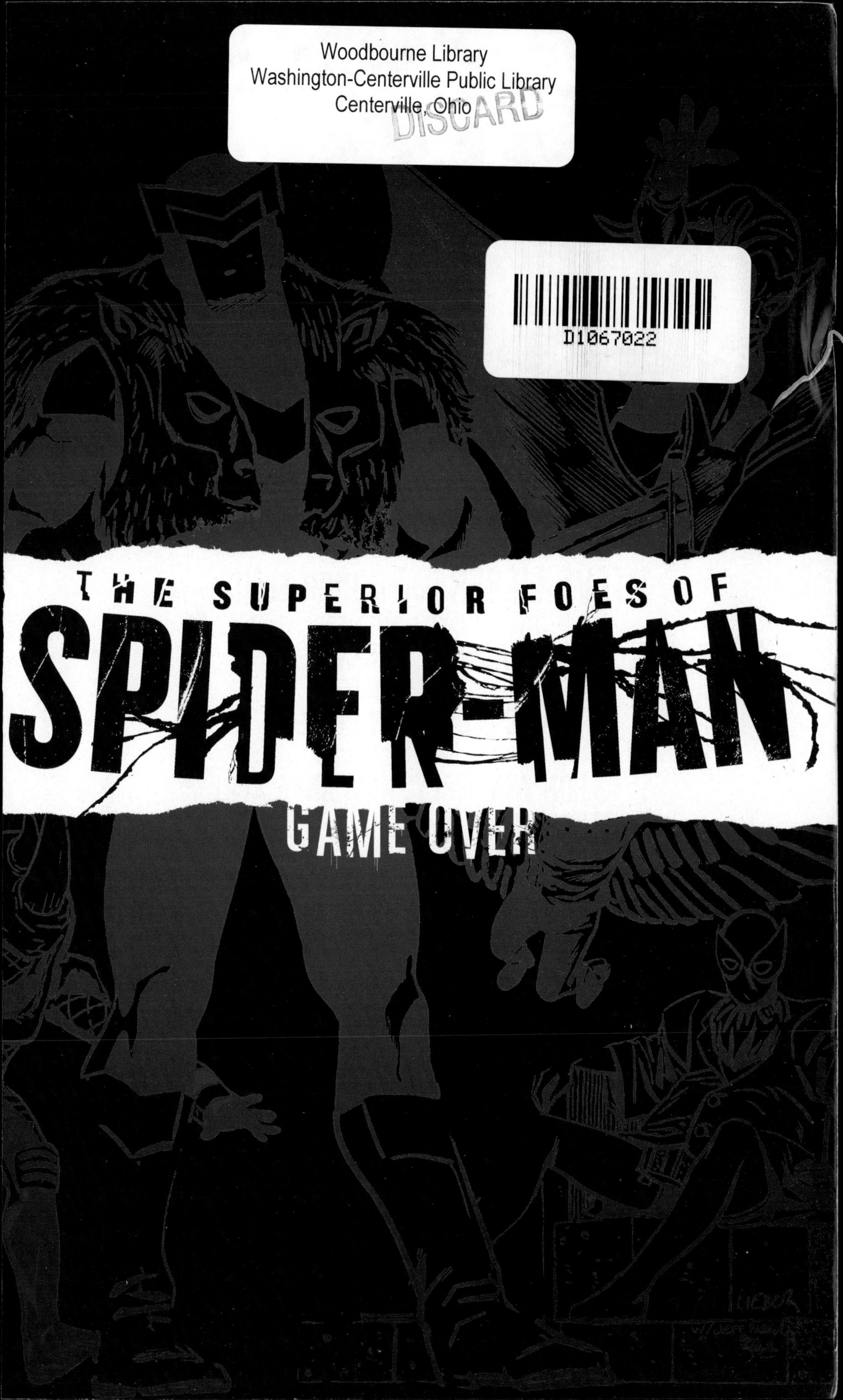
THE SUPERIOR FOES OF
SPIDER-MAN
GAME OVER

THE SUPERIOR FOES OF SPIDER-MAN

GAME OVER

WRITER
NICK SPENCER

ARTISTS
STEVE LIEBER WITH RICH ELLIS (#14)

COLOR ARTIST
RACHELLE ROSENBERG

LETTERER
VC'S CLAYTON COWLES

COVER ARTISTS
RON WIMBERLY, KRIS ANKA AND
STEVE LIEBER & RACHELLE ROSENBERG

ASSISTANT EDITOR
JON MOISAN

EDITOR
LAUREN SANKOVITCH

Collection Editor: **Alex Starbuck**
Assistant Editor: **Sarah Brunstad**
Editors, Special Projects: **Jennifer Grünwald & Mark D. Beazley**
Senior Editor, Special Projects: **Jeff Youngquist**
SVP Print, Sales & Marketing: **David Gabriel**
Book Design: **Nelson Ribeiro**

Editor in Chief: **Axel Alonso**
Chief Creative Officer: **Joe Quesada**
Publisher: **Dan Buckley**
Executive Producer: **Alan Fine**

THE SUPERIOR FOES OF SPIDER-MAN VOL. 3: GAME OVER. Contains material originally published in magazine form as THE SUPERIOR FOES OF SPIDER-MAN #12-17. First printing 2015. ISBN# 978-0-7851-9170-
Published by MARVEL WORLDWIDE, INC., a subsidiary of MARVEL ENTERTAINMENT, LLC. OFFICE OF PUBLICATION: 135 West 50th Street, New York, NY 10020. Copyright © 2014 and 2015 Marvel Characters, Inc.
rights reserved. All characters featured in this issue and the distinctive names and likenesses thereof, and all related indicia are trademarks of Marvel Characters, Inc. No similarity between any of the names, characte
persons, and/or institutions in this magazine with those of any living or dead person or institution is intended, and any such similarity which may exist is purely coincidental. **Printed in Canada.** ALAN FINE, EVP - Offi
of the President, Marvel Worldwide, Inc. and EVP & CMO Marvel Characters B.V.; DAN BUCKLEY, Publisher & President - Print, Animation & Digital Divisions; JOE QUESADA, Chief Creative Officer; TOM BREVOORT, S
of Publishing; DAVID BOGART, SVP of Operations & Procurement, Publishing; C.B. CEBULSKI, SVP of Creator & Content Development; DAVID GABRIEL, SVP Print, Sales & Marketing; JIM O'KEEFE, VP of Operations
Logistics; DAN CARR, Executive Director of Publishing Technology; SUSAN CRESPI, Editorial Operations Manager; ALEX MORALES, Publishing Operations Manager; STAN LEE, Chairman Emeritus. For information regardi
advertising in Marvel Comics or on Marvel.com, please contact Niza Disla, Director of Marvel Partnerships, at ndisla@marvel.com. For Marvel subscription inquiries, please call 800-217-9158. **Manufactured betwe**
12/5/2014 and 1/12/2015 by SOLISCO PRINTERS, SCOTT, QC, CANADA.

10 9 8 7 6 5 4 3 2 1

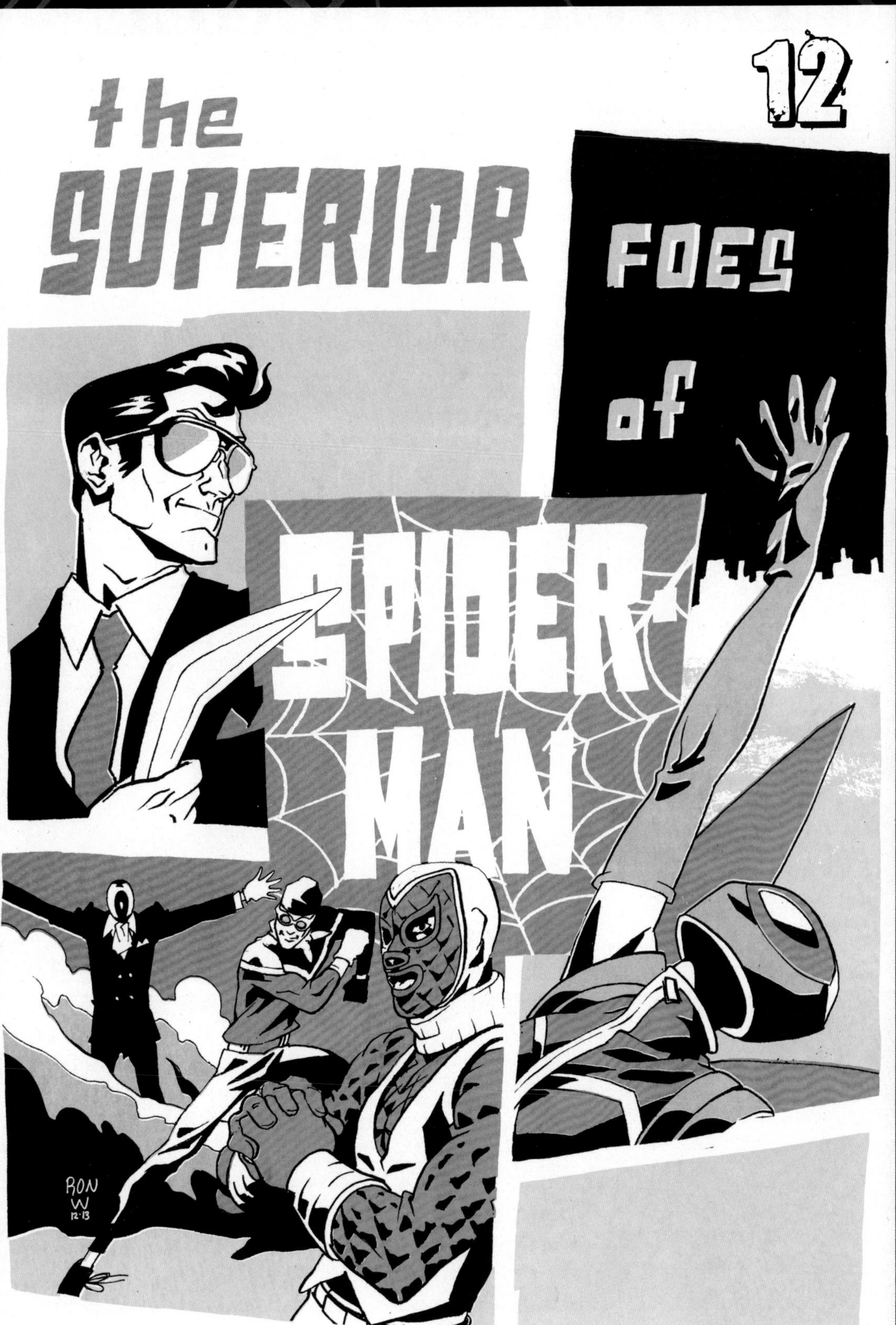
12
the SUPERIOR
FOES
of
SPIDER-MAN
RON W 12·13

FINAL ☆☆☆☆

DAILY BUGLE®

NEW YORK'S FINEST DAILY NEWSPAPER

SINCE 1897 ☆☆☆
$1.00 (in NY
$1.50 (outside c

INSIDE: LUNAR LUNACY - WHAT ARE THE EARTH'S HEROES DOING ON THE MOON? BULL IN THE BOARDROOM – HOW ROXXON'S DARIO AGGER PLANS TO CHANGE THE WORLD! GAME OVER – OUR EXPERTS WEIGH IN ON THE FOOTAGE OF ARCADE'S MUR

DEPARTMENT OF REVENGE-UCATION

In a seriously twisted (and not terribly intelligent) scheme, Boomerang left the Sinister Six, stole a painting of Dr. Doom with his mask off from the Owl, got the painting stolen from him by the Chameleon, and managed to convince the Owl that the Chameleon was the original thief. Fresh off this 'success,' Boomerang was confronted by ex-teammates Beetle, Overdrive...and a souped-up school bus full of children armed to the teeth. Public education ain't what it used to be.

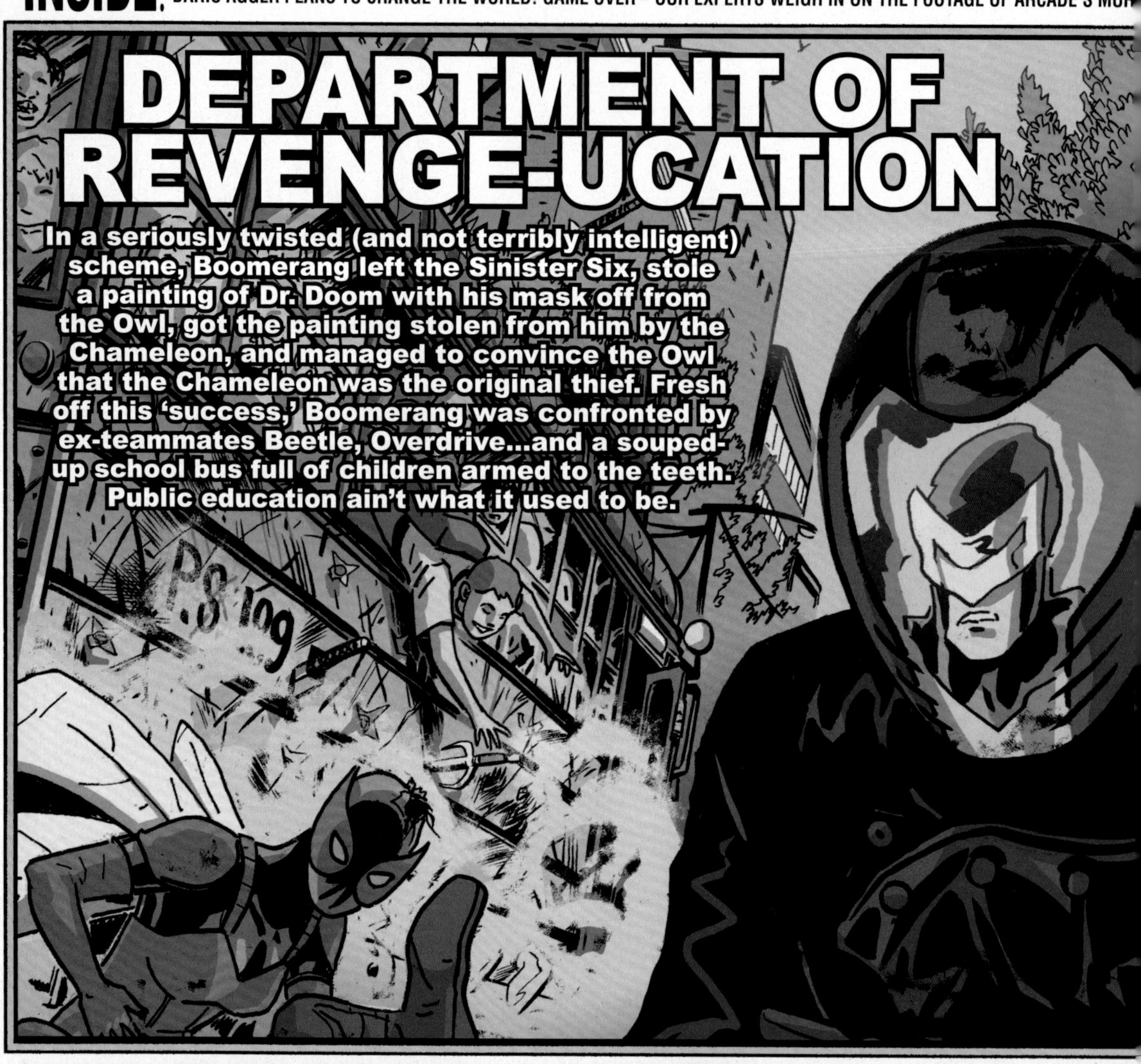
P.S. 109

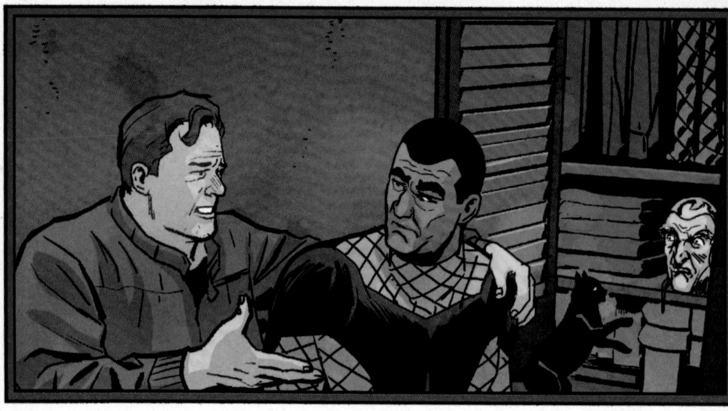

SHOCKED!

Unbeknownst to pretty much everyone, The Shocker has the cybernetic head of Maggia don Silvermane in his possession... and he was able to keep the mechanical curmudgeon a secre until Hydro-Man showed up for movie night. Looks like this urba legend is about to become a known fact!

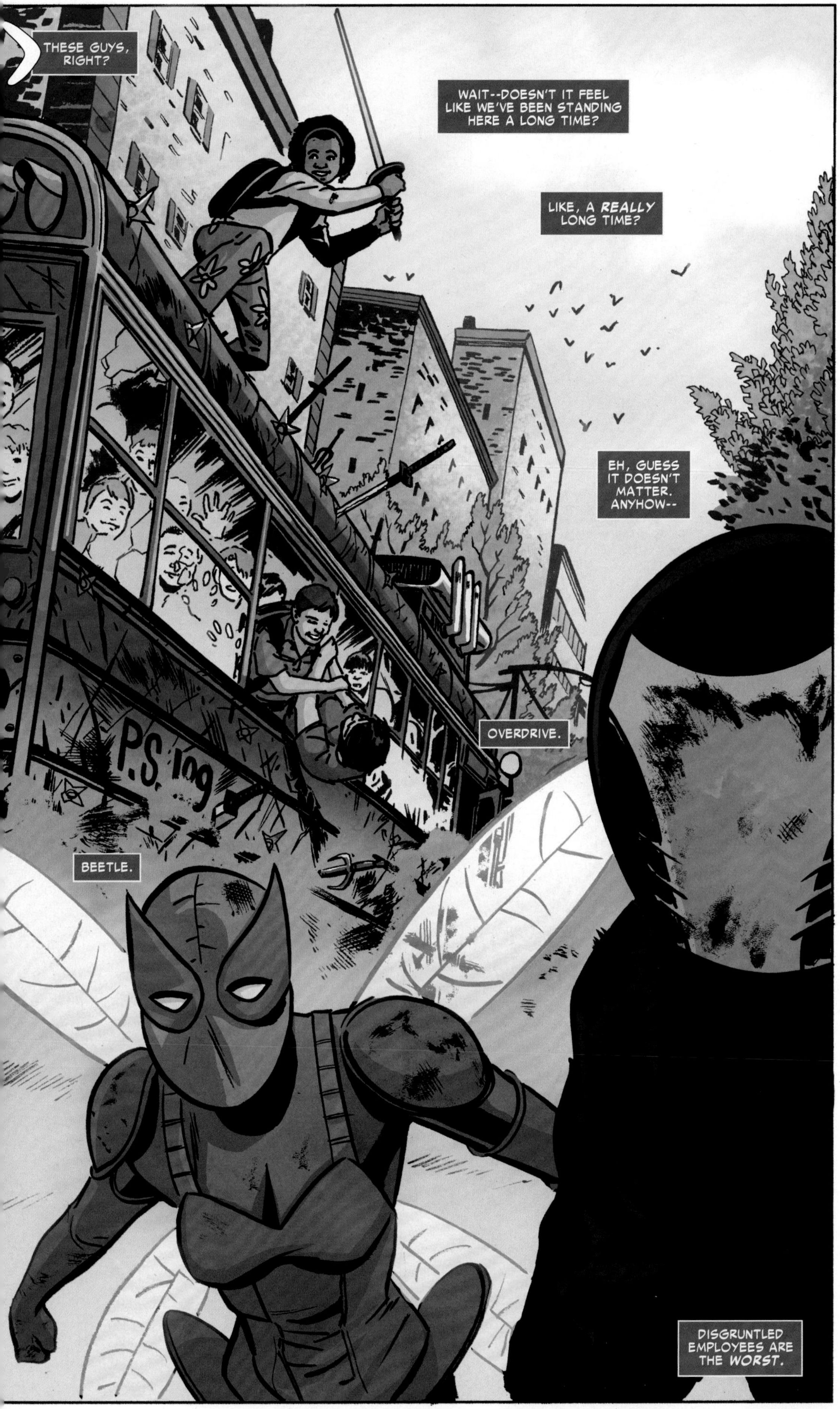
THESE GUYS, RIGHT?
WAIT--DOESN'T IT FEEL LIKE WE'VE BEEN STANDING HERE A LONG TIME?
LIKE, A *REALLY* LONG TIME?
EH, GUESS IT DOESN'T MATTER. ANYHOW--
P.S. 109
OVERDRIVE.
BEETLE.
DISGRUNTLED EMPLOYEES ARE THE *WORST*.

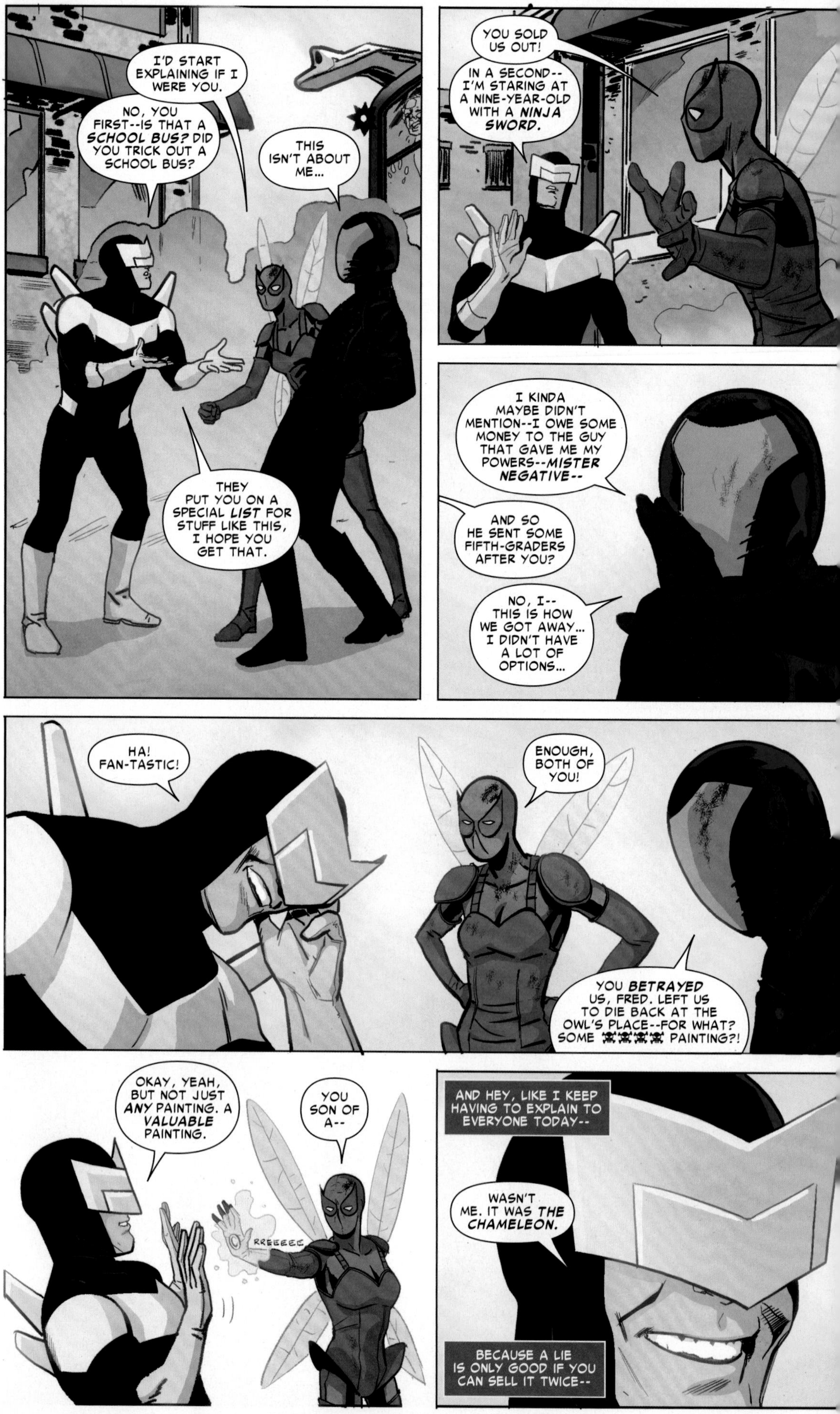
I'D START EXPLAINING IF I WERE YOU.
NO, YOU FIRST--IS THAT A SCHOOL BUS? DID YOU TRICK OUT A SCHOOL BUS?
THIS ISN'T ABOUT ME...
THEY PUT YOU ON A SPECIAL LIST FOR STUFF LIKE THIS, I HOPE YOU GET THAT.
YOU SOLD US OUT!
IN A SECOND--I'M STARING AT A NINE-YEAR-OLD WITH A NINJA SWORD.
I KINDA MAYBE DIDN'T MENTION--I OWE SOME MONEY TO THE GUY THAT GAVE ME MY POWERS--MISTER NEGATIVE--
AND SO HE SENT SOME FIFTH-GRADERS AFTER YOU?
NO, I--THIS IS HOW WE GOT AWAY... I DIDN'T HAVE A LOT OF OPTIONS...
HA! FAN-TASTIC!
ENOUGH, BOTH OF YOU!
YOU BETRAYED US, FRED. LEFT US TO DIE BACK AT THE OWL'S PLACE--FOR WHAT? SOME ☠☠☠☠ PAINTING?!
OKAY, YEAH, BUT NOT JUST ANY PAINTING. A VALUABLE PAINTING.
YOU SON OF A--
RREEEEEE
AND HEY, LIKE I KEEP HAVING TO EXPLAIN TO EVERYONE TODAY--
WASN'T ME. IT WAS THE CHAMELEON.
BECAUSE A LIE IS ONLY GOOD IF YOU CAN SELL IT TWICE--

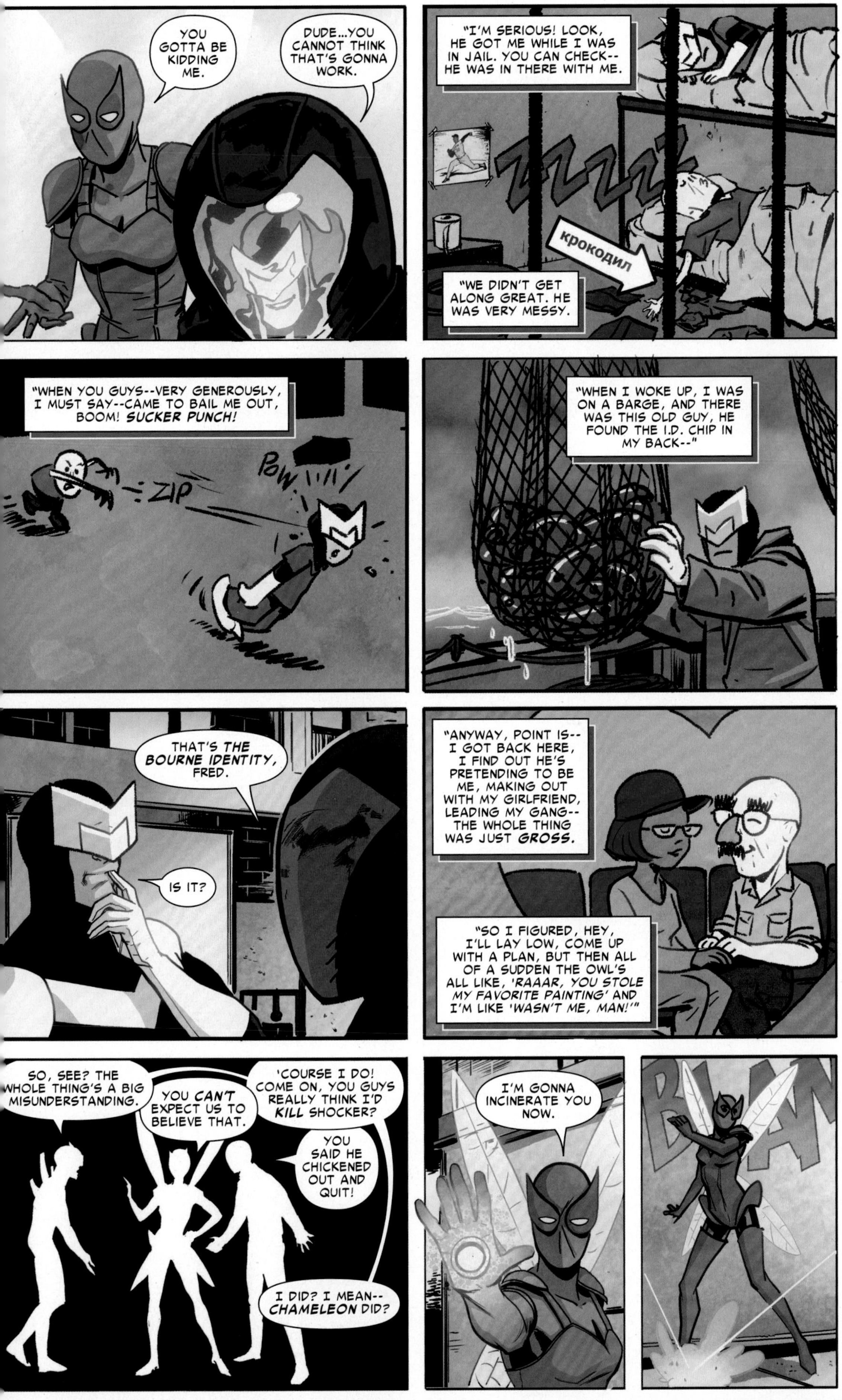

YOU GOTTA BE KIDDING ME.
DUDE...YOU CANNOT THINK THAT'S GONNA WORK.
"I'M SERIOUS! LOOK, HE GOT ME WHILE I WAS IN JAIL. YOU CAN CHECK--HE WAS IN THERE WITH ME.
ZZZZZ
КРОКОДИЛ
"WE DIDN'T GET ALONG GREAT. HE WAS VERY MESSY.
"WHEN YOU GUYS--VERY GENEROUSLY, I MUST SAY--CAME TO BAIL ME OUT, BOOM! SUCKER PUNCH!
ZIP
POW
"WHEN I WOKE UP, I WAS ON A BARGE, AND THERE WAS THIS OLD GUY, HE FOUND THE I.D. CHIP IN MY BACK--"
THAT'S THE BOURNE IDENTITY, FRED.
IS IT?
"ANYWAY, POINT IS--I GOT BACK HERE, I FIND OUT HE'S PRETENDING TO BE ME, MAKING OUT WITH MY GIRLFRIEND, LEADING MY GANG--THE WHOLE THING WAS JUST GROSS.
"SO I FIGURED, HEY, I'LL LAY LOW, COME UP WITH A PLAN, BUT THEN ALL OF A SUDDEN THE OWL'S ALL LIKE, 'RAAAR, YOU STOLE MY FAVORITE PAINTING' AND I'M LIKE 'WASN'T ME, MAN!'"
SO, SEE? THE WHOLE THING'S A BIG MISUNDERSTANDING.
YOU CAN'T EXPECT US TO BELIEVE THAT.
'COURSE I DO! COME ON, YOU GUYS REALLY THINK I'D KILL SHOCKER?
YOU SAID HE CHICKENED OUT AND QUIT!
I DID? I MEAN--CHAMELEON DID?
I'M GONNA INCINERATE YOU NOW.
BLAM

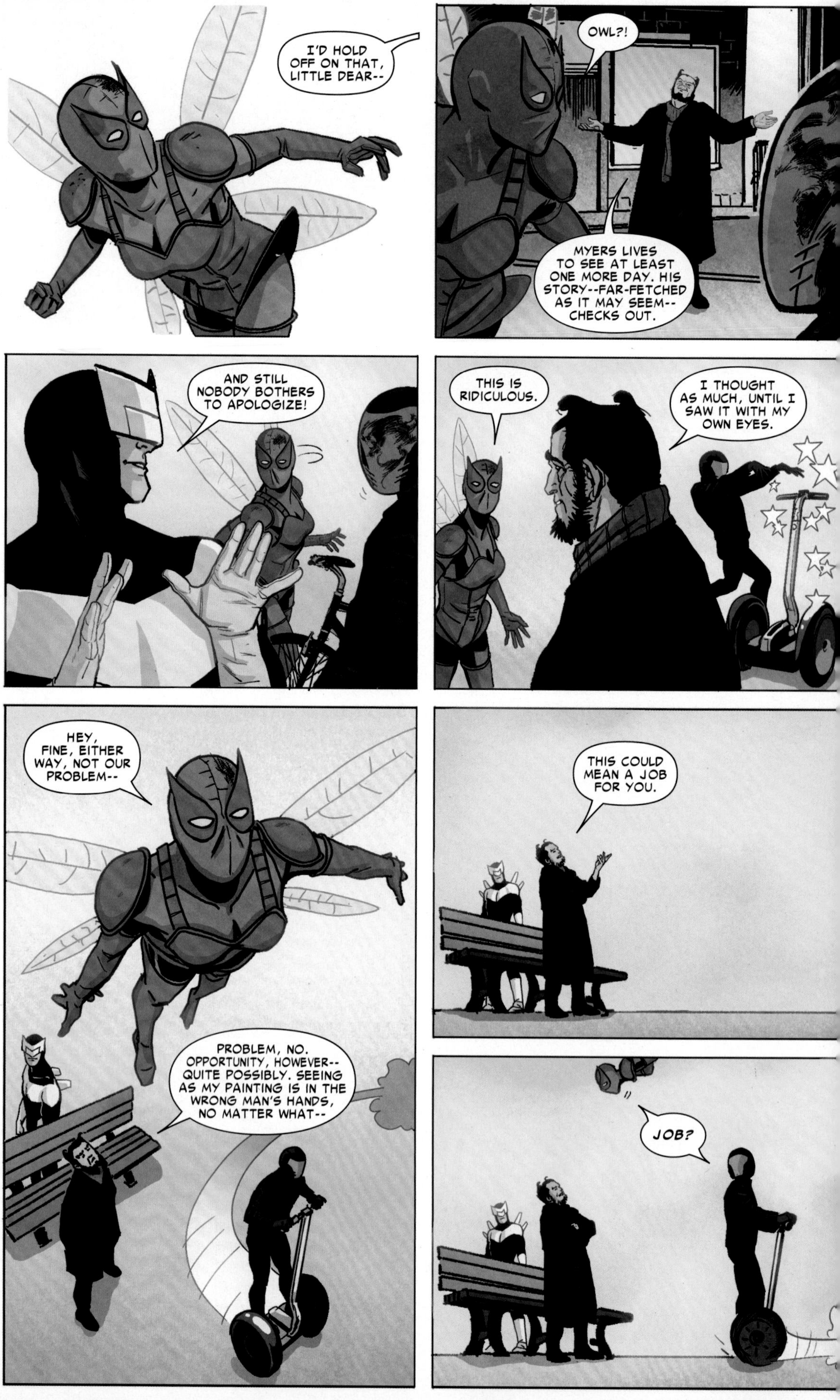
I'D HOLD OFF ON THAT, LITTLE DEAR--
OWL?!
MYERS LIVES TO SEE AT LEAST ONE MORE DAY. HIS STORY--FAR-FETCHED AS IT MAY SEEM--CHECKS OUT.
AND STILL NOBODY BOTHERS TO APOLOGIZE!
THIS IS RIDICULOUS.
I THOUGHT AS MUCH, UNTIL I SAW IT WITH MY OWN EYES.
HEY, FINE, EITHER WAY, NOT OUR PROBLEM--
PROBLEM, NO. OPPORTUNITY, HOWEVER--QUITE POSSIBLY. SEEING AS MY PAINTING IS IN THE WRONG MAN'S HANDS, NO MATTER WHAT--
THIS COULD MEAN A JOB FOR YOU.
JOB?

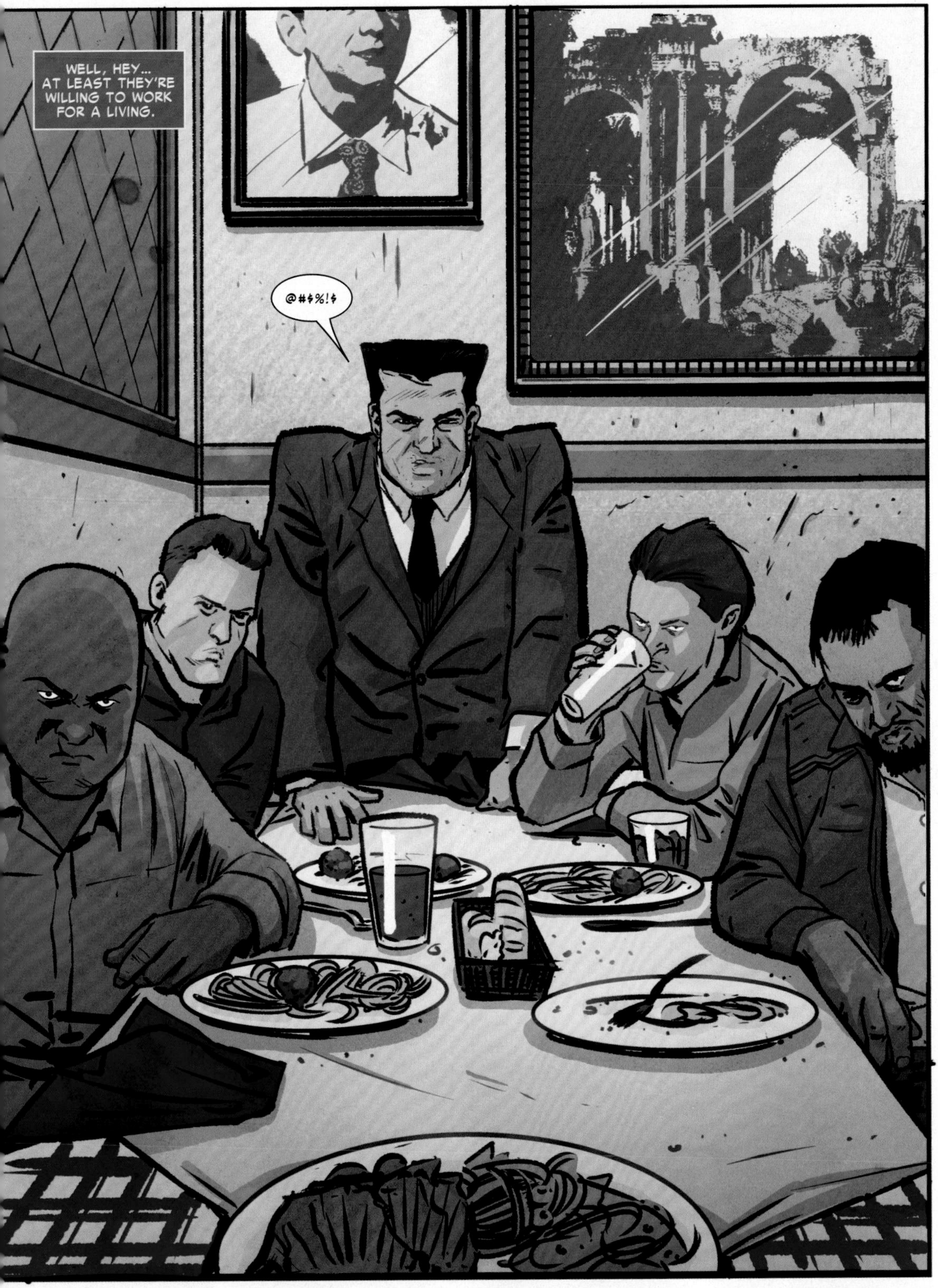
WELL, HEY... AT LEAST THEY'RE WILLING TO WORK FOR A LIVING.
@#$%!$

HAMMERHEAD OF THE FAMILY

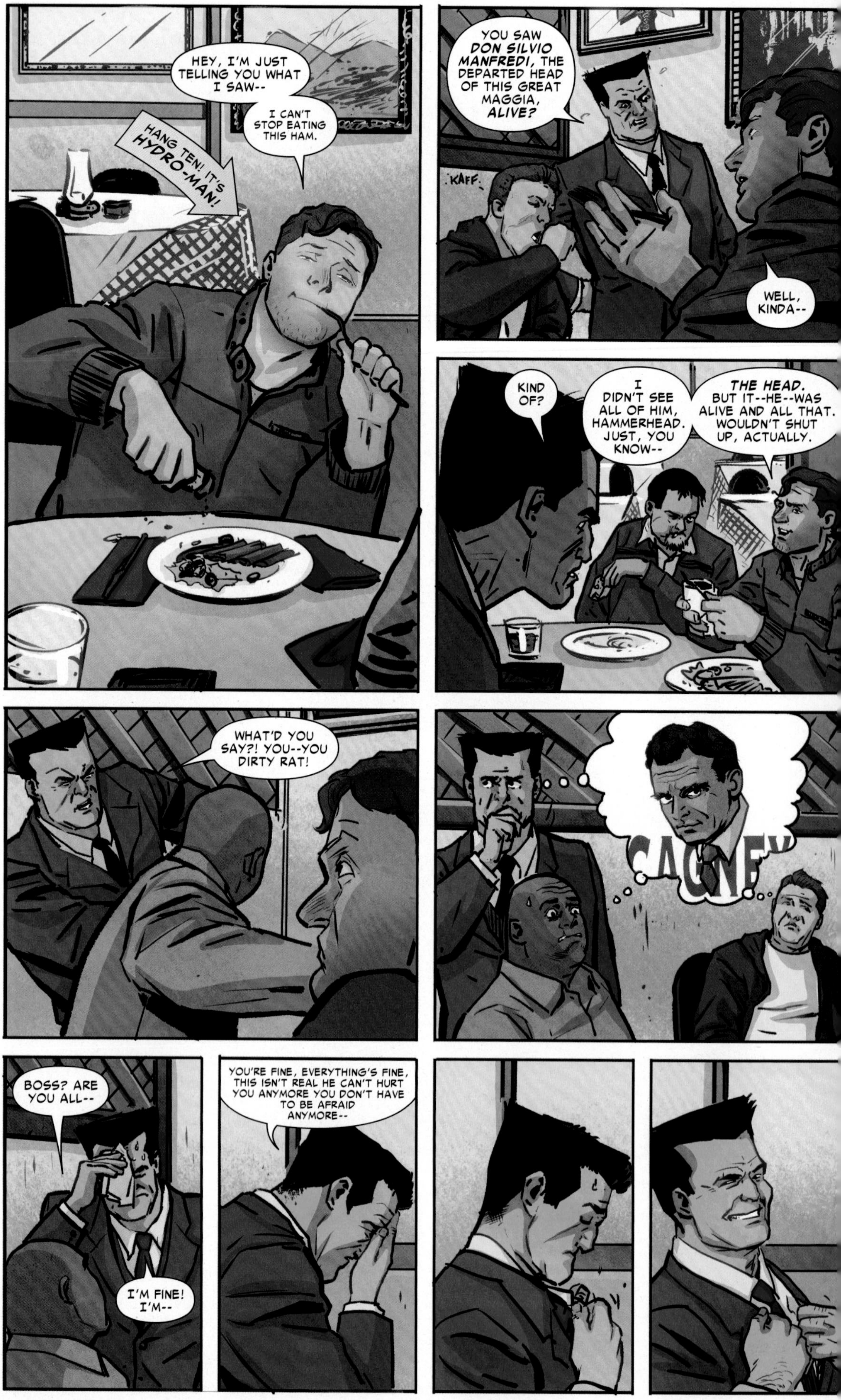
HEY, I'M JUST TELLING YOU WHAT I SAW--
I CAN'T STOP EATING THIS HAM.
HANG TEN! IT'S HYDRO-MAN!
YOU SAW DON SILVIO MANFREDI, THE DEPARTED HEAD OF THIS GREAT MAGGIA, ALIVE?
KAFF
WELL, KINDA--
KIND OF?
I DIDN'T SEE ALL OF HIM, HAMMERHEAD. JUST, YOU KNOW--
THE HEAD. BUT IT--HE--WAS ALIVE AND ALL THAT. WOULDN'T SHUT UP, ACTUALLY.
WHAT'D YOU SAY?! YOU--YOU DIRTY RAT!
CAGNEY
BOSS? ARE YOU ALL--
I'M FINE! I'M--
YOU'RE FINE, EVERYTHING'S FINE, THIS ISN'T REAL HE CAN'T HURT YOU ANYMORE YOU DON'T HAVE TO BE AFRAID ANYMORE--

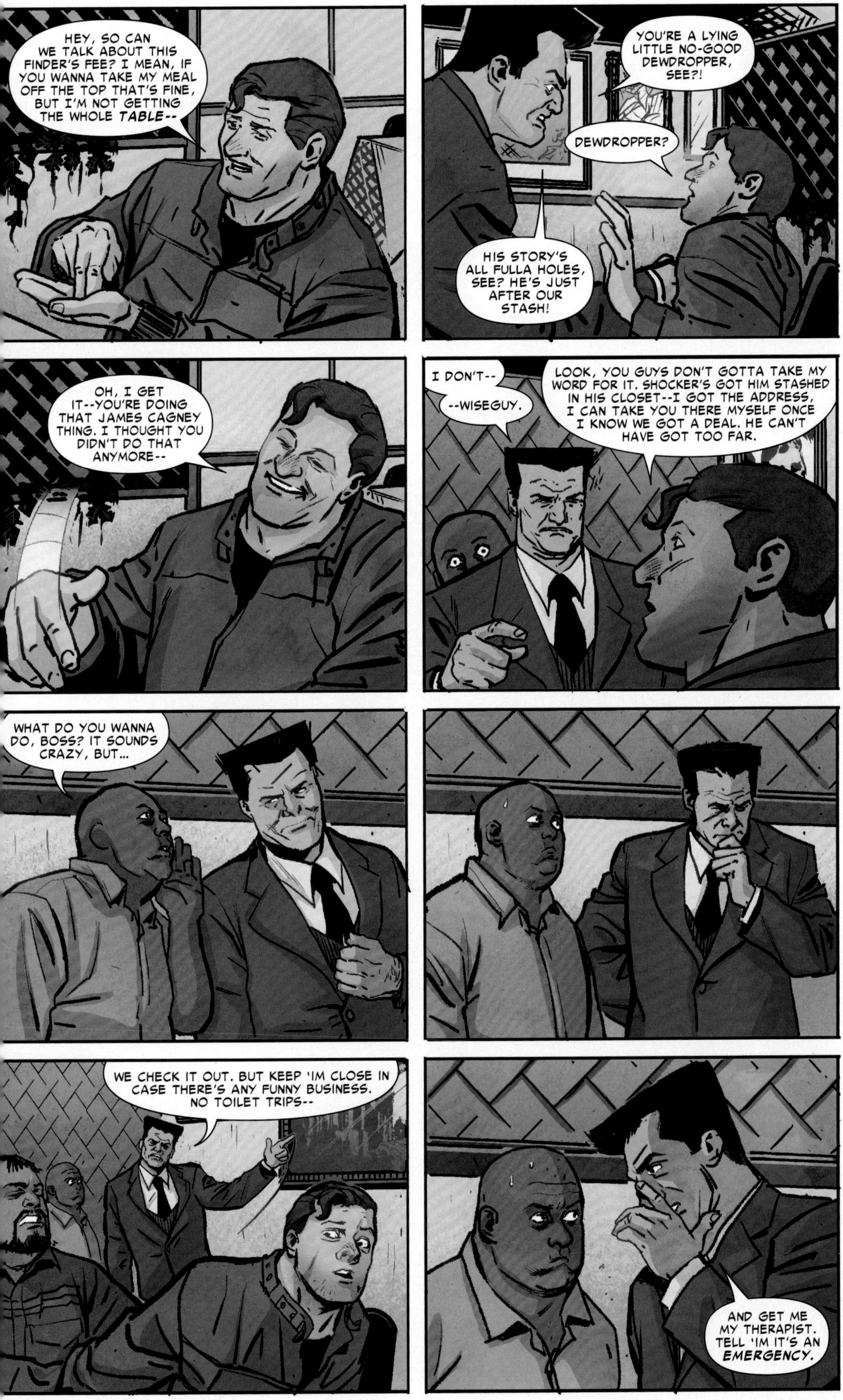

HEY, SO CAN WE TALK ABOUT THIS FINDER'S FEE? I MEAN, IF YOU WANNA TAKE MY MEAL OFF THE TOP THAT'S FINE, BUT I'M NOT GETTING THE WHOLE *TABLE*--
YOU'RE A LYING LITTLE NO-GOOD DEWDROPPER, SEE?!
DEWDROPPER?
HIS STORY'S ALL FULLA HOLES, SEE? HE'S JUST AFTER OUR STASH!
OH, I GET IT--YOU'RE DOING THAT JAMES CAGNEY THING. I THOUGHT YOU DIDN'T DO THAT ANYMORE--
I DON'T--
--WISEGUY.
LOOK, YOU GUYS DON'T GOTTA TAKE MY WORD FOR IT. SHOCKER'S GOT HIM STASHED IN HIS CLOSET--I GOT THE ADDRESS, I CAN TAKE YOU THERE MYSELF ONCE I KNOW WE GOT A DEAL. HE CAN'T HAVE GOT TOO FAR.
WHAT DO YOU WANNA DO, BOSS? IT SOUNDS CRAZY, BUT...
WE CHECK IT OUT. BUT KEEP 'IM CLOSE IN CASE THERE'S ANY FUNNY BUSINESS. NO TOILET TRIPS--
AND GET ME MY THERAPIST. TELL 'IM IT'S AN *EMERGENCY*.

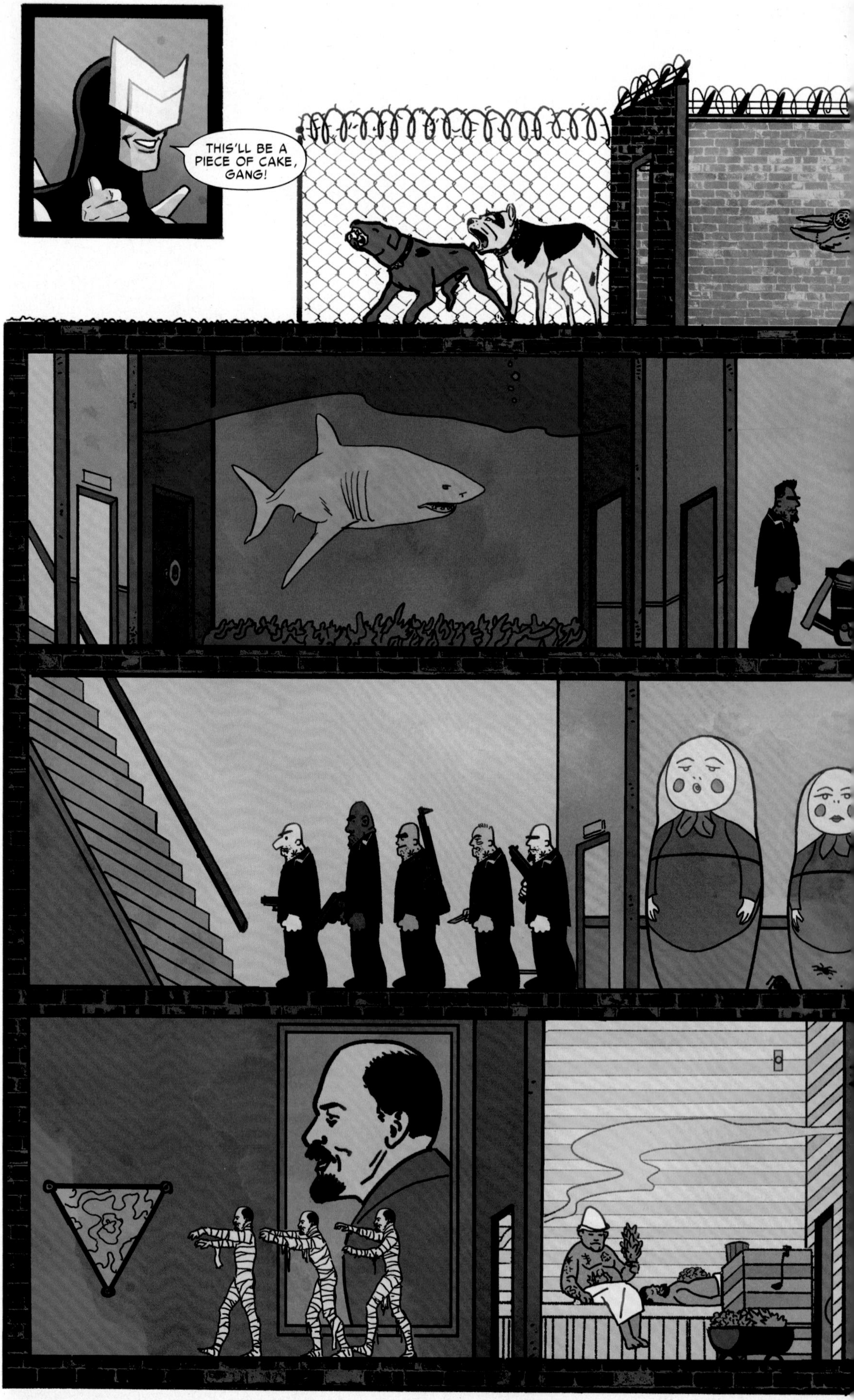
THIS'LL BE A PIECE OF CAKE, GANG!

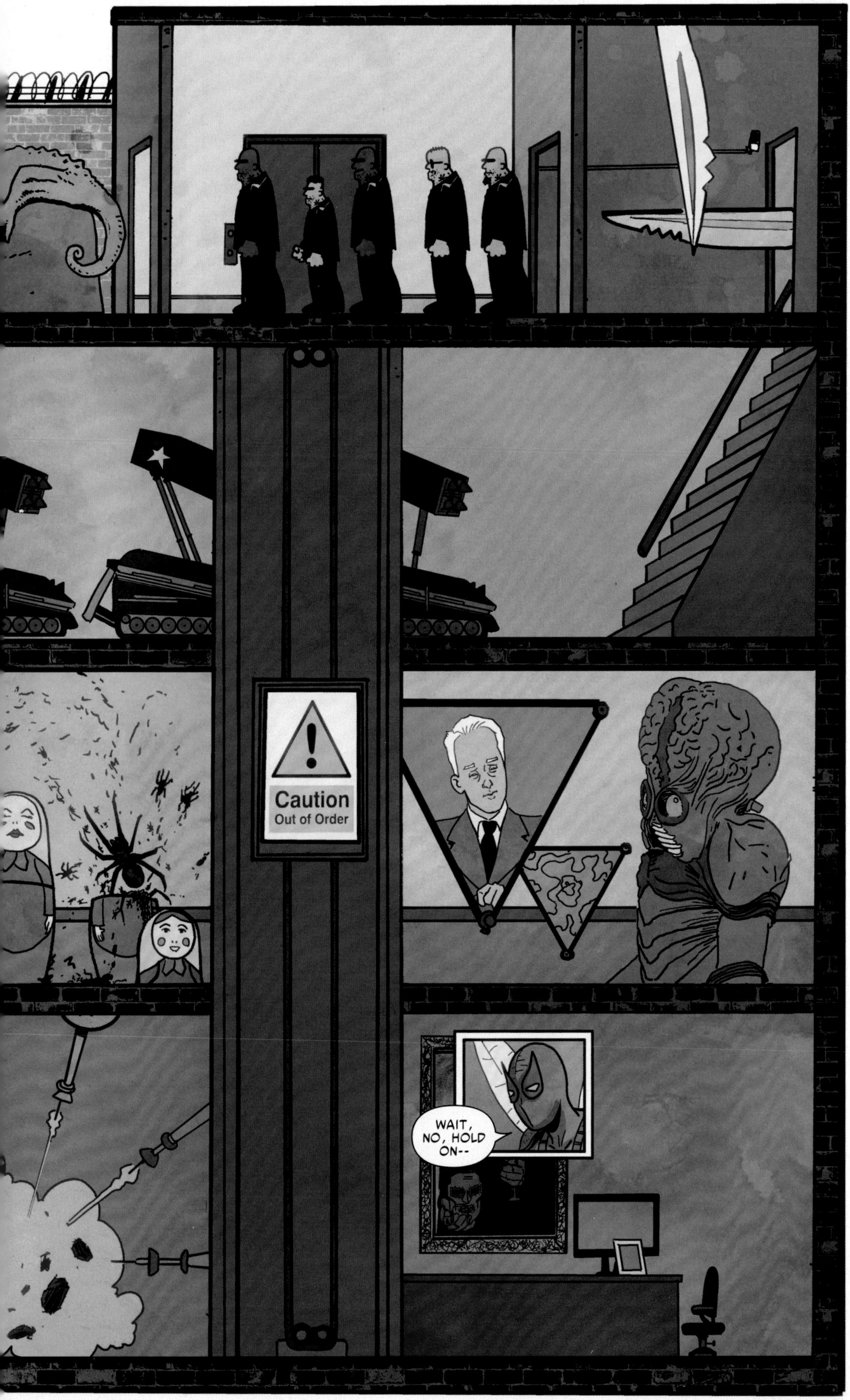
Caution
Out of Order
WAIT, NO, HOLD ON--

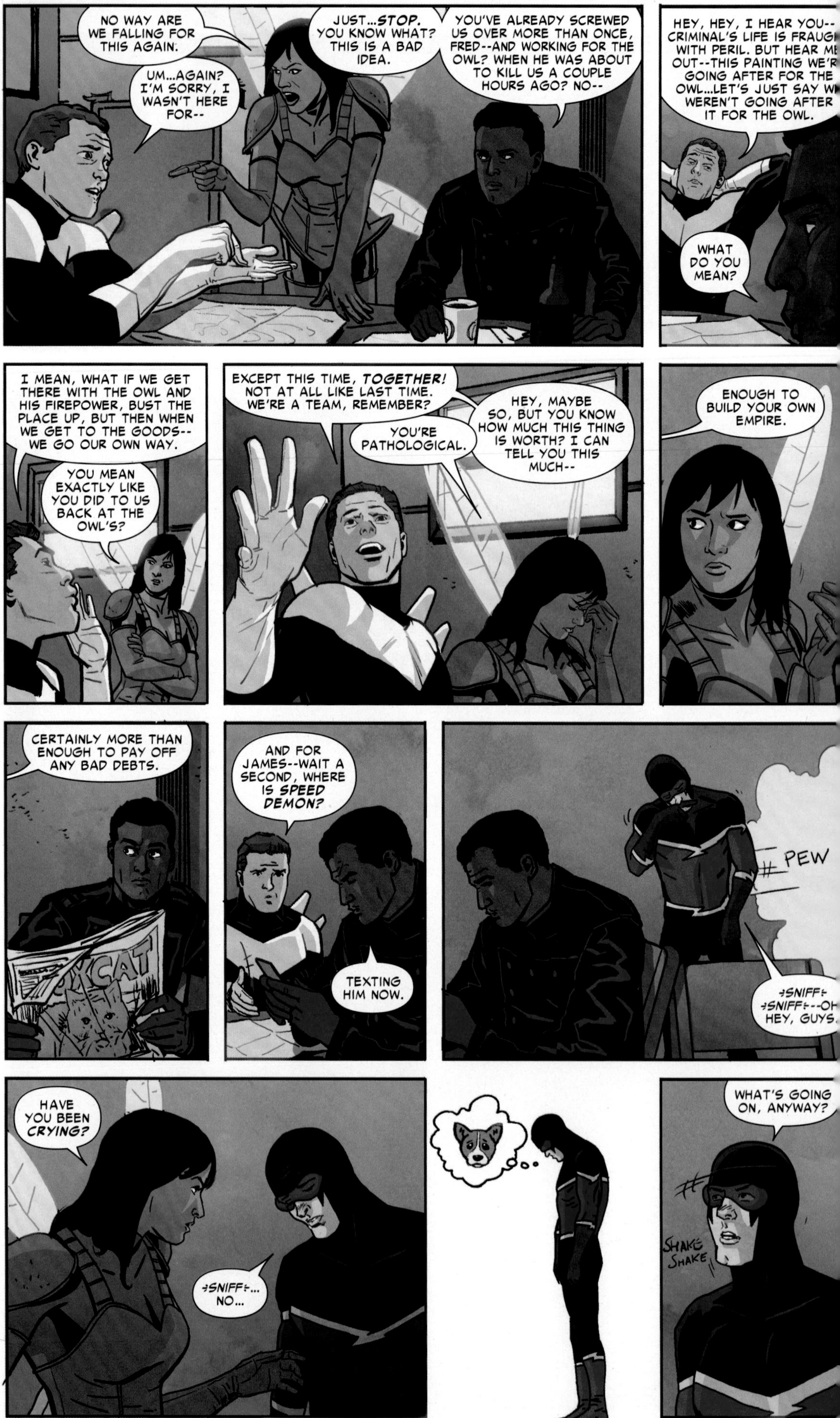
NO WAY ARE WE FALLING FOR THIS AGAIN.
UM...AGAIN? I'M SORRY, I WASN'T HERE FOR--
JUST...STOP. YOU KNOW WHAT? THIS IS A BAD IDEA.
YOU'VE ALREADY SCREWED US OVER MORE THAN ONCE, FRED--AND WORKING FOR THE OWL? WHEN HE WAS ABOUT TO KILL US A COUPLE HOURS AGO? NO--
HEY, HEY, I HEAR YOU-- CRIMINAL'S LIFE IS FRAUG WITH PERIL. BUT HEAR M OUT--THIS PAINTING WE'R GOING AFTER FOR THE OWL...LET'S JUST SAY W WEREN'T GOING AFTER IT FOR THE OWL.
WHAT DO YOU MEAN?
I MEAN, WHAT IF WE GET THERE WITH THE OWL AND HIS FIREPOWER, BUST THE PLACE UP, BUT THEN WHEN WE GET TO THE GOODS-- WE GO OUR OWN WAY.
YOU MEAN EXACTLY LIKE YOU DID TO US BACK AT THE OWL'S?
EXCEPT THIS TIME, TOGETHER! NOT AT ALL LIKE LAST TIME. WE'RE A TEAM, REMEMBER?
YOU'RE PATHOLOGICAL.
HEY, MAYBE SO, BUT YOU KNOW HOW MUCH THIS THING IS WORTH? I CAN TELL YOU THIS MUCH--
ENOUGH TO BUILD YOUR OWN EMPIRE.
CERTAINLY MORE THAN ENOUGH TO PAY OFF ANY BAD DEBTS.
AND FOR JAMES--WAIT A SECOND, WHERE IS SPEED DEMON?
TEXTING HIM NOW.
PEW
SNIFF SNIFF--OH HEY, GUYS.
HAVE YOU BEEN CRYING?
SNIFF... NO...
WHAT'S GOING ON, ANYWAY?
SHAKE SHAKE

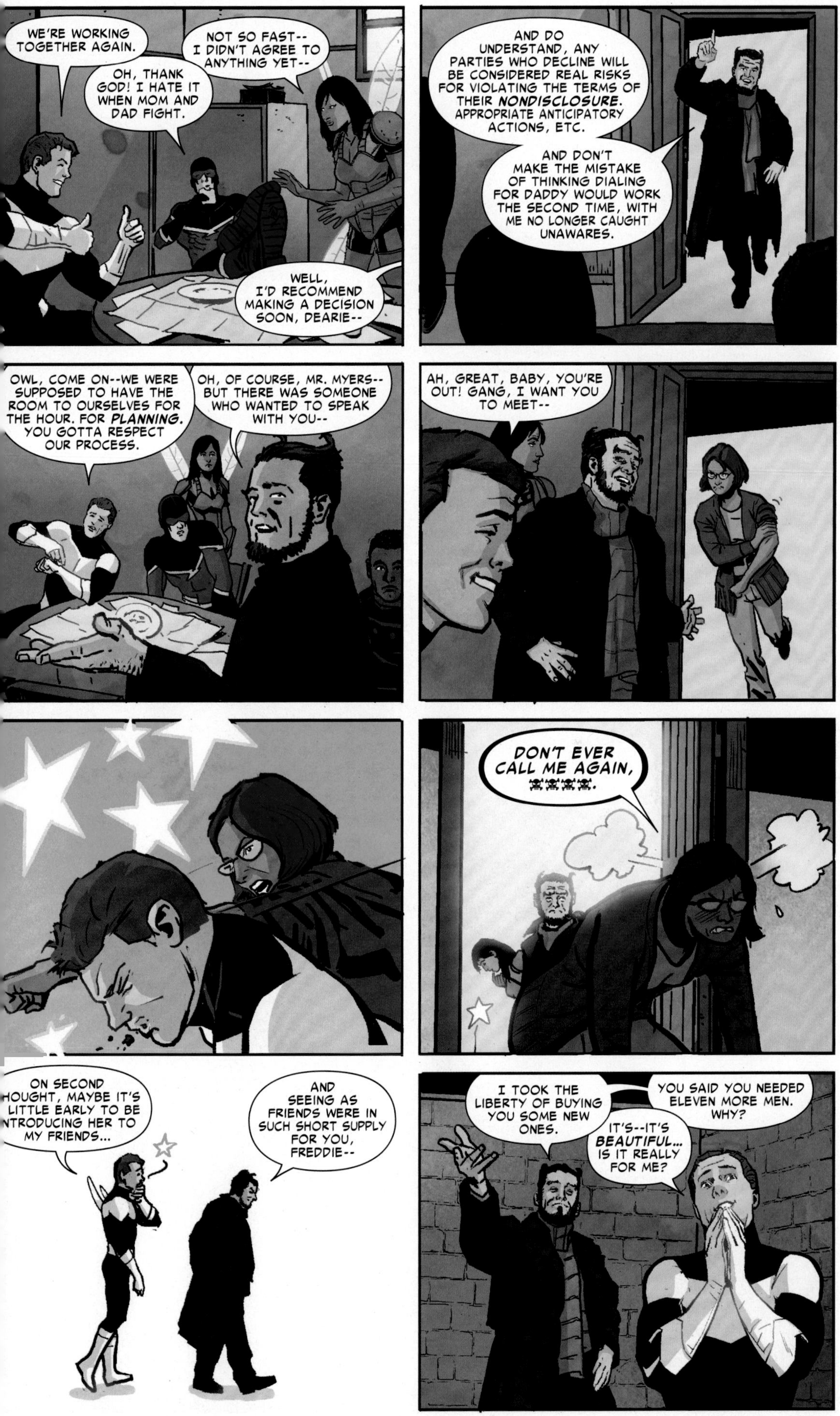
WE'RE WORKING TOGETHER AGAIN.
NOT SO FAST-- I DIDN'T AGREE TO ANYTHING YET--
OH, THANK GOD! I HATE IT WHEN MOM AND DAD FIGHT.
WELL, I'D RECOMMEND MAKING A DECISION SOON, DEARIE--
AND DO UNDERSTAND, ANY PARTIES WHO DECLINE WILL BE CONSIDERED REAL RISKS FOR VIOLATING THE TERMS OF THEIR NONDISCLOSURE. APPROPRIATE ANTICIPATORY ACTIONS, ETC.
AND DON'T MAKE THE MISTAKE OF THINKING DIALING FOR DADDY WOULD WORK THE SECOND TIME, WITH ME NO LONGER CAUGHT UNAWARES.
OWL, COME ON--WE WERE SUPPOSED TO HAVE THE ROOM TO OURSELVES FOR THE HOUR. FOR PLANNING. YOU GOTTA RESPECT OUR PROCESS.
OH, OF COURSE, MR. MYERS-- BUT THERE WAS SOMEONE WHO WANTED TO SPEAK WITH YOU--
AH, GREAT, BABY, YOU'RE OUT! GANG, I WANT YOU TO MEET--
DON'T EVER CALL ME AGAIN,
ON SECOND THOUGHT, MAYBE IT'S A LITTLE EARLY TO BE INTRODUCING HER TO MY FRIENDS...
AND SEEING AS FRIENDS WERE IN SUCH SHORT SUPPLY FOR YOU, FREDDIE--
I TOOK THE LIBERTY OF BUYING YOU SOME NEW ONES.
YOU SAID YOU NEEDED ELEVEN MORE MEN. WHY?
IT'S--IT'S BEAUTIFUL... IS IT REALLY FOR ME?

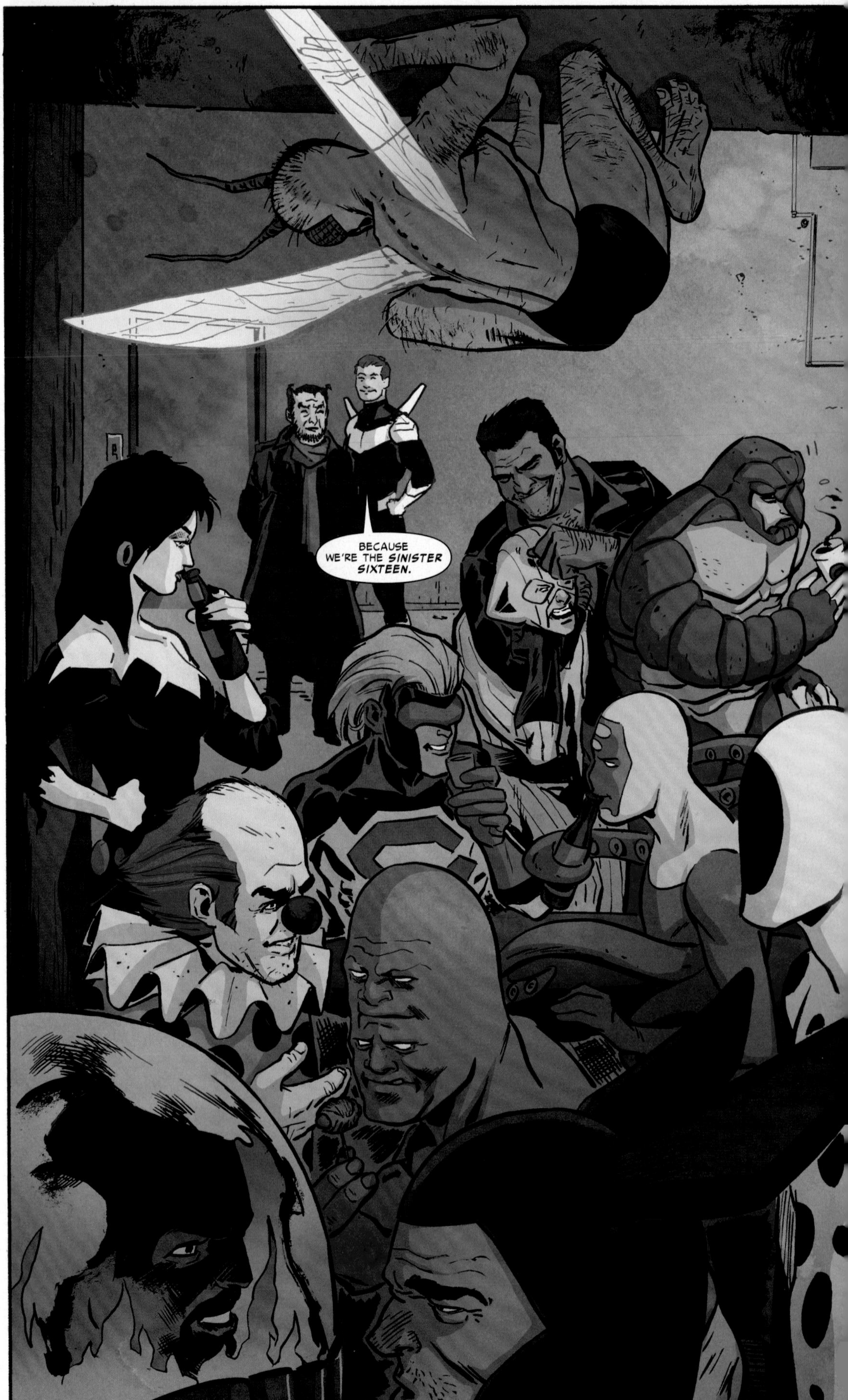
BECAUSE WE'RE THE SINISTER SIXTEEN.

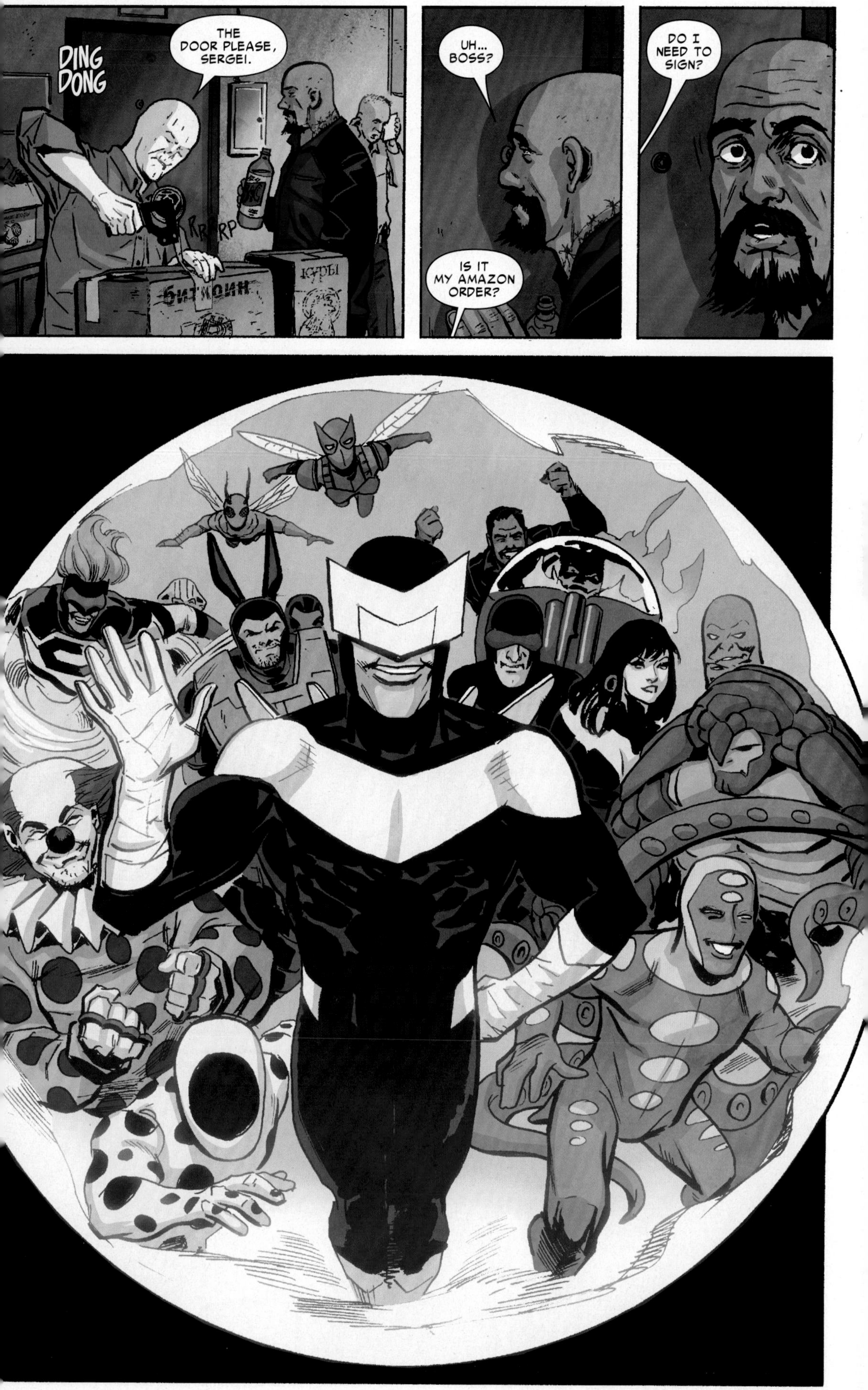
DING DONG
THE DOOR PLEASE, SERGEI.
UH... BOSS?
IS IT MY AMAZON ORDER?
DO I NEED TO SIGN?

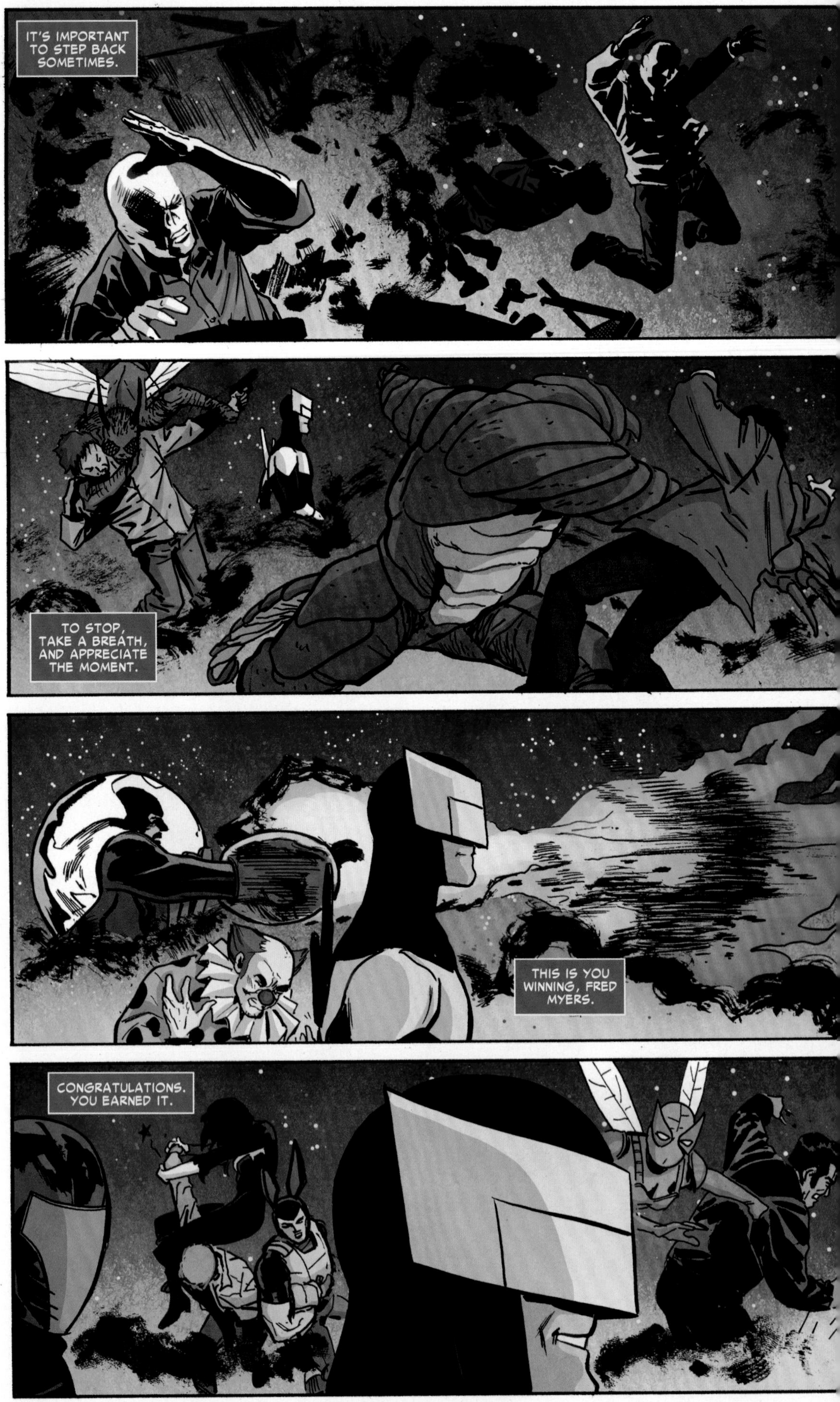
IT'S IMPORTANT TO STEP BACK SOMETIMES.
TO STOP, TAKE A BREATH, AND APPRECIATE THE MOMENT.
THIS IS YOU WINNING, FRED MYERS.
CONGRATULATIONS. YOU EARNED IT.

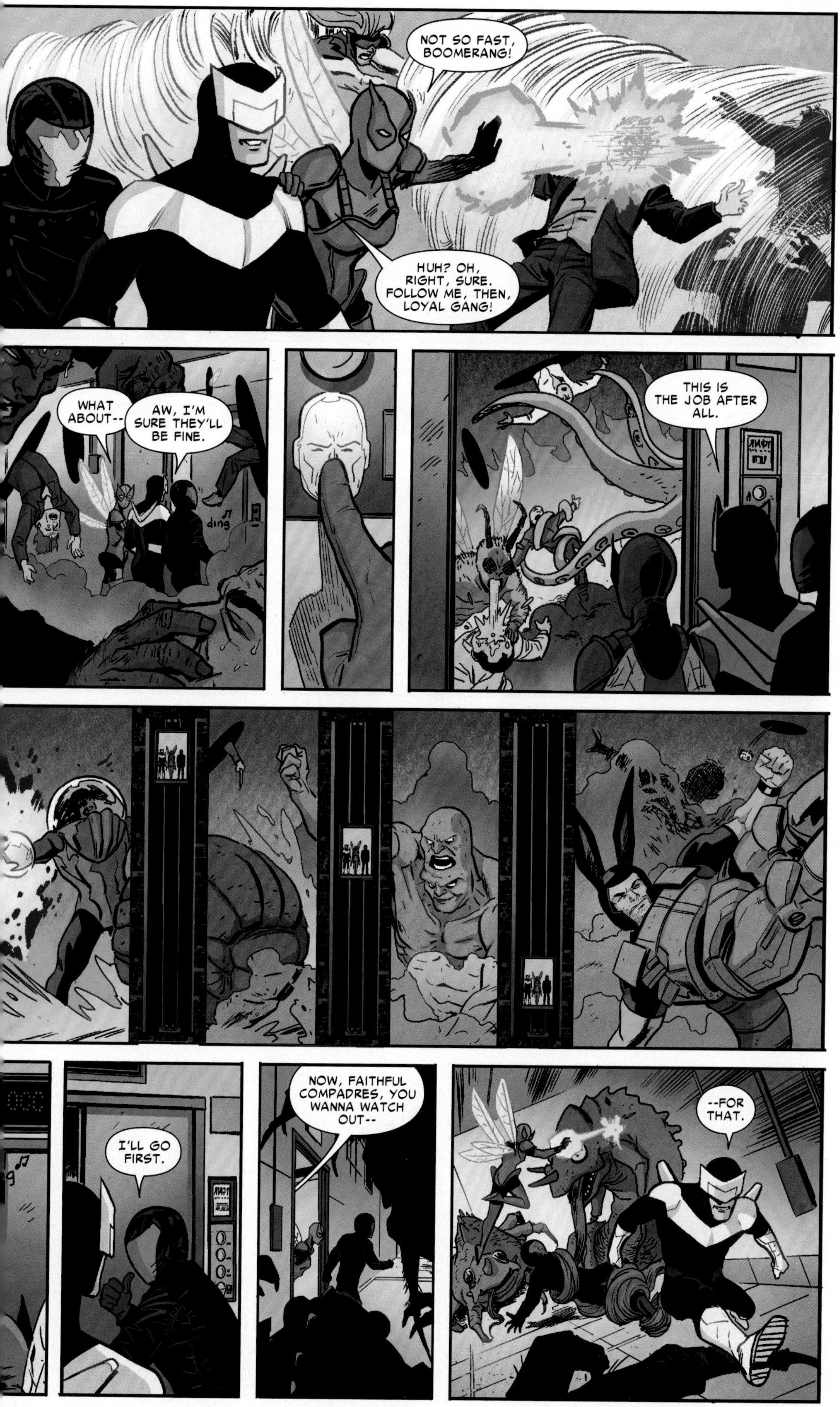
NOT SO FAST, BOOMERANG!
HUH? OH, RIGHT, SURE. FOLLOW ME, THEN, LOYAL GANG!
WHAT ABOUT--
AW, I'M SURE THEY'LL BE FINE.
ding
THIS IS THE JOB AFTER ALL.
I'LL GO FIRST.
NOW, FAITHFUL COMPADRES, YOU WANNA WATCH OUT--
--FOR THAT.

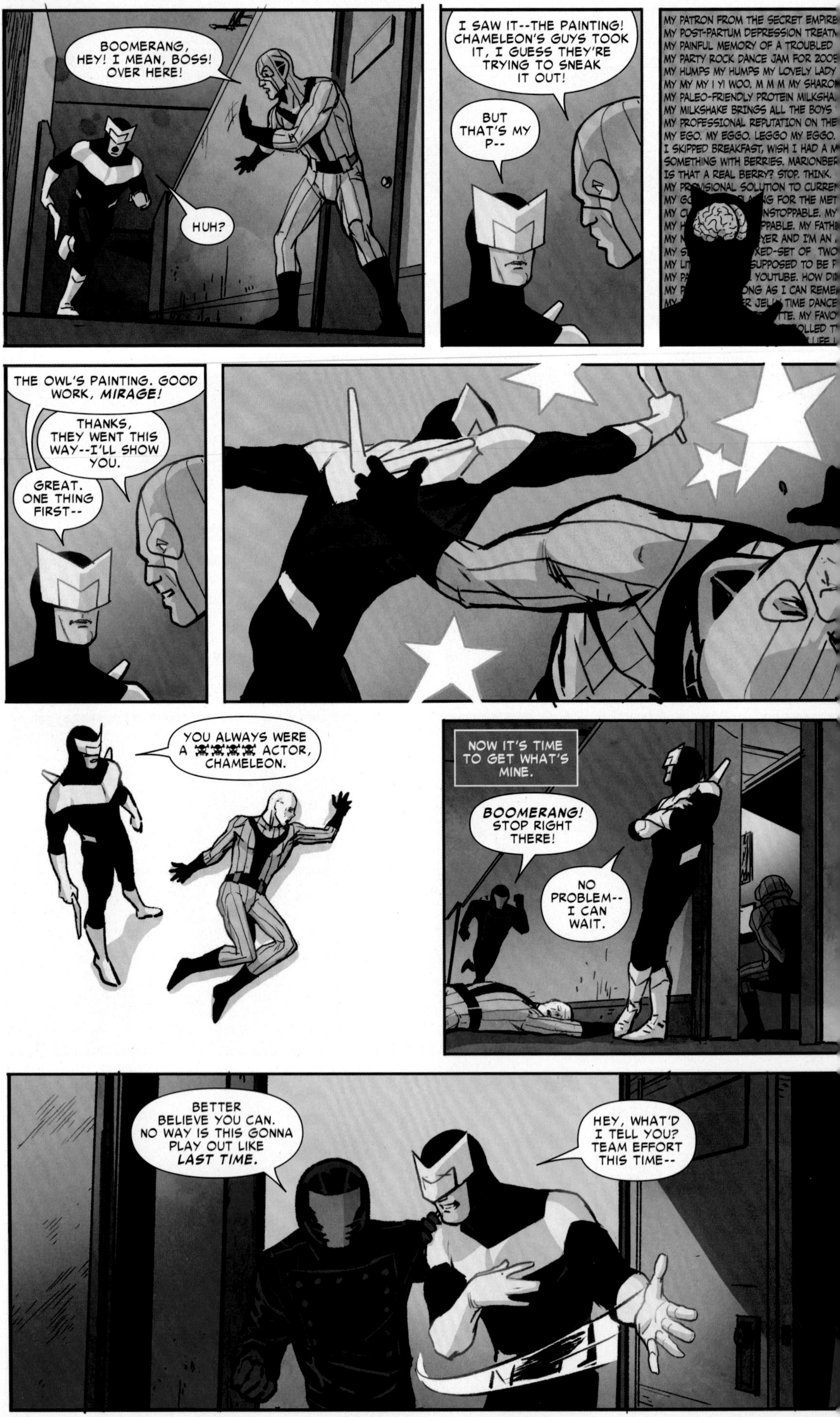
BOOMERANG, HEY! I MEAN, BOSS! OVER HERE!
HUH?
I SAW IT--THE PAINTING! CHAMELEON'S GUYS TOOK IT, I GUESS THEY'RE TRYING TO SNEAK IT OUT!
BUT THAT'S MY P--
MY PATRON FROM THE SECRET
MY POST-PARTUM DEPRESSION
MY PAINFUL MEMORY OF A TROUBLED
MY PARTY ROCK DANCE JAM FOR
MY HUMPS MY HUMPS MY LOVELY LADY
MY MY MY I YI WOO. M M M MY
MY PALEO-FRIENDLY PROTEIN
MY MILKSHAKE BRINGS ALL THE BOYS
MY PROFESSIONAL REPUTATION ON
MY EGO. MY EGGO. LEGGO MY EGGO.
I SKIPPED BREAKFAST, WISH I HAD A
SOMETHING WITH BERRIES.
IS THAT A REAL BERRY? STOP. THINK.
THE OWL'S PAINTING. GOOD WORK, *MIRAGE!*
THANKS, THEY WENT THIS WAY--I'LL SHOW YOU.
GREAT. ONE THING FIRST--
YOU ALWAYS WERE A ☠☠☠ ACTOR, CHAMELEON.
NOW IT'S TIME TO GET WHAT'S MINE.
BOOMERANG! STOP RIGHT THERE!
NO PROBLEM-- I CAN WAIT.
BETTER BELIEVE YOU CAN. NO WAY IS THIS GONNA PLAY OUT LIKE *LAST TIME.*
HEY, WHAT'D I TELL YOU? TEAM EFFORT THIS TIME--

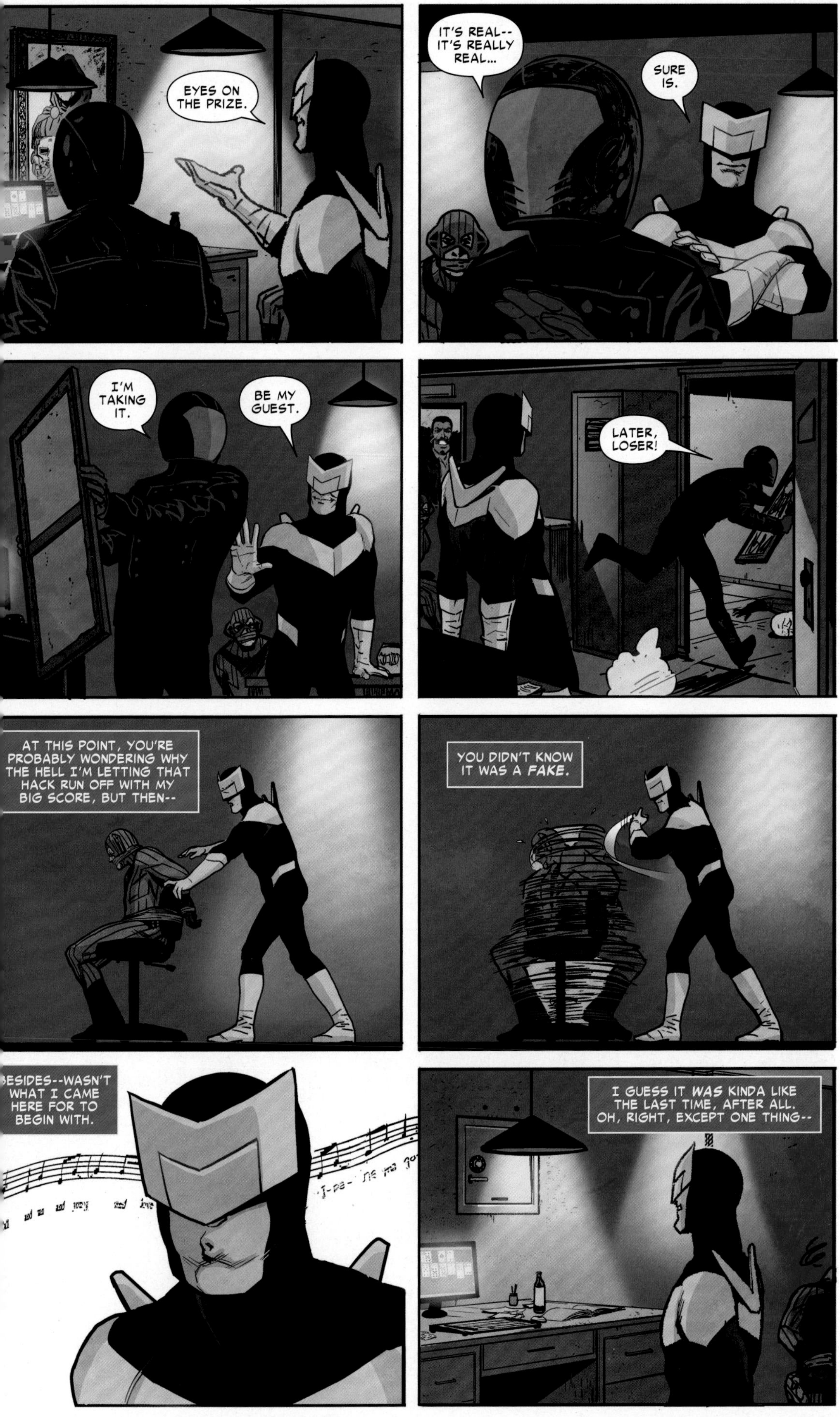
EYES ON THE PRIZE.
IT'S REAL-- IT'S REALLY REAL...
SURE IS.
I'M TAKING IT.
BE MY GUEST.
LATER, LOSER!
AT THIS POINT, YOU'RE PROBABLY WONDERING WHY THE HELL I'M LETTING THAT HACK RUN OFF WITH MY BIG SCORE, BUT THEN--
YOU DIDN'T KNOW IT WAS A FAKE.
BESIDES--WASN'T WHAT I CAME HERE FOR TO BEGIN WITH.
I GUESS IT WAS KINDA LIKE THE LAST TIME, AFTER ALL. OH, RIGHT, EXCEPT ONE THING--

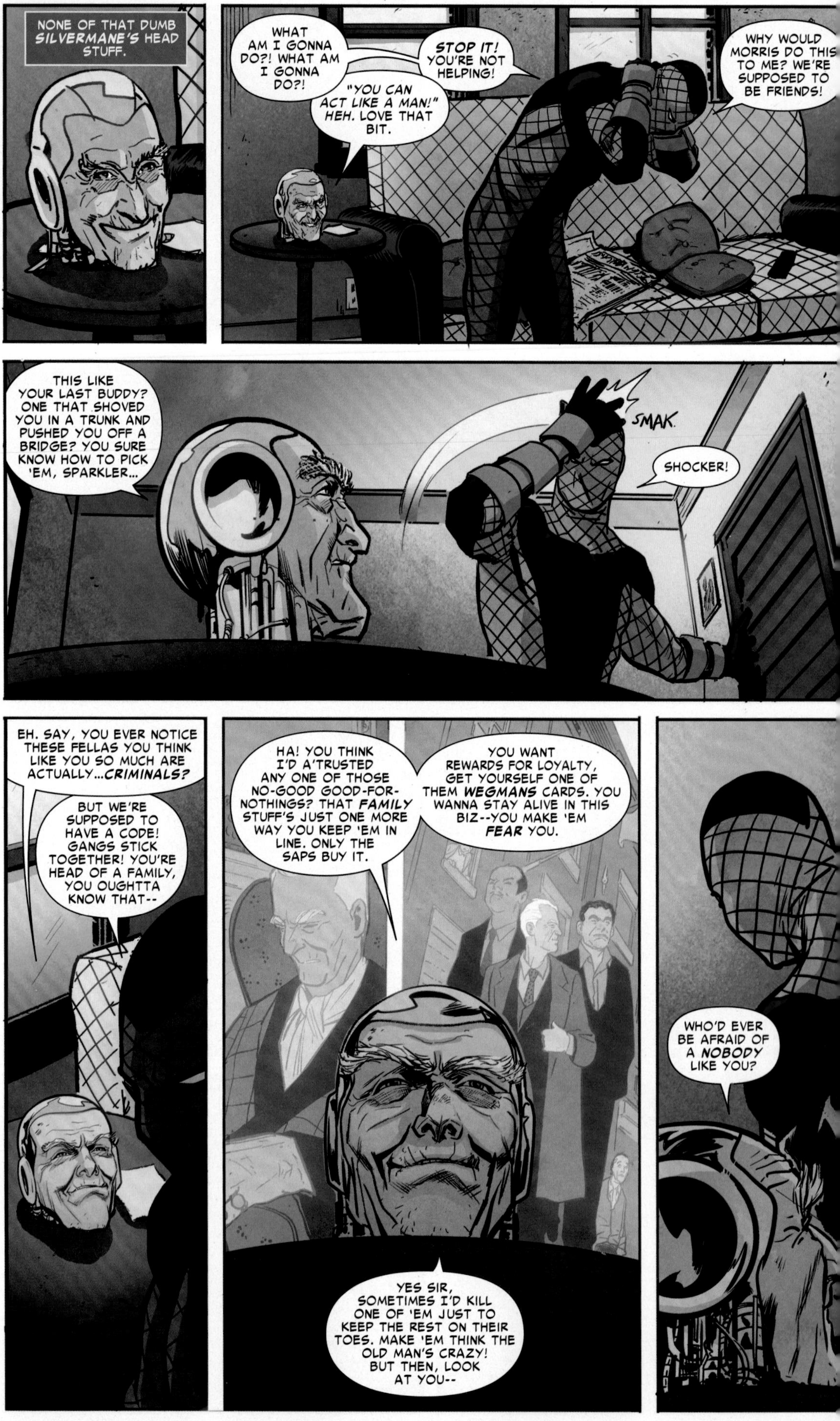
NONE OF THAT DUMB SILVERMANE'S HEAD STUFF.
WHAT AM I GONNA DO?! WHAT AM I GONNA DO?!
STOP IT! YOU'RE NOT HELPING!
"YOU CAN ACT LIKE A MAN!" HEH. LOVE THAT BIT.
WHY WOULD MORRIS DO THIS TO ME? WE'RE SUPPOSED TO BE FRIENDS!
THIS LIKE YOUR LAST BUDDY? ONE THAT SHOVED YOU IN A TRUNK AND PUSHED YOU OFF A BRIDGE? YOU SURE KNOW HOW TO PICK 'EM, SPARKLER...
SMAK
SHOCKER!
EH. SAY, YOU EVER NOTICE THESE FELLAS YOU THINK LIKE YOU SO MUCH ARE ACTUALLY...CRIMINALS?
BUT WE'RE SUPPOSED TO HAVE A CODE! GANGS STICK TOGETHER! YOU'RE HEAD OF A FAMILY, YOU OUGHTTA KNOW THAT--
HA! YOU THINK I'D A'TRUSTED ANY ONE OF THOSE NO-GOOD GOOD-FOR-NOTHINGS? THAT FAMILY STUFF'S JUST ONE MORE WAY YOU KEEP 'EM IN LINE. ONLY THE SAPS BUY IT.
YOU WANT REWARDS FOR LOYALTY, GET YOURSELF ONE OF THEM WEGMANS CARDS. YOU WANNA STAY ALIVE IN THIS BIZ--YOU MAKE 'EM FEAR YOU.
YES SIR, SOMETIMES I'D KILL ONE OF 'EM JUST TO KEEP THE REST ON THEIR TOES. MAKE 'EM THINK THE OLD MAN'S CRAZY! BUT THEN, LOOK AT YOU--
WHO'D EVER BE AFRAID OF A NOBODY LIKE YOU?

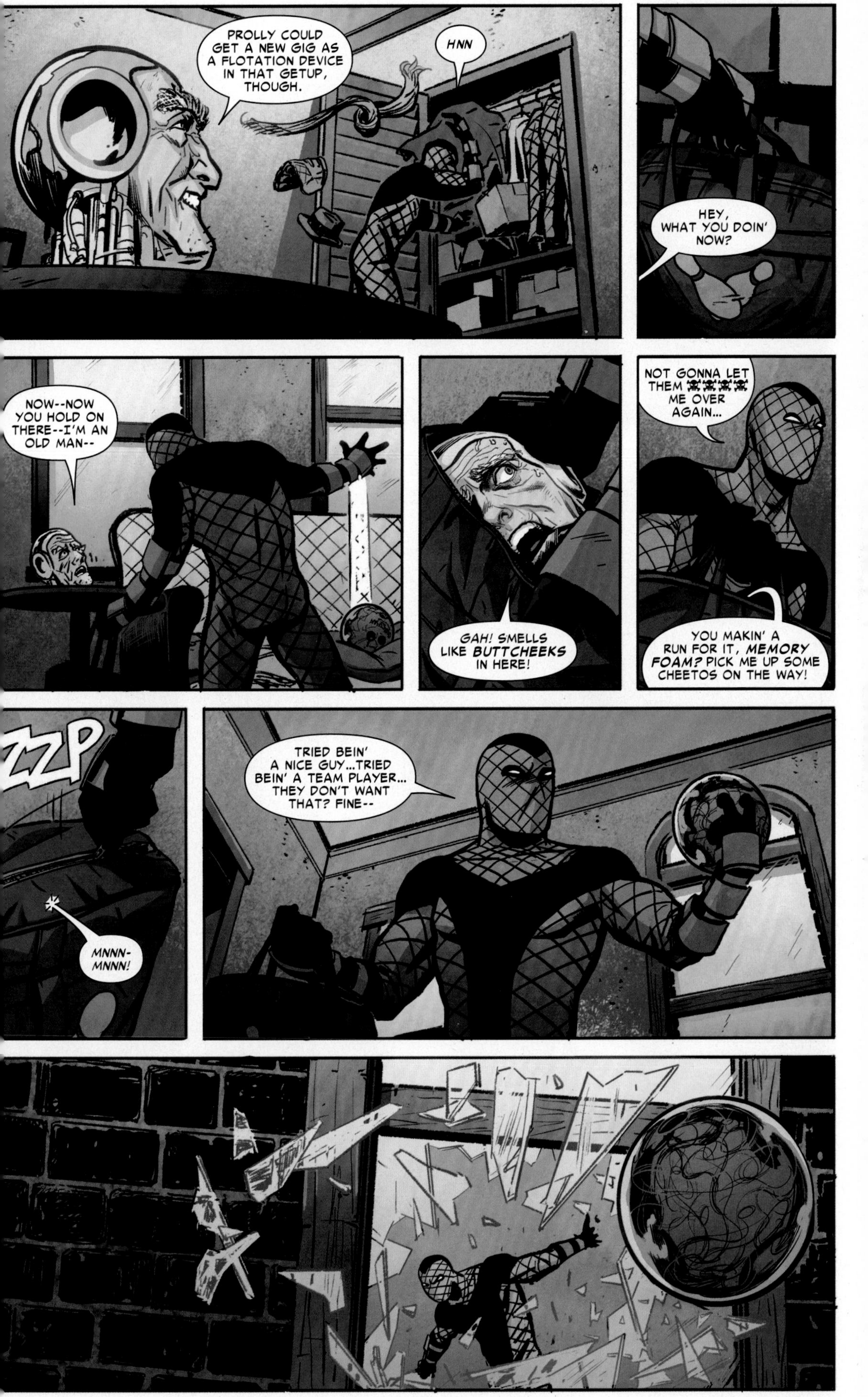
PROLLY COULD GET A NEW GIG AS A FLOTATION DEVICE IN THAT GETUP, THOUGH.
HNN
HEY, WHAT YOU DOIN' NOW?
NOW--NOW YOU HOLD ON THERE--I'M AN OLD MAN--
GAH! SMELLS LIKE BUTTCHEEKS IN HERE!
NOT GONNA LET THEM ☠☠☠☠ ME OVER AGAIN...
YOU MAKIN' A RUN FOR IT, MEMORY FOAM? PICK ME UP SOME CHEETOS ON THE WAY!
ZZP
MNNN-MNNN!
TRIED BEIN' A NICE GUY...TRIED BEIN' A TEAM PLAYER... THEY DON'T WANT THAT? FINE--

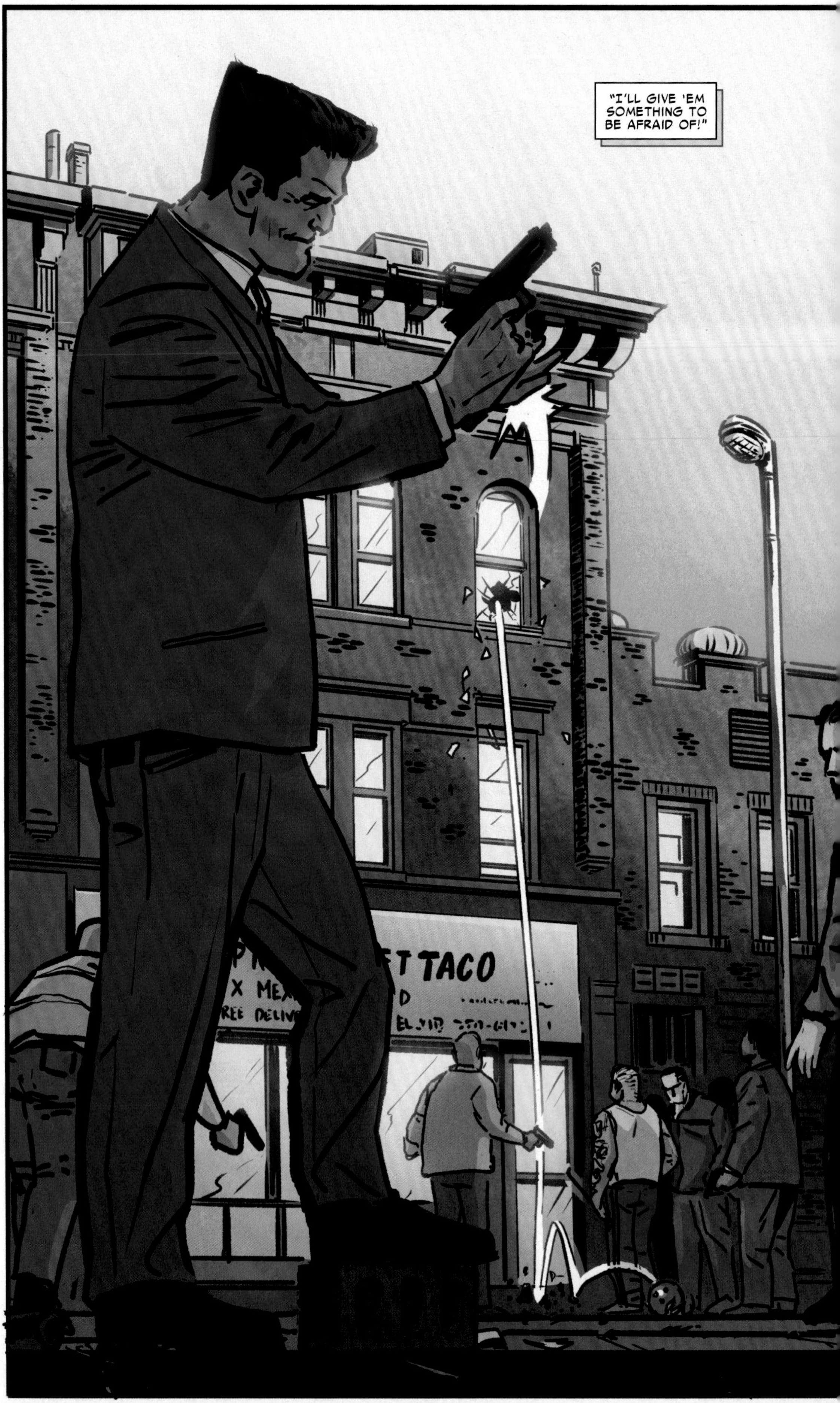
"I'LL GIVE 'EM SOMETHING TO BE AFRAID OF!"

13

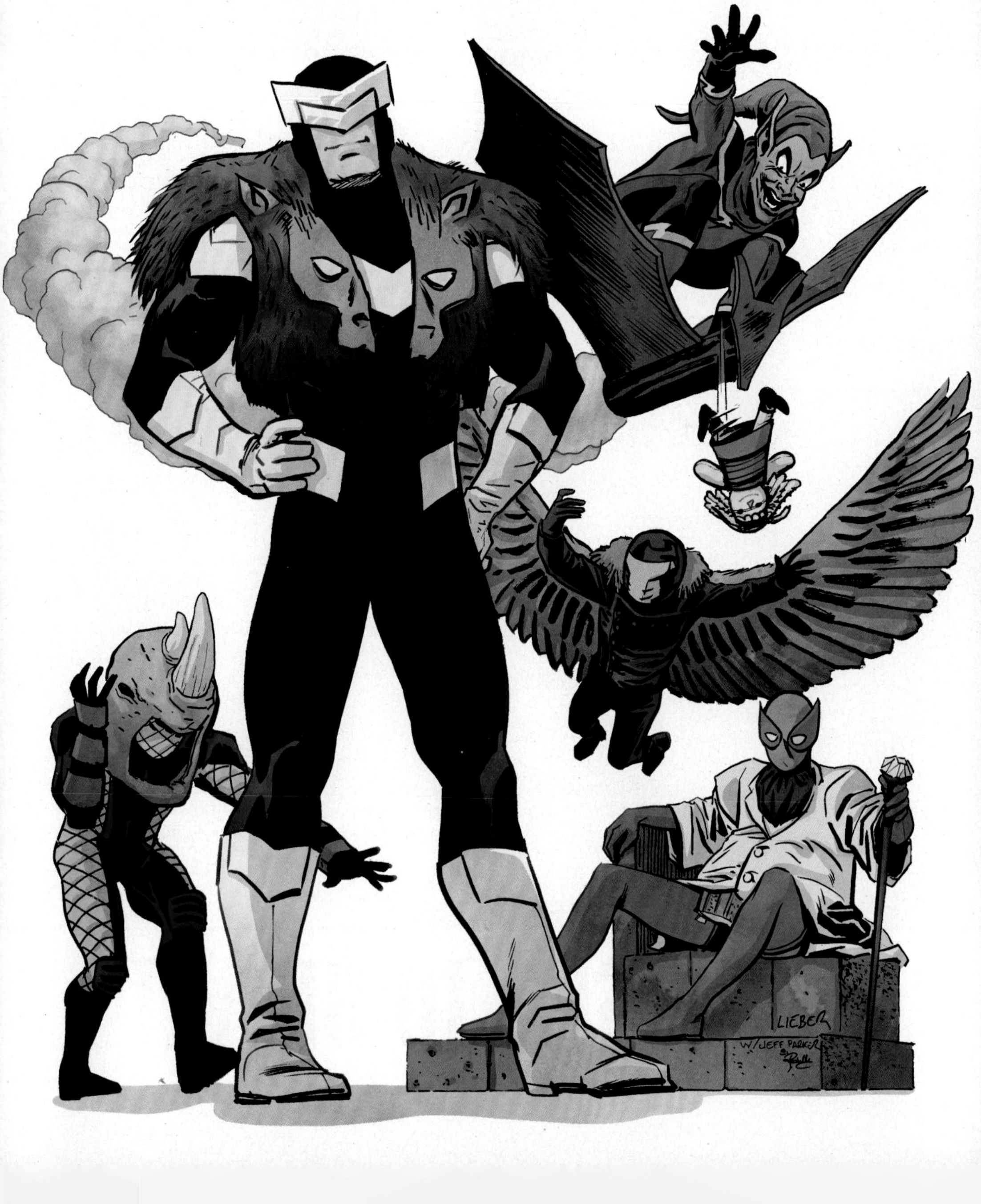
LIEBER
W/JEFF PARKER

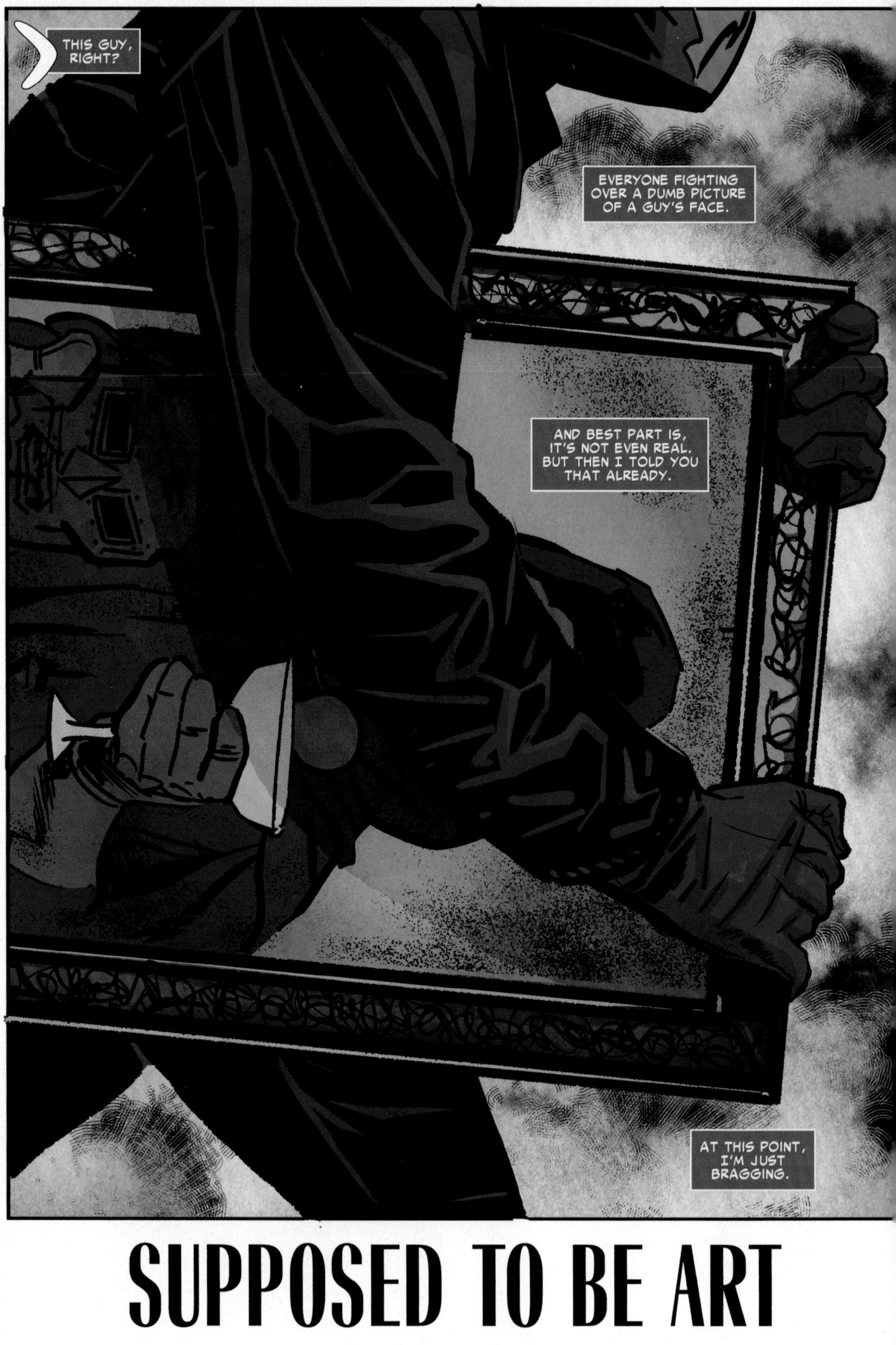
THIS GUY, RIGHT?
EVERYONE FIGHTING OVER A DUMB PICTURE OF A GUY'S FACE.
AND BEST PART IS, IT'S NOT EVEN REAL. BUT THEN I TOLD YOU THAT ALREADY.
AT THIS POINT, I'M JUST BRAGGING.

SUPPOSED TO BE ART

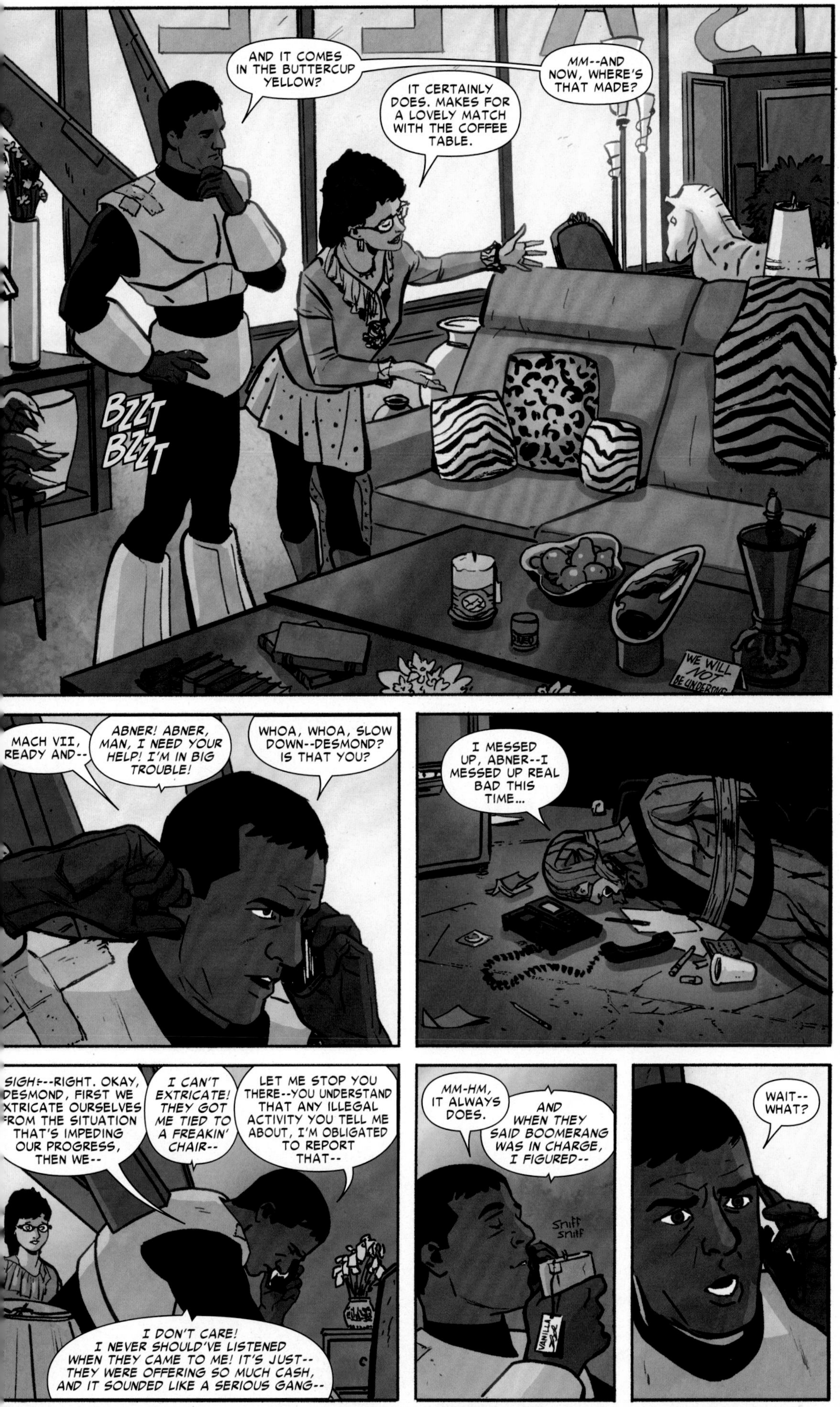

AND IT COMES IN THE BUTTERCUP YELLOW?
IT CERTAINLY DOES. MAKES FOR A LOVELY MATCH WITH THE COFFEE TABLE.
MM--AND NOW, WHERE'S THAT MADE?
BZZT BZZT
WE WILL NOT BE UNDERSOLD
MACH VII, READY AND--
ABNER! ABNER, MAN, I NEED YOUR HELP! I'M IN BIG TROUBLE!
WHOA, WHOA, SLOW DOWN--DESMOND? IS THAT YOU?
I MESSED UP, ABNER--I MESSED UP REAL BAD THIS TIME...
SIGH--RIGHT. OKAY, DESMOND, FIRST WE EXTRICATE OURSELVES FROM THE SITUATION THAT'S IMPEDING OUR PROGRESS, THEN WE--
I CAN'T EXTRICATE! THEY GOT ME TIED TO A FREAKIN' CHAIR--
LET ME STOP YOU THERE--YOU UNDERSTAND THAT ANY ILLEGAL ACTIVITY YOU TELL ME ABOUT, I'M OBLIGATED TO REPORT THAT--
I DON'T CARE! I NEVER SHOULD'VE LISTENED WHEN THEY CAME TO ME! IT'S JUST--THEY WERE OFFERING SO MUCH CASH, AND IT SOUNDED LIKE A SERIOUS GANG--
MM-HM, IT ALWAYS DOES.
AND WHEN THEY SAID BOOMERANG WAS IN CHARGE, I FIGURED--
SNIFF SNIFF
VANILLA
WAIT--WHAT?

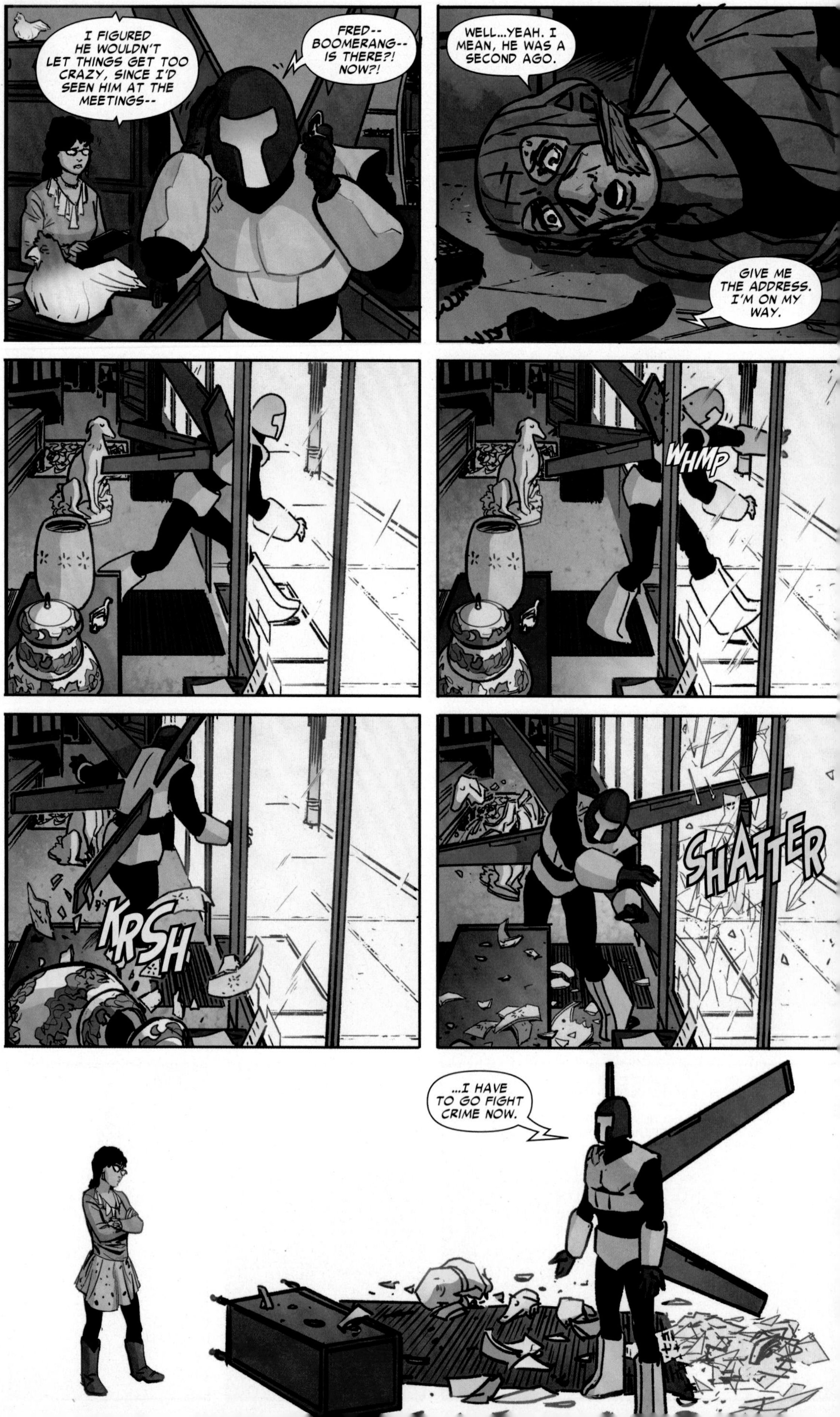
I FIGURED HE WOULDN'T LET THINGS GET TOO CRAZY, SINCE I'D SEEN HIM AT THE MEETINGS--
FRED-- BOOMERANG-- IS THERE?! NOW?!
WELL...YEAH. I MEAN, HE WAS A SECOND AGO.
GIVE ME THE ADDRESS. I'M ON MY WAY.
WHMP
KRSH
SHATTER
...I HAVE TO GO FIGHT CRIME NOW.

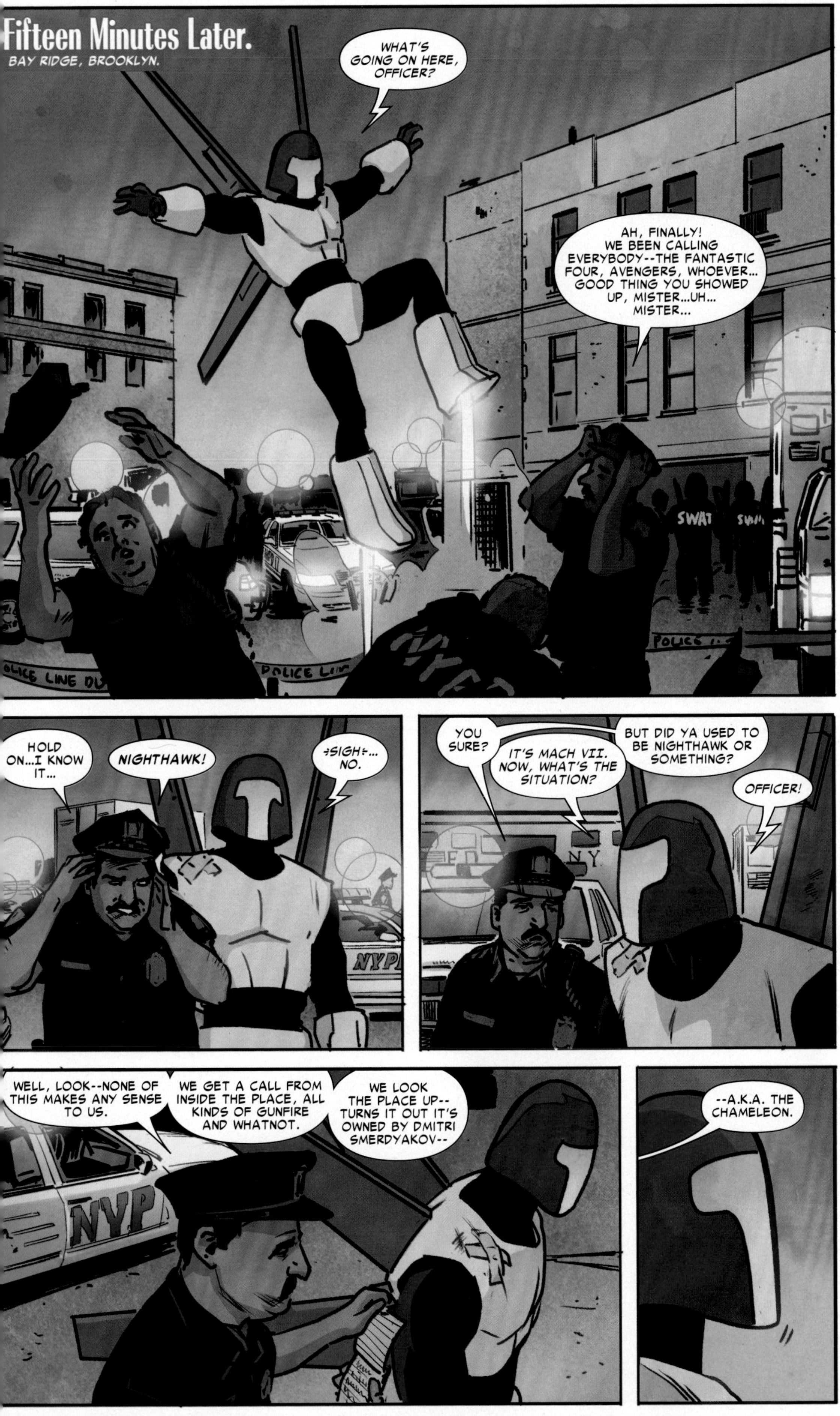
Fifteen Minutes Later.
BAY RIDGE, BROOKLYN.
WHAT'S GOING ON HERE, OFFICER?
AH, FINALLY! WE BEEN CALLING EVERYBODY--THE FANTASTIC FOUR, AVENGERS, WHOEVER... GOOD THING YOU SHOWED UP, MISTER...UH... MISTER...
SWAT
POLICE LINE DO
POLICE LIN
HOLD ON...I KNOW IT...
NIGHTHAWK!
SIGH... NO.
YOU SURE?
IT'S MACH VII. NOW, WHAT'S THE SITUATION?
BUT DID YA USED TO BE NIGHTHAWK OR SOMETHING?
OFFICER!
WELL, LOOK--NONE OF THIS MAKES ANY SENSE TO US.
WE GET A CALL FROM INSIDE THE PLACE, ALL KINDS OF GUNFIRE AND WHATNOT.
WE LOOK THE PLACE UP--TURNS IT OUT IT'S OWNED BY DMITRI SMERDYAKOV--
--A.K.A. THE CHAMELEON.

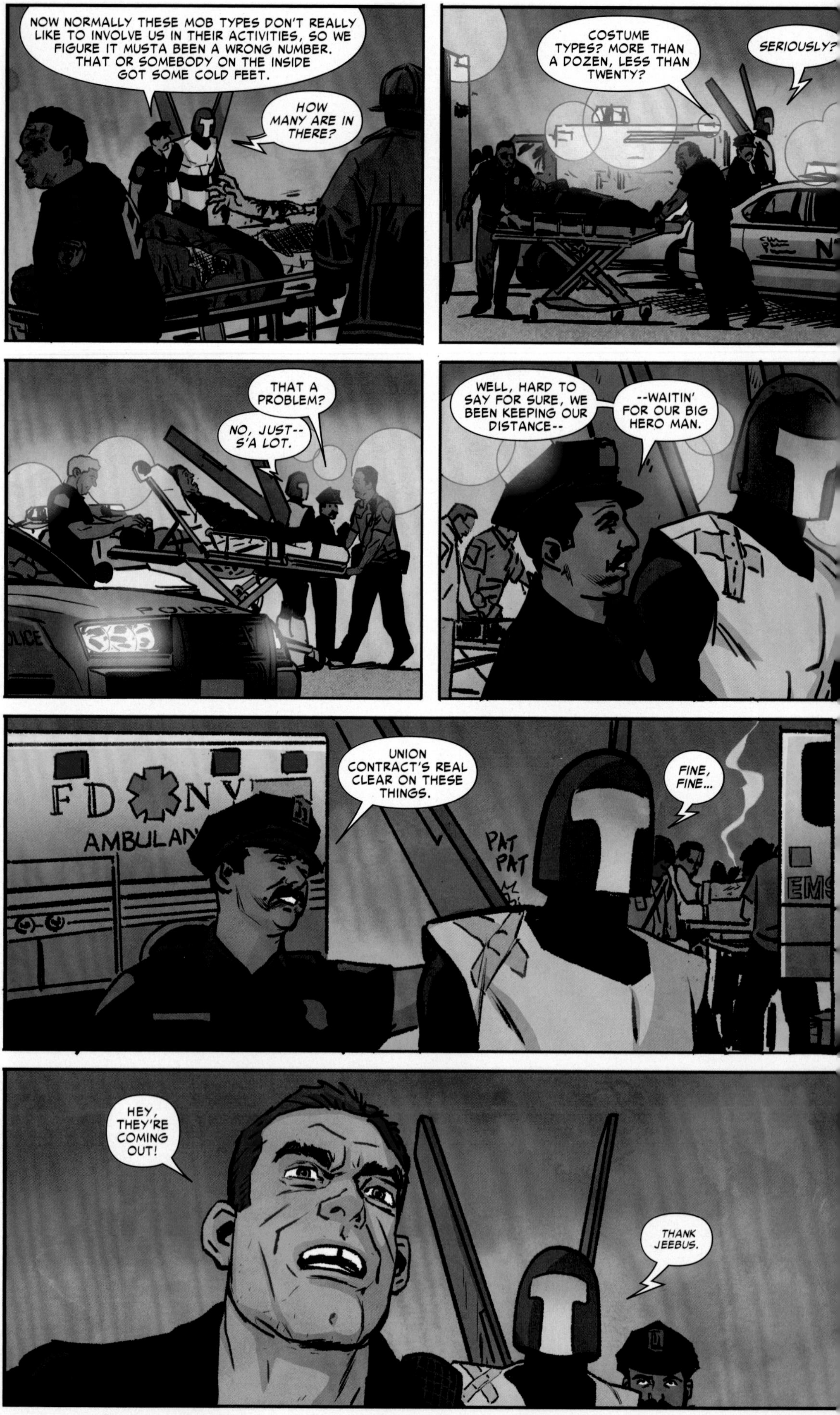
NOW NORMALLY THESE MOB TYPES DON'T REALLY LIKE TO INVOLVE US IN THEIR ACTIVITIES, SO WE FIGURE IT MUSTA BEEN A WRONG NUMBER. THAT OR SOMEBODY ON THE INSIDE GOT SOME COLD FEET.
HOW MANY ARE IN THERE?
COSTUME TYPES? MORE THAN A DOZEN, LESS THAN TWENTY?
SERIOUSLY?
THAT A PROBLEM?
NO, JUST-- S'A LOT.
WELL, HARD TO SAY FOR SURE, WE BEEN KEEPING OUR DISTANCE--
--WAITIN' FOR OUR BIG HERO MAN.
FD NY
AMBULAN
UNION CONTRACT'S REAL CLEAR ON THESE THINGS.
PAT PAT
FINE, FINE...
EMS
HEY, THEY'RE COMING OUT!
THANK JEEBUS.

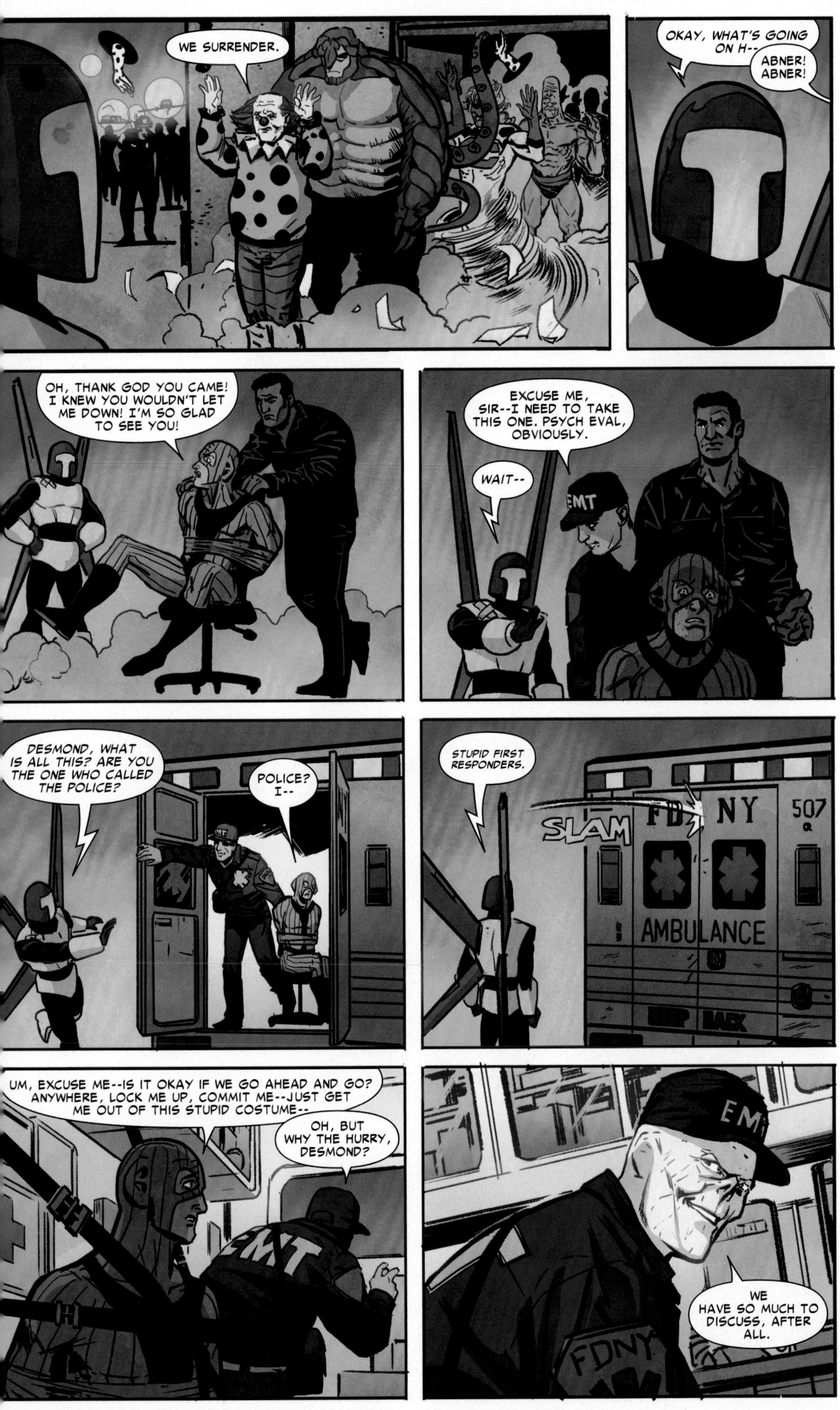
WE SURRENDER.
OKAY, WHAT'S GOING ON H--
ABNER! ABNER!
OH, THANK GOD YOU CAME! I KNEW YOU WOULDN'T LET ME DOWN! I'M SO GLAD TO SEE YOU!
EXCUSE ME, SIR--I NEED TO TAKE THIS ONE. PSYCH EVAL, OBVIOUSLY.
WAIT--
EMT
DESMOND, WHAT IS ALL THIS? ARE YOU THE ONE WHO CALLED THE POLICE?
POLICE? I--
STUPID FIRST RESPONDERS.
SLAM
FDNY
507
AMBULANCE
UM, EXCUSE ME--IS IT OKAY IF WE GO AHEAD AND GO? ANYWHERE, LOCK ME UP, COMMIT ME--JUST GET ME OUT OF THIS STUPID COSTUME--
OH, BUT WHY THE HURRY, DESMOND?
EMT
WE HAVE SO MUCH TO DISCUSS, AFTER ALL.
FDNY

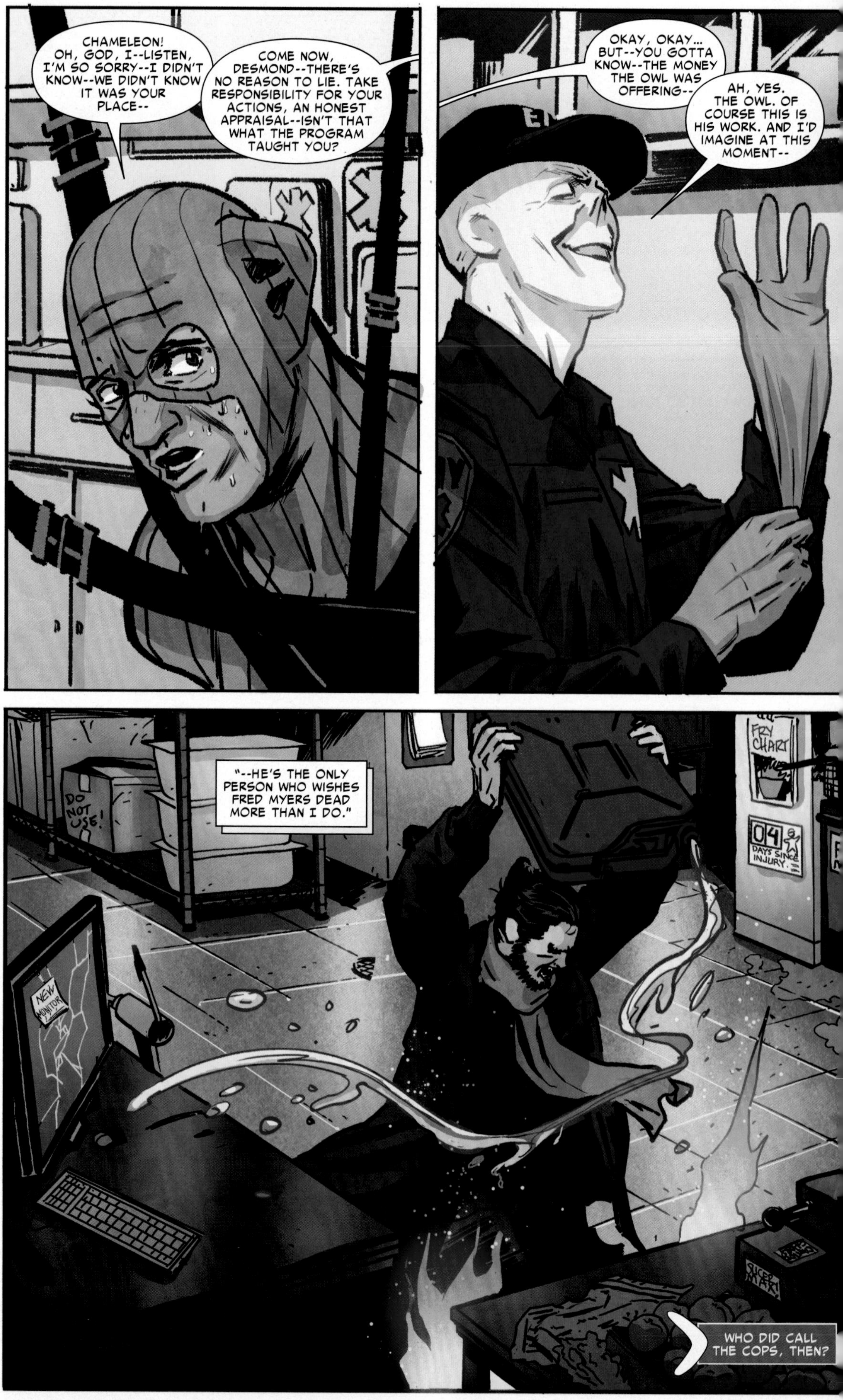

CHAMELEON! OH, GOD, I--LISTEN, I'M SO SORRY--I DIDN'T KNOW--WE DIDN'T KNOW IT WAS YOUR PLACE--
COME NOW, DESMOND--THERE'S NO REASON TO LIE. TAKE RESPONSIBILITY FOR YOUR ACTIONS, AN HONEST APPRAISAL--ISN'T THAT WHAT THE PROGRAM TAUGHT YOU?
OKAY, OKAY... BUT--YOU GOTTA KNOW--THE MONEY THE OWL WAS OFFERING--
AH, YES. THE OWL. OF COURSE THIS IS HIS WORK. AND I'D IMAGINE AT THIS MOMENT--
"--HE'S THE ONLY PERSON WHO WISHES FRED MYERS DEAD MORE THAN I DO."
DO NOT USE!
FRY CHART
04 DAYS SINCE INJURY.
NEW MONITOR
WHO DID CALL THE COPS, THEN?

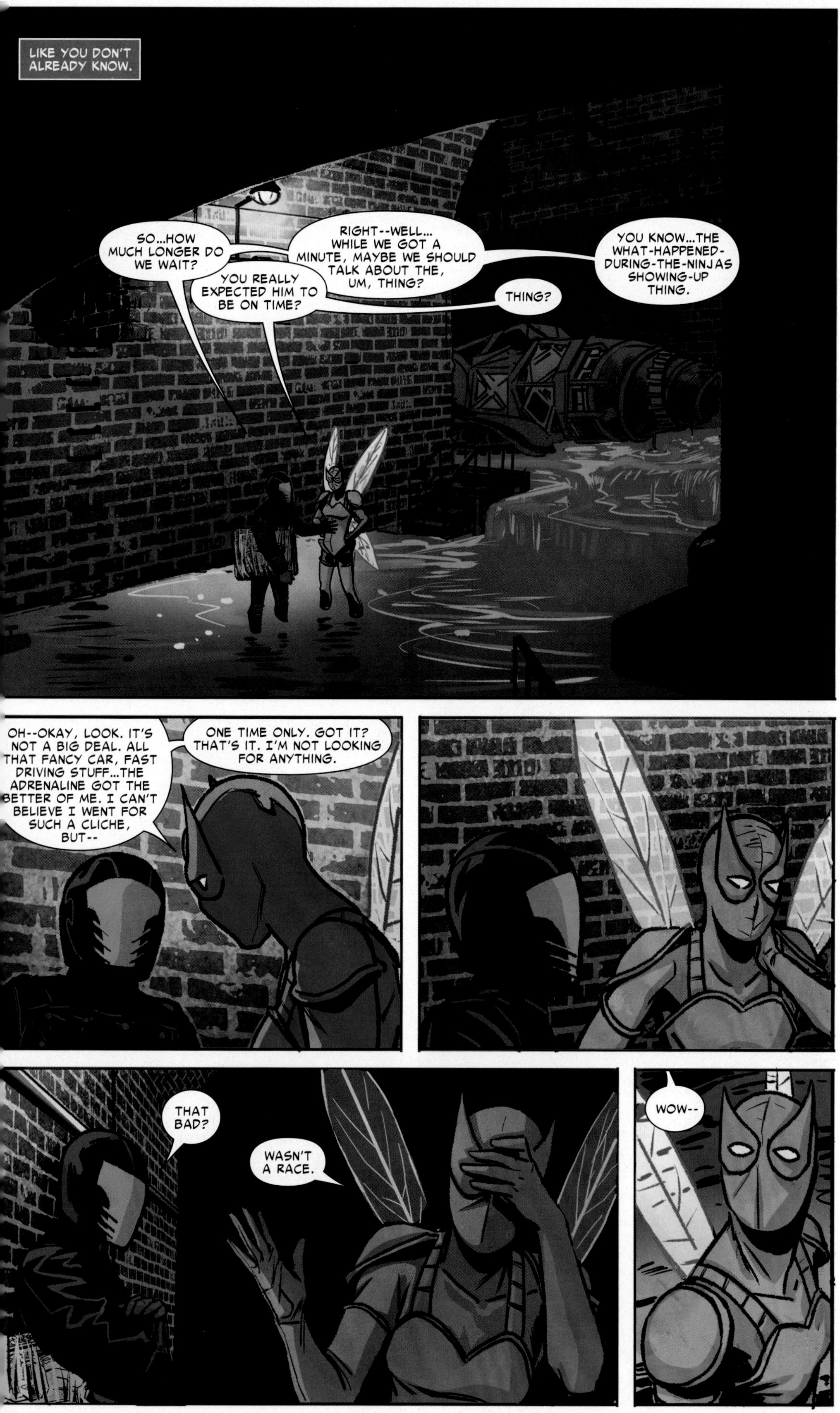

LIKE YOU DON'T ALREADY KNOW.
SO...HOW MUCH LONGER DO WE WAIT?
YOU REALLY EXPECTED HIM TO BE ON TIME?
RIGHT--WELL... WHILE WE GOT A MINUTE, MAYBE WE SHOULD TALK ABOUT THE, UM, THING?
THING?
YOU KNOW...THE WHAT-HAPPENED-DURING-THE-NINJAS SHOWING-UP THING.
OH--OKAY, LOOK. IT'S NOT A BIG DEAL. ALL THAT FANCY CAR, FAST DRIVING STUFF...THE ADRENALINE GOT THE BETTER OF ME. I CAN'T BELIEVE I WENT FOR SUCH A CLICHE, BUT--
ONE TIME ONLY. GOT IT? THAT'S IT. I'M NOT LOOKING FOR ANYTHING.
THAT BAD?
WASN'T A RACE.
WOW--

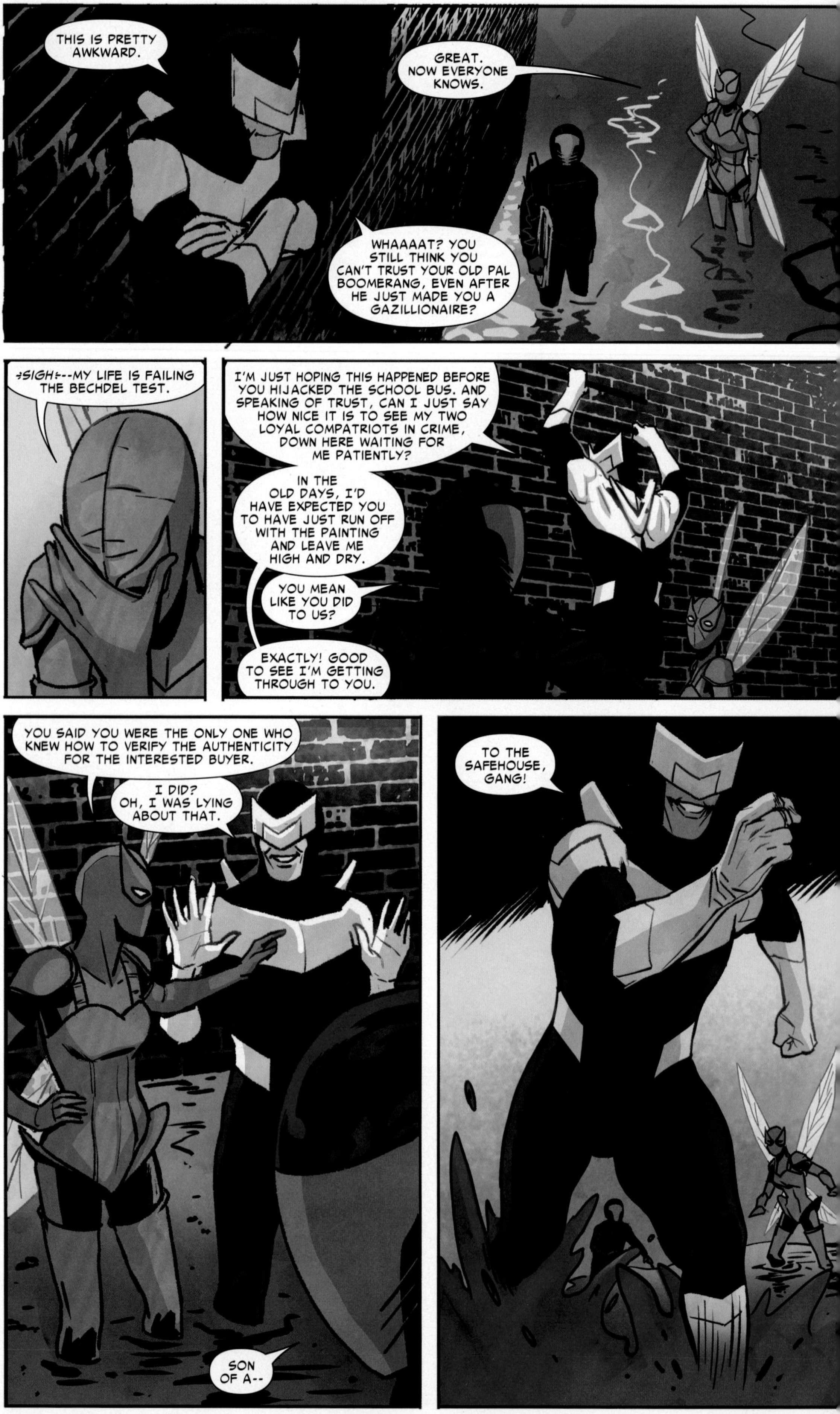
THIS IS PRETTY AWKWARD.
GREAT. NOW EVERYONE KNOWS.
WHAAAAT? YOU STILL THINK YOU CAN'T TRUST YOUR OLD PAL BOOMERANG, EVEN AFTER HE JUST MADE YOU A GAZILLIONAIRE?
=SIGH=--MY LIFE IS FAILING THE BECHDEL TEST.
I'M JUST HOPING THIS HAPPENED BEFORE YOU HIJACKED THE SCHOOL BUS. AND SPEAKING OF TRUST, CAN I JUST SAY HOW NICE IT IS TO SEE MY TWO LOYAL COMPATRIOTS IN CRIME, DOWN HERE WAITING FOR ME PATIENTLY?
IN THE OLD DAYS, I'D HAVE EXPECTED YOU TO HAVE JUST RUN OFF WITH THE PAINTING AND LEAVE ME HIGH AND DRY.
YOU MEAN LIKE YOU DID TO US?
EXACTLY! GOOD TO SEE I'M GETTING THROUGH TO YOU.
YOU SAID YOU WERE THE ONLY ONE WHO KNEW HOW TO VERIFY THE AUTHENTICITY FOR THE INTERESTED BUYER.
I DID? OH, I WAS LYING ABOUT THAT.
SON OF A--
TO THE SAFEHOUSE, GANG!

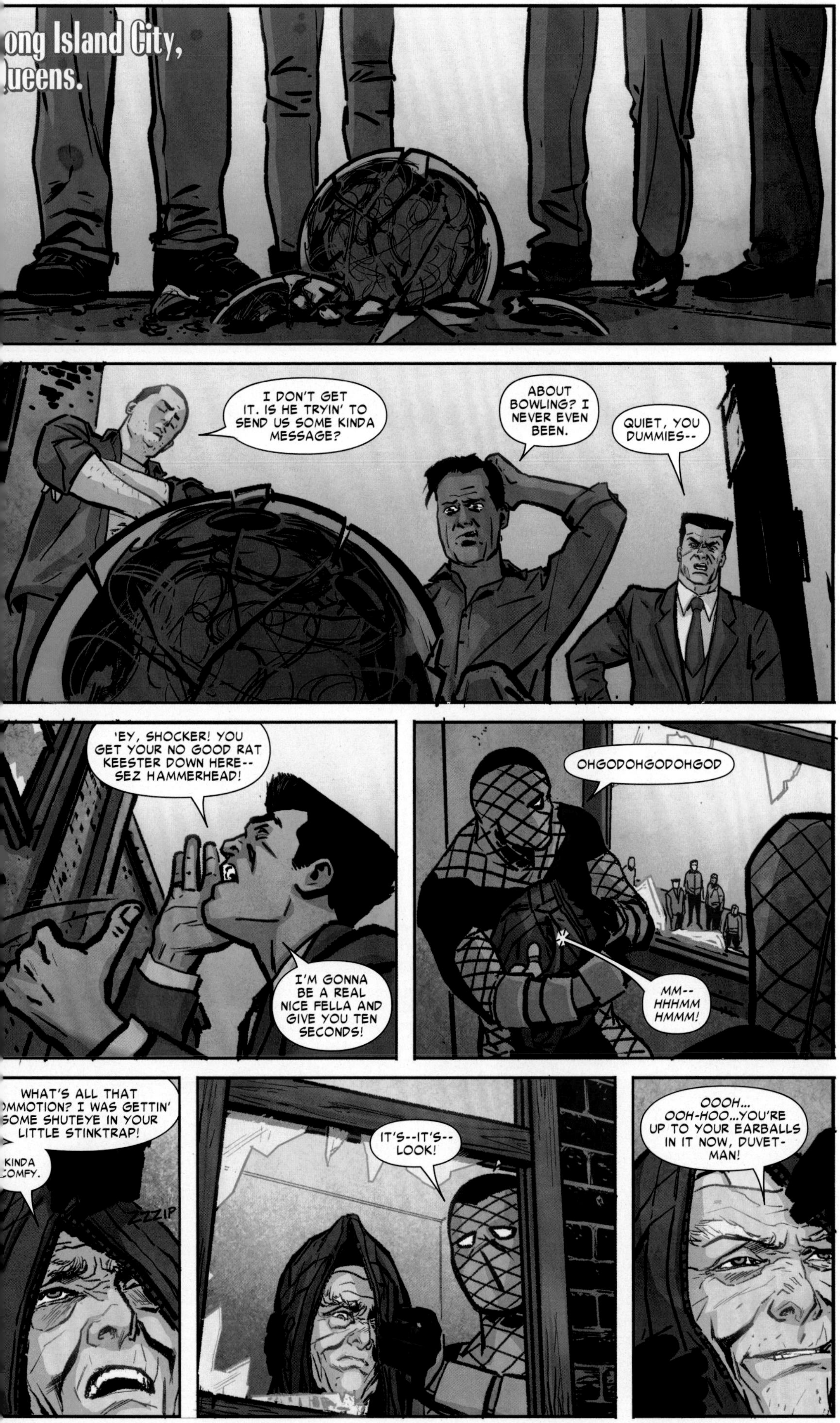
ong Island City,
ueens.
I DON'T GET IT. IS HE TRYIN' TO SEND US SOME KINDA MESSAGE?
ABOUT BOWLING? I NEVER EVEN BEEN.
QUIET, YOU DUMMIES--
'EY, SHOCKER! YOU GET YOUR NO GOOD RAT KEESTER DOWN HERE-- SEZ HAMMERHEAD!
I'M GONNA BE A REAL NICE FELLA AND GIVE YOU TEN SECONDS!
OHGODOHGODOHGOD
MM-- HHHMM HMMM!
WHAT'S ALL THAT OMMOTION? I WAS GETTIN' SOME SHUTEYE IN YOUR LITTLE STINKTRAP!
KINDA COMFY.
ZZZIP
IT'S--IT'S-- LOOK!
OOOH... OOH-HOO...YOU'RE UP TO YOUR EARBALLS IN IT NOW, DUVET-MAN!

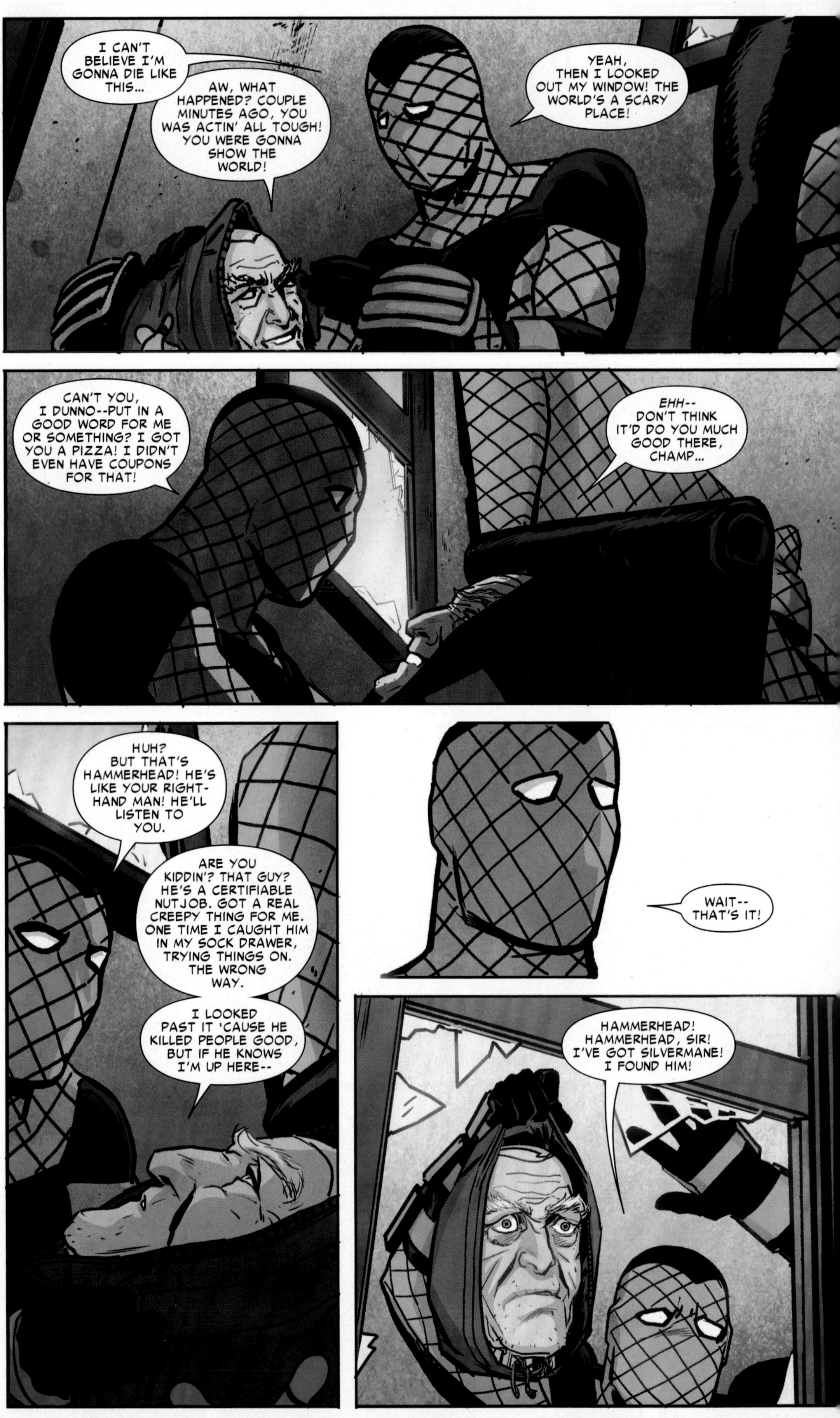
I CAN'T BELIEVE I'M GONNA DIE LIKE THIS...
AW, WHAT HAPPENED? COUPLE MINUTES AGO, YOU WAS ACTIN' ALL TOUGH! YOU WERE GONNA SHOW THE WORLD!
YEAH, THEN I LOOKED OUT MY WINDOW! THE WORLD'S A SCARY PLACE!
CAN'T YOU, I DUNNO--PUT IN A GOOD WORD FOR ME OR SOMETHING? I GOT YOU A PIZZA! I DIDN'T EVEN HAVE COUPONS FOR THAT!
EHH-- DON'T THINK IT'D DO YOU MUCH GOOD THERE, CHAMP...
HUH? BUT THAT'S HAMMERHEAD! HE'S LIKE YOUR RIGHT-HAND MAN! HE'LL LISTEN TO YOU.
ARE YOU KIDDIN'? THAT GUY? HE'S A CERTIFIABLE NUTJOB. GOT A REAL CREEPY THING FOR ME. ONE TIME I CAUGHT HIM IN MY SOCK DRAWER, TRYING THINGS ON. THE WRONG WAY.
I LOOKED PAST IT 'CAUSE HE KILLED PEOPLE GOOD, BUT IF HE KNOWS I'M UP HERE--
WAIT-- THAT'S IT!
HAMMERHEAD! HAMMERHEAD, SIR! I'VE GOT SILVERMANE! I FOUND HIM!

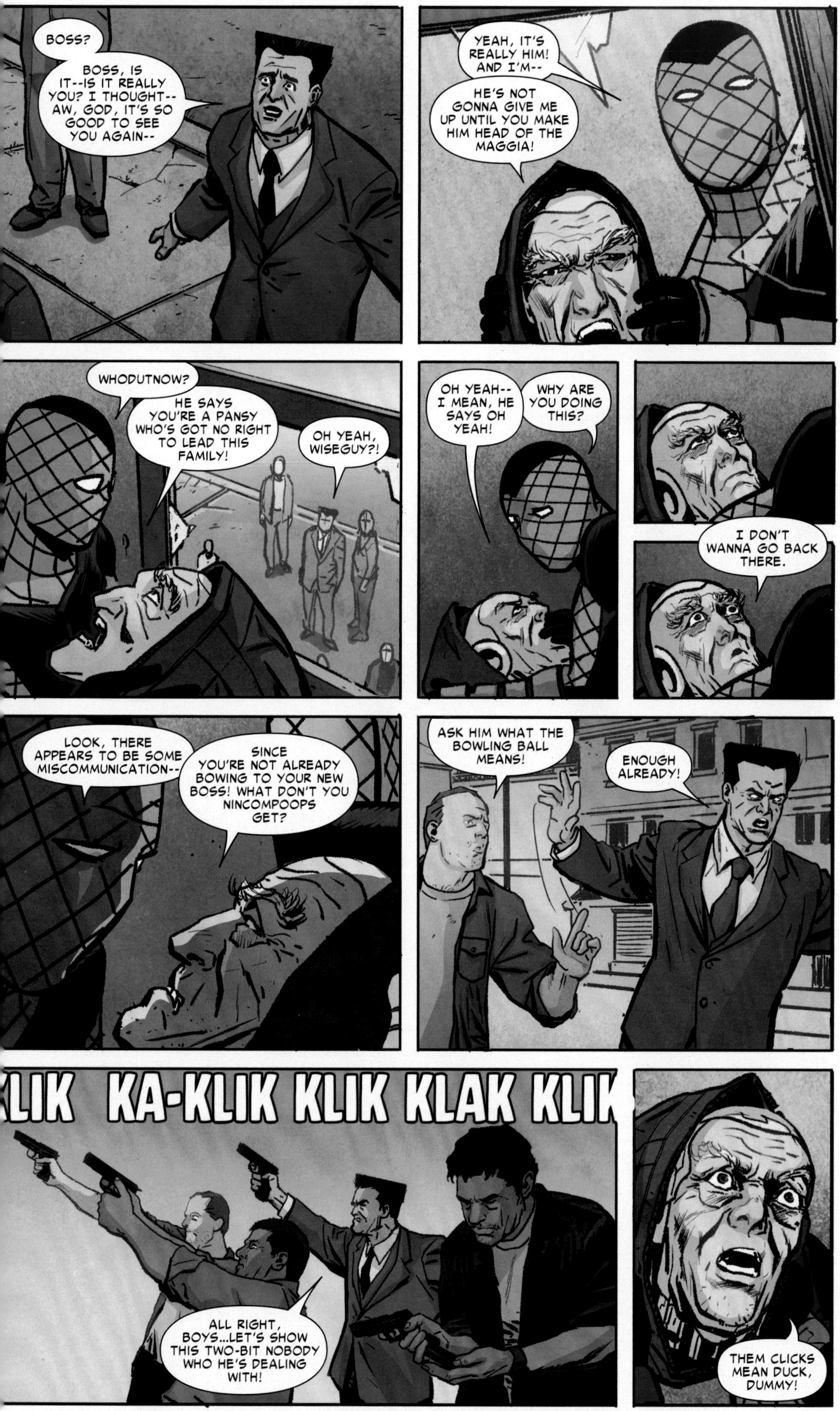

BOSS?
BOSS, IS IT--IS IT REALLY YOU? I THOUGHT-- AW, GOD, IT'S SO GOOD TO SEE YOU AGAIN--
YEAH, IT'S REALLY HIM! AND I'M--
HE'S NOT GONNA GIVE ME UP UNTIL YOU MAKE HIM HEAD OF THE MAGGIA!
WHODUTNOW?
HE SAYS YOU'RE A PANSY WHO'S GOT NO RIGHT TO LEAD THIS FAMILY!
OH YEAH, WISEGUY?!
OH YEAH-- I MEAN, HE SAYS OH YEAH!
WHY ARE YOU DOING THIS?
I DON'T WANNA GO BACK THERE.
LOOK, THERE APPEARS TO BE SOME MISCOMMUNICATION--
SINCE YOU'RE NOT ALREADY BOWING TO YOUR NEW BOSS! WHAT DON'T YOU NINCOMPOOPS GET?
ASK HIM WHAT THE BOWLING BALL MEANS!
ENOUGH ALREADY!
KLIK KA-KLIK KLIK KLAK KLIK
ALL RIGHT, BOYS...LET'S SHOW THIS TWO-BIT NOBODY WHO HE'S DEALING WITH!
THEM CLICKS MEAN DUCK, DUMMY!

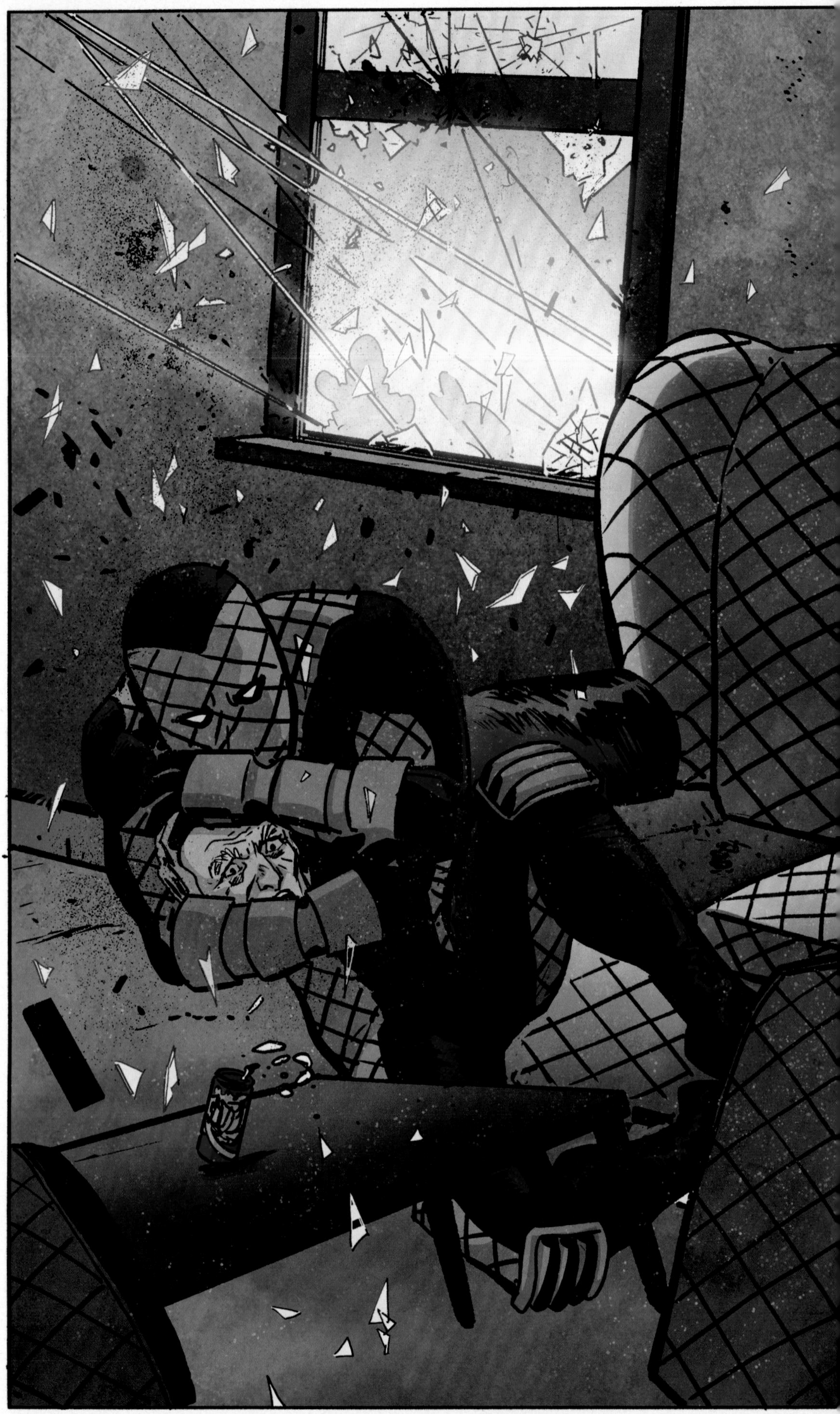

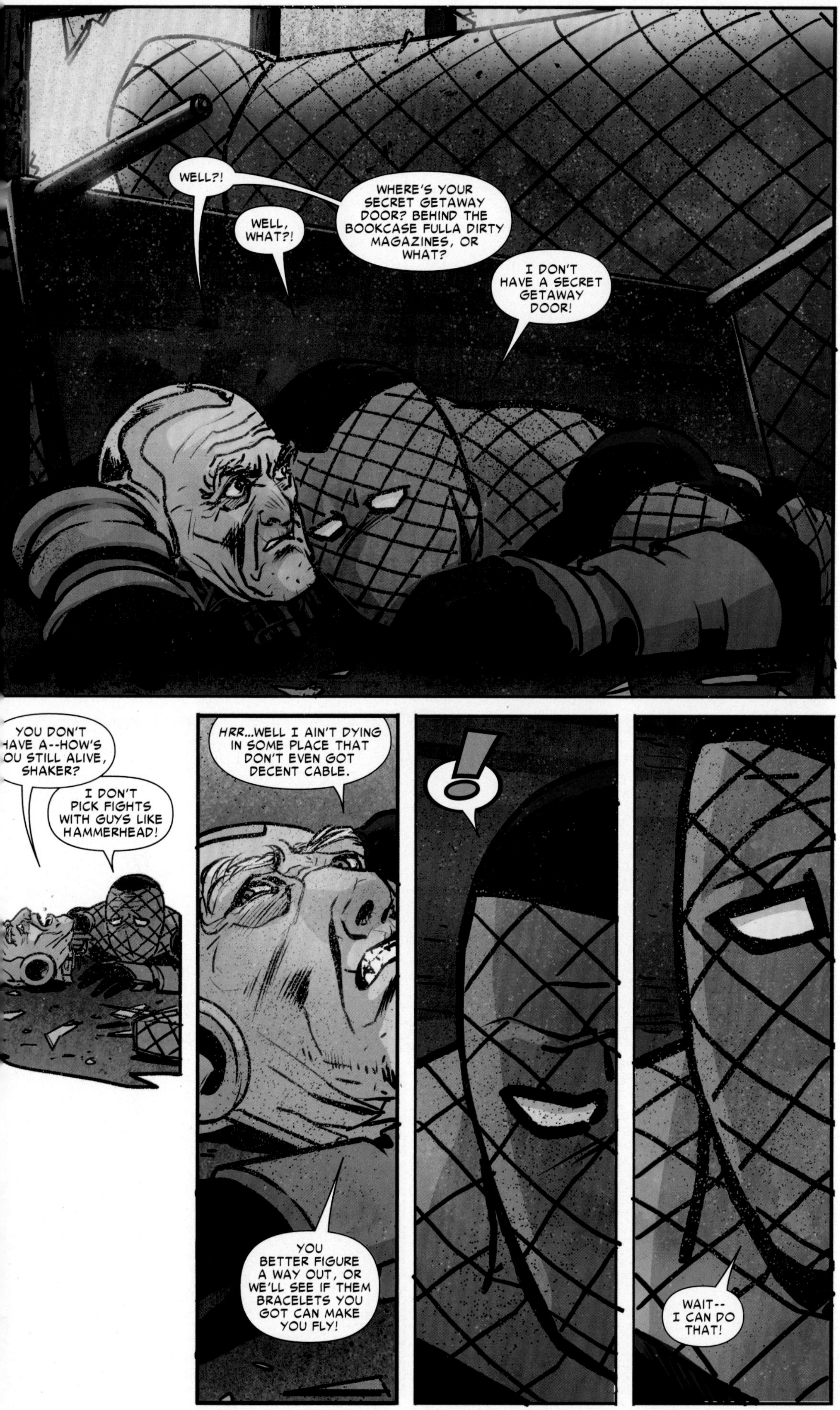
WELL?!
WELL, WHAT?!
WHERE'S YOUR SECRET GETAWAY DOOR? BEHIND THE BOOKCASE FULLA DIRTY MAGAZINES, OR WHAT?
I DON'T HAVE A SECRET GETAWAY DOOR!
YOU DON'T HAVE A--HOW'S YOU STILL ALIVE, SHAKER?
I DON'T PICK FIGHTS WITH GUYS LIKE HAMMERHEAD!
HRR...WELL I AIN'T DYING IN SOME PLACE THAT DON'T EVEN GOT DECENT CABLE.
YOU BETTER FIGURE A WAY OUT, OR WE'LL SEE IF THEM BRACELETS YOU GOT CAN MAKE YOU FLY!
!
WAIT-- I CAN DO THAT!

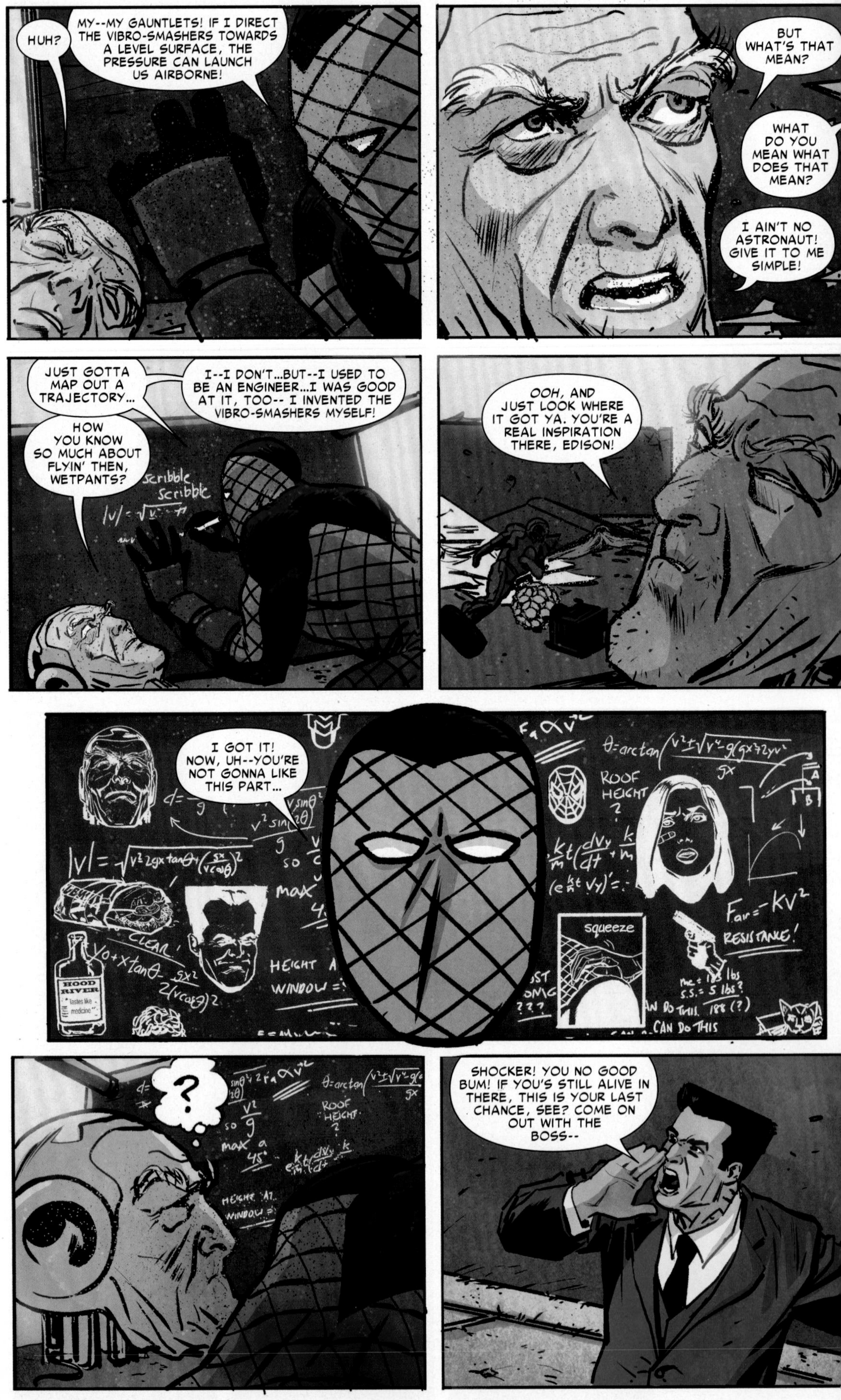
HUH?
MY--MY GAUNTLETS! IF I DIRECT THE VIBRO-SMASHERS TOWARDS A LEVEL SURFACE, THE PRESSURE CAN LAUNCH US AIRBORNE!
BUT WHAT'S THAT MEAN?
WHAT DO YOU MEAN WHAT DOES THAT MEAN?
I AIN'T NO ASTRONAUT! GIVE IT TO ME SIMPLE!
JUST GOTTA MAP OUT A TRAJECTORY...
HOW YOU KNOW SO MUCH ABOUT FLYIN' THEN, WETPANTS?
I--I DON'T...BUT--I USED TO BE AN ENGINEER...I WAS GOOD AT IT, TOO-- I INVENTED THE VIBRO-SMASHERS MYSELF!
scribble scribble
OOH, AND JUST LOOK WHERE IT GOT YA. YOU'RE A REAL INSPIRATION THERE, EDISON!
I GOT IT! NOW, UH--YOU'RE NOT GONNA LIKE THIS PART...
ROOF HEIGHT ?
RESISTANCE!
squeeze
CLEAR
HOOD RIVER "tastes like medicine"
CAN DO THIS
?
SHOCKER! YOU NO GOOD BUM! IF YOU'S STILL ALIVE IN THERE, THIS IS YOUR LAST CHANCE, SEE? COME ON OUT WITH THE BOSS--

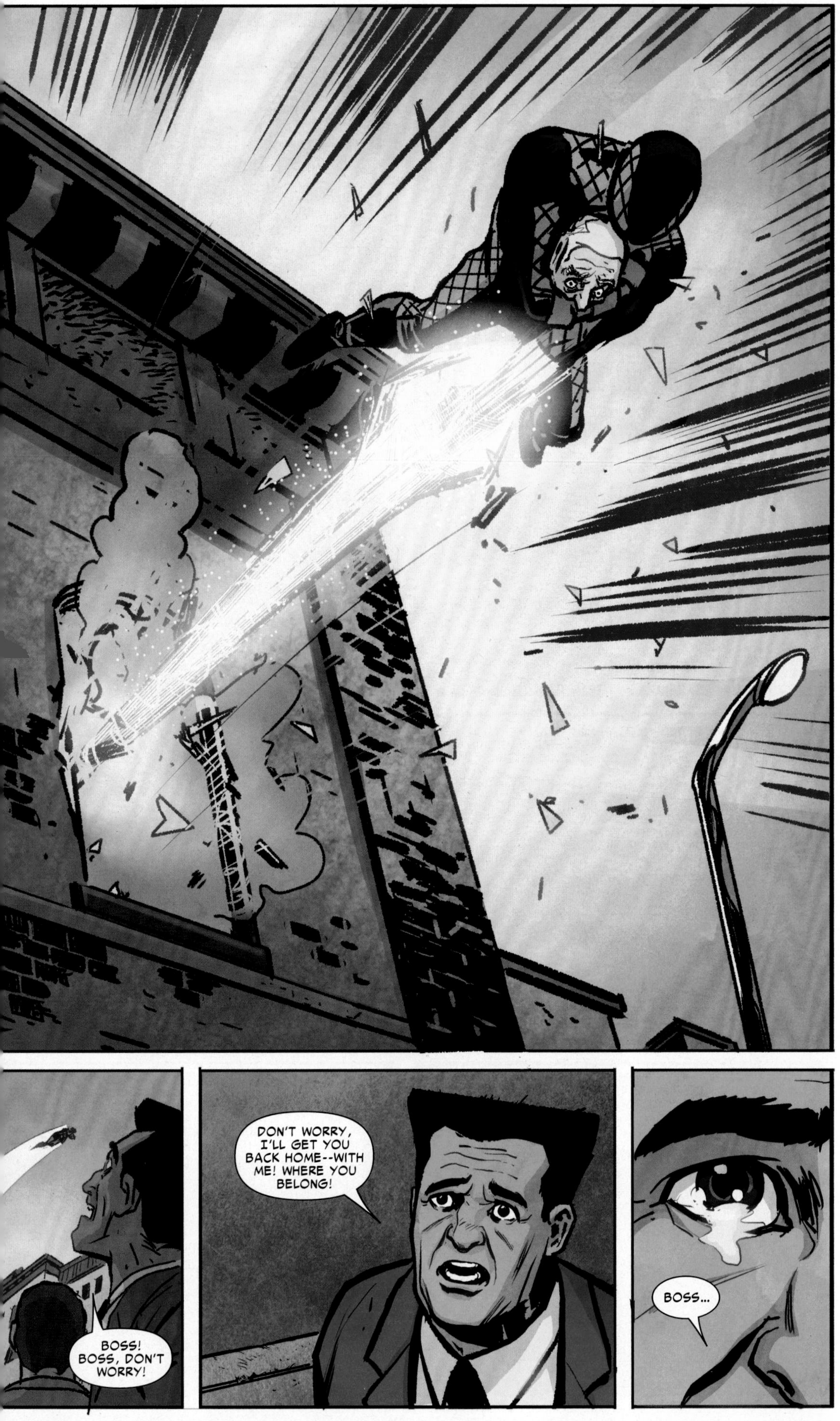
BOSS! BOSS, DON'T WORRY!
DON'T WORRY, I'LL GET YOU BACK HOME--WITH ME! WHERE YOU BELONG!
BOSS...

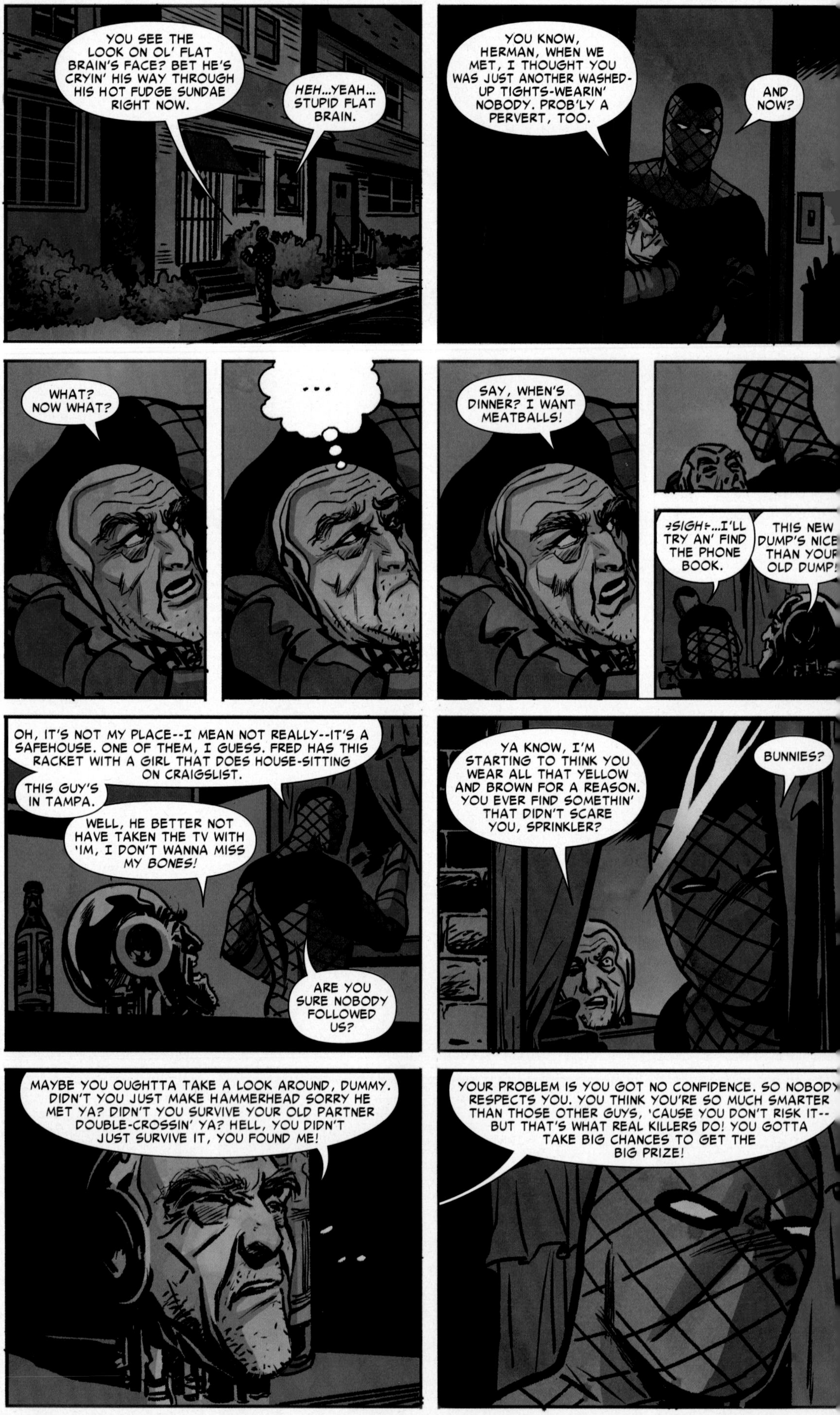

YOU SEE THE LOOK ON OL' FLAT BRAIN'S FACE? BET HE'S CRYIN' HIS WAY THROUGH HIS HOT FUDGE SUNDAE RIGHT NOW.
HEH...YEAH... STUPID FLAT BRAIN.
YOU KNOW, HERMAN, WHEN WE MET, I THOUGHT YOU WAS JUST ANOTHER WASHED-UP TIGHTS-WEARIN' NOBODY. PROB'LY A PERVERT, TOO.
AND NOW?
WHAT? NOW WHAT?
...
SAY, WHEN'S DINNER? I WANT MEATBALLS!
⇉SIGH⇇...I'LL TRY AN' FIND THE PHONE BOOK.
THIS NEW DUMP'S NICE THAN YOUR OLD DUMP!
OH, IT'S NOT MY PLACE--I MEAN NOT REALLY--IT'S A SAFEHOUSE. ONE OF THEM, I GUESS. FRED HAS THIS RACKET WITH A GIRL THAT DOES HOUSE-SITTING ON CRAIGSLIST.
THIS GUY'S IN TAMPA.
WELL, HE BETTER NOT HAVE TAKEN THE TV WITH 'IM, I DON'T WANNA MISS MY BONES!
ARE YOU SURE NOBODY FOLLOWED US?
YA KNOW, I'M STARTING TO THINK YOU WEAR ALL THAT YELLOW AND BROWN FOR A REASON. YOU EVER FIND SOMETHIN' THAT DIDN'T SCARE YOU, SPRINKLER?
BUNNIES?
MAYBE YOU OUGHTTA TAKE A LOOK AROUND, DUMMY. DIDN'T YOU JUST MAKE HAMMERHEAD SORRY HE MET YA? DIDN'T YOU SURVIVE YOUR OLD PARTNER DOUBLE-CROSSIN' YA? HELL, YOU DIDN'T JUST SURVIVE IT, YOU FOUND ME!
YOUR PROBLEM IS YOU GOT NO CONFIDENCE. SO NOBODY RESPECTS YOU. YOU THINK YOU'RE SO MUCH SMARTER THAN THOSE OTHER GUYS, 'CAUSE YOU DON'T RISK IT--BUT THAT'S WHAT REAL KILLERS DO! YOU GOTTA TAKE BIG CHANCES TO GET THE BIG PRIZE!

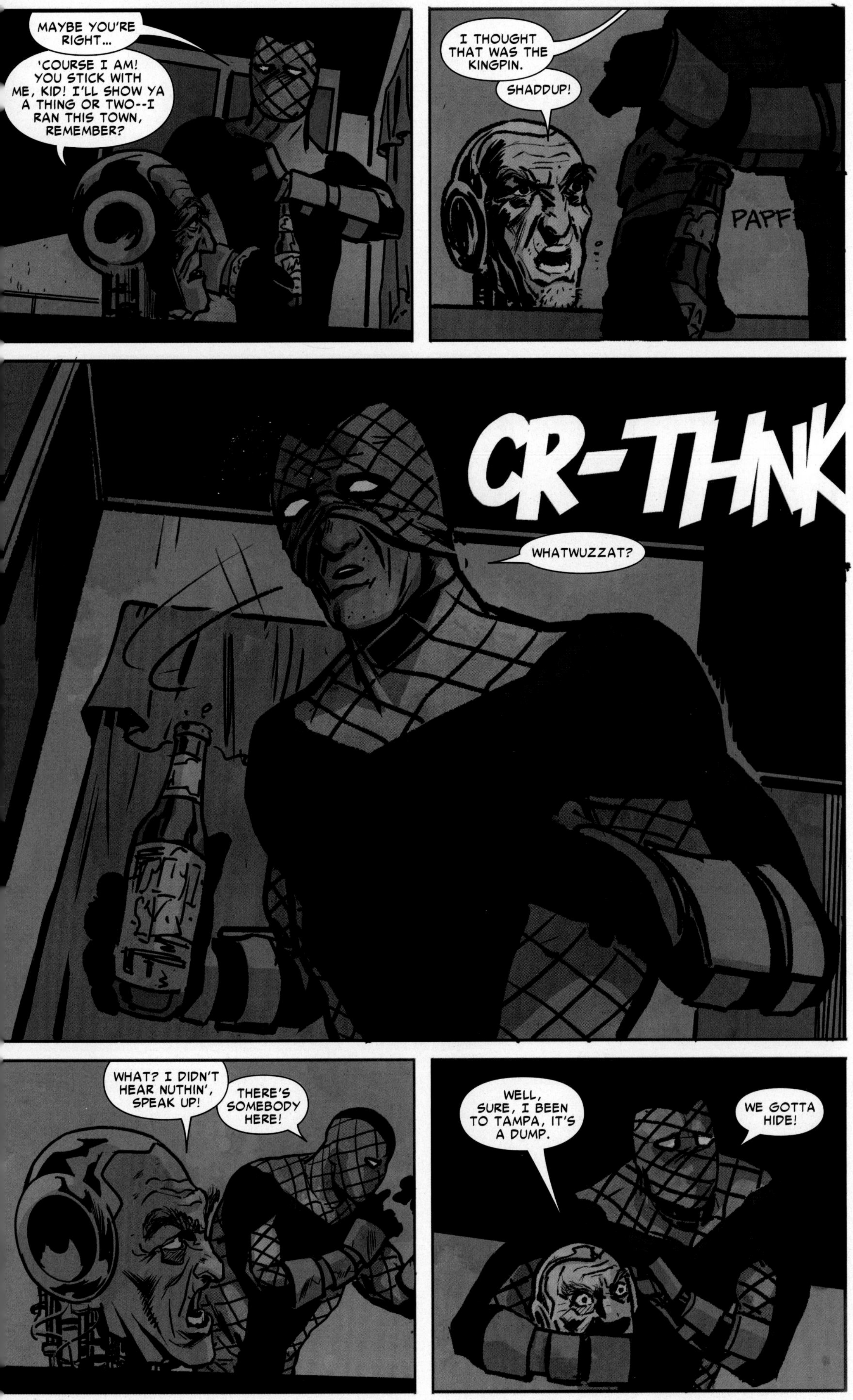
MAYBE YOU'RE RIGHT...
'COURSE I AM! YOU STICK WITH ME, KID! I'LL SHOW YA A THING OR TWO--I RAN THIS TOWN, REMEMBER?
I THOUGHT THAT WAS THE KINGPIN.
SHADDUP!
PAPF
CR-THNK
WHATWUZZAT?
WHAT? I DIDN'T HEAR NUTHIN', SPEAK UP!
THERE'S SOMEBODY HERE!
WELL, SURE, I BEEN TO TAMPA, IT'S A DUMP.
WE GOTTA HIDE!

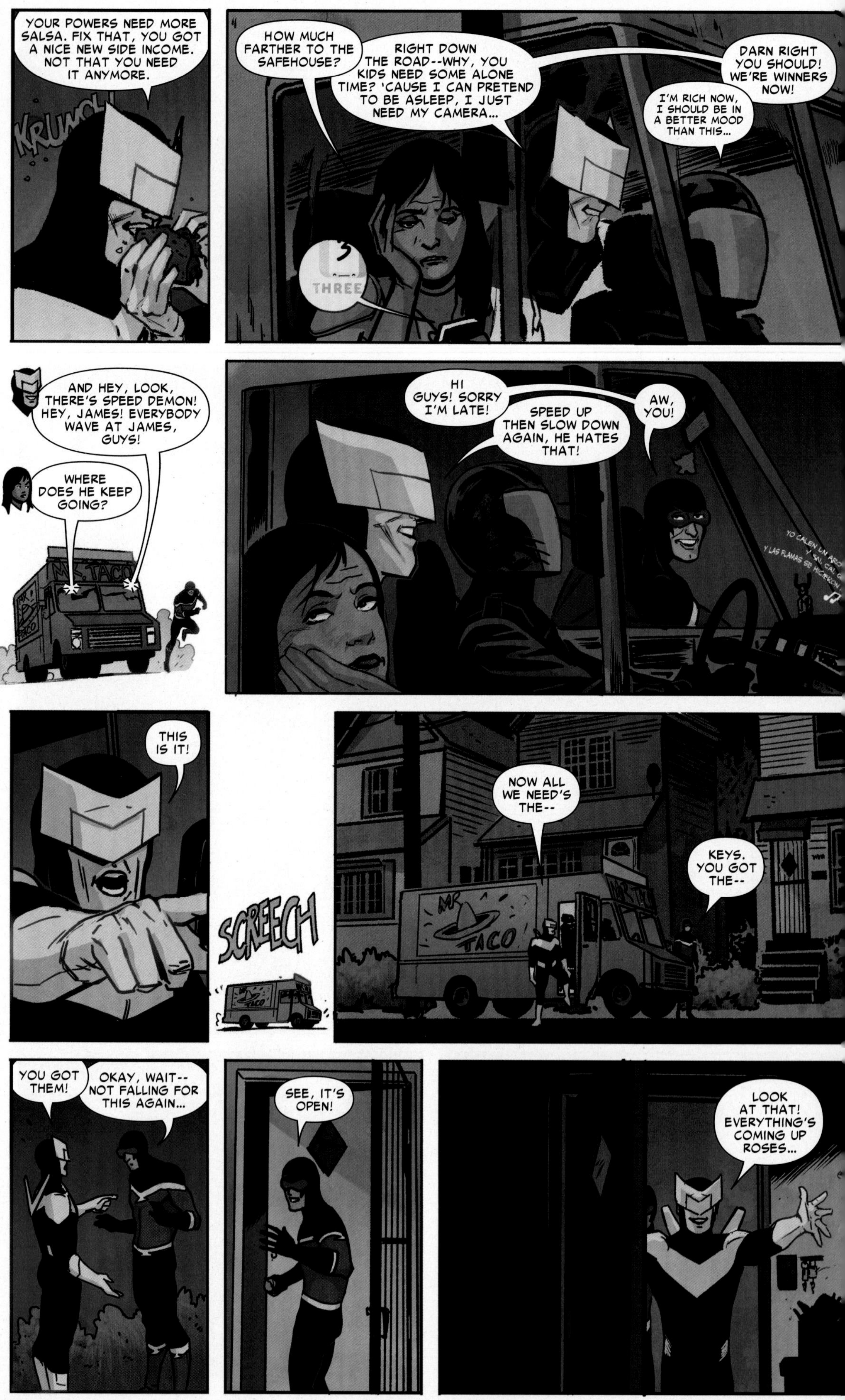
YOUR POWERS NEED MORE SALSA. FIX THAT, YOU GOT A NICE NEW SIDE INCOME. NOT THAT YOU NEED IT ANYMORE.
HOW MUCH FARTHER TO THE SAFEHOUSE?
RIGHT DOWN THE ROAD--WHY, YOU KIDS NEED SOME ALONE TIME? 'CAUSE I CAN PRETEND TO BE ASLEEP, I JUST NEED MY CAMERA...
DARN RIGHT YOU SHOULD! WE'RE WINNERS NOW!
I'M RICH NOW, I SHOULD BE IN A BETTER MOOD THAN THIS...
THREE
AND HEY, LOOK, THERE'S SPEED DEMON! HEY, JAMES! EVERYBODY WAVE AT JAMES, GUYS!
WHERE DOES HE KEEP GOING?
HI GUYS! SORRY I'M LATE!
SPEED UP THEN SLOW DOWN AGAIN, HE HATES THAT!
AW, YOU!
YO CALEN UN ARO
Y LAS FLAMAS SE HICIERON
THIS IS IT!
SCREECH
NOW ALL WE NEED'S THE--
KEYS. YOU GOT THE--
YOU GOT THEM!
OKAY, WAIT-- NOT FALLING FOR THIS AGAIN...
SEE, IT'S OPEN!
LOOK AT THAT! EVERYTHING'S COMING UP ROSES...

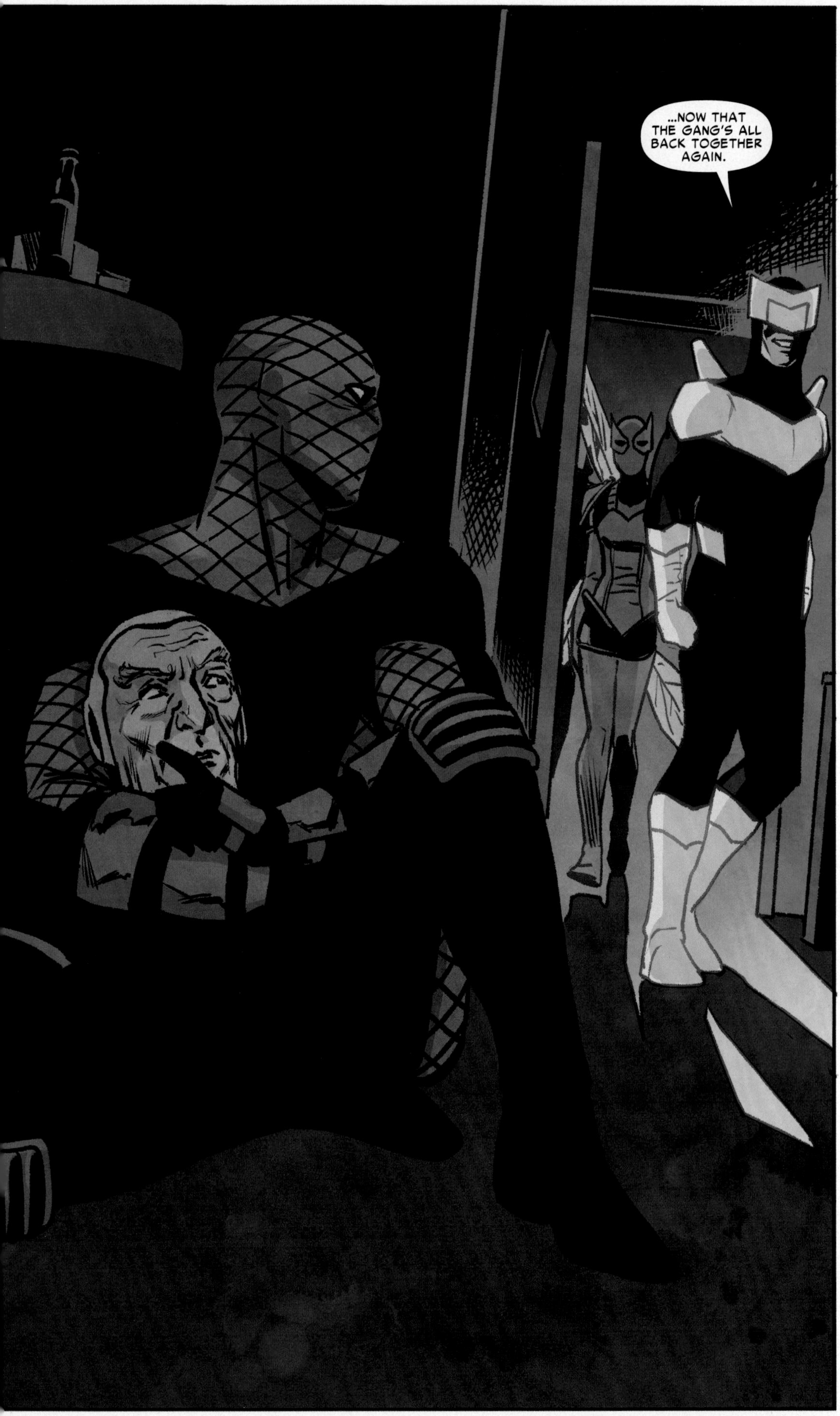
...NOW THAT THE GANG'S ALL BACK TOGETHER AGAIN.

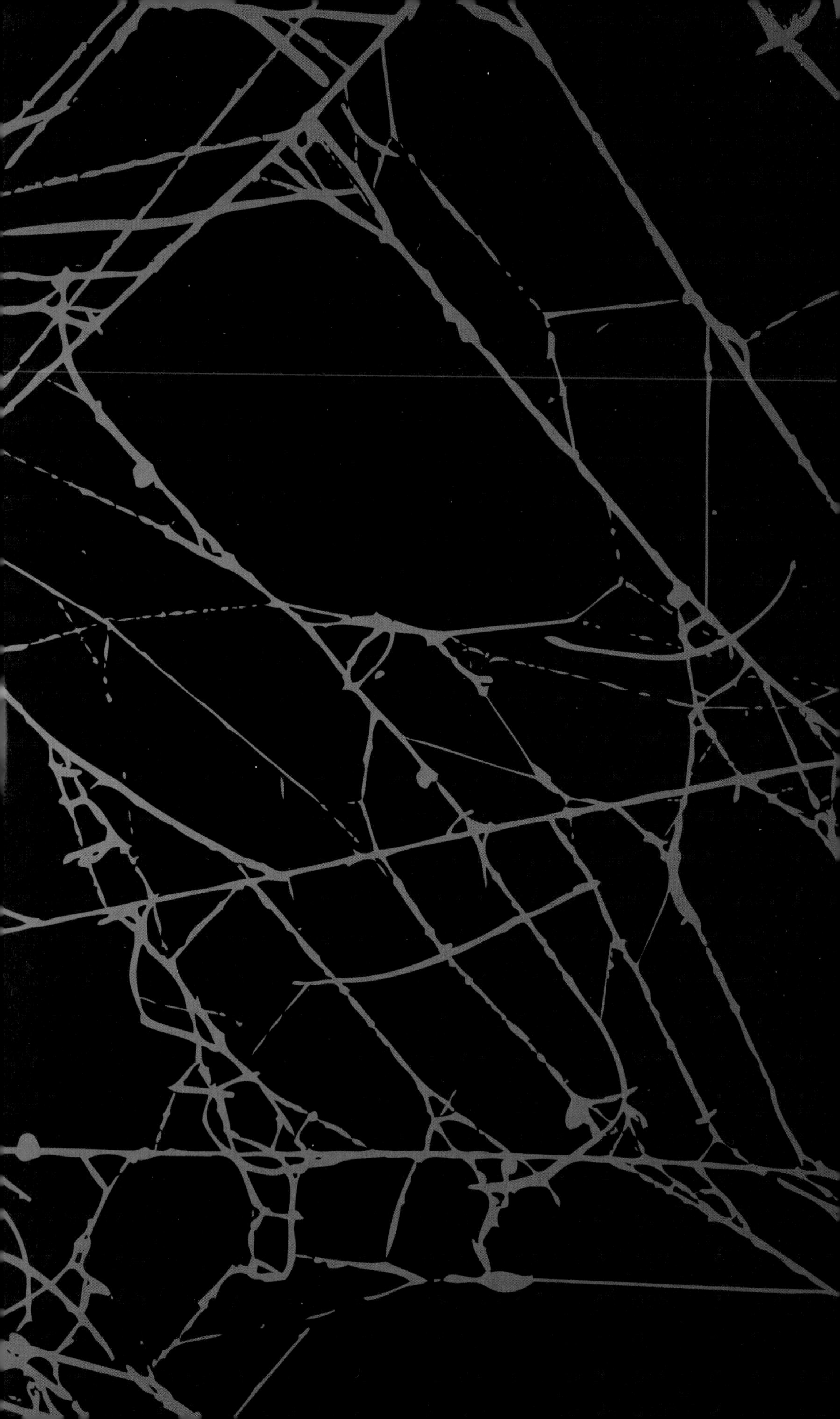

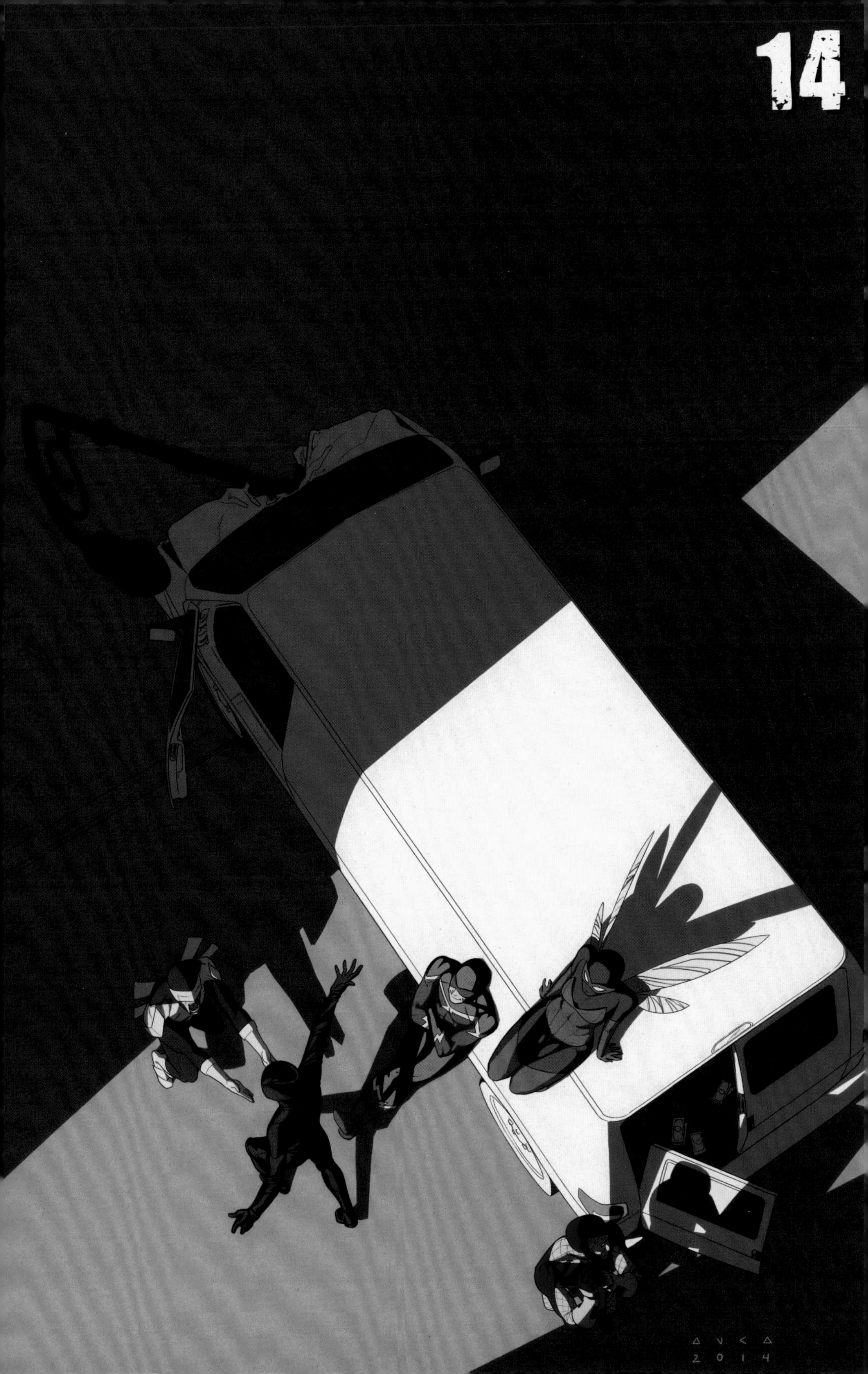
14

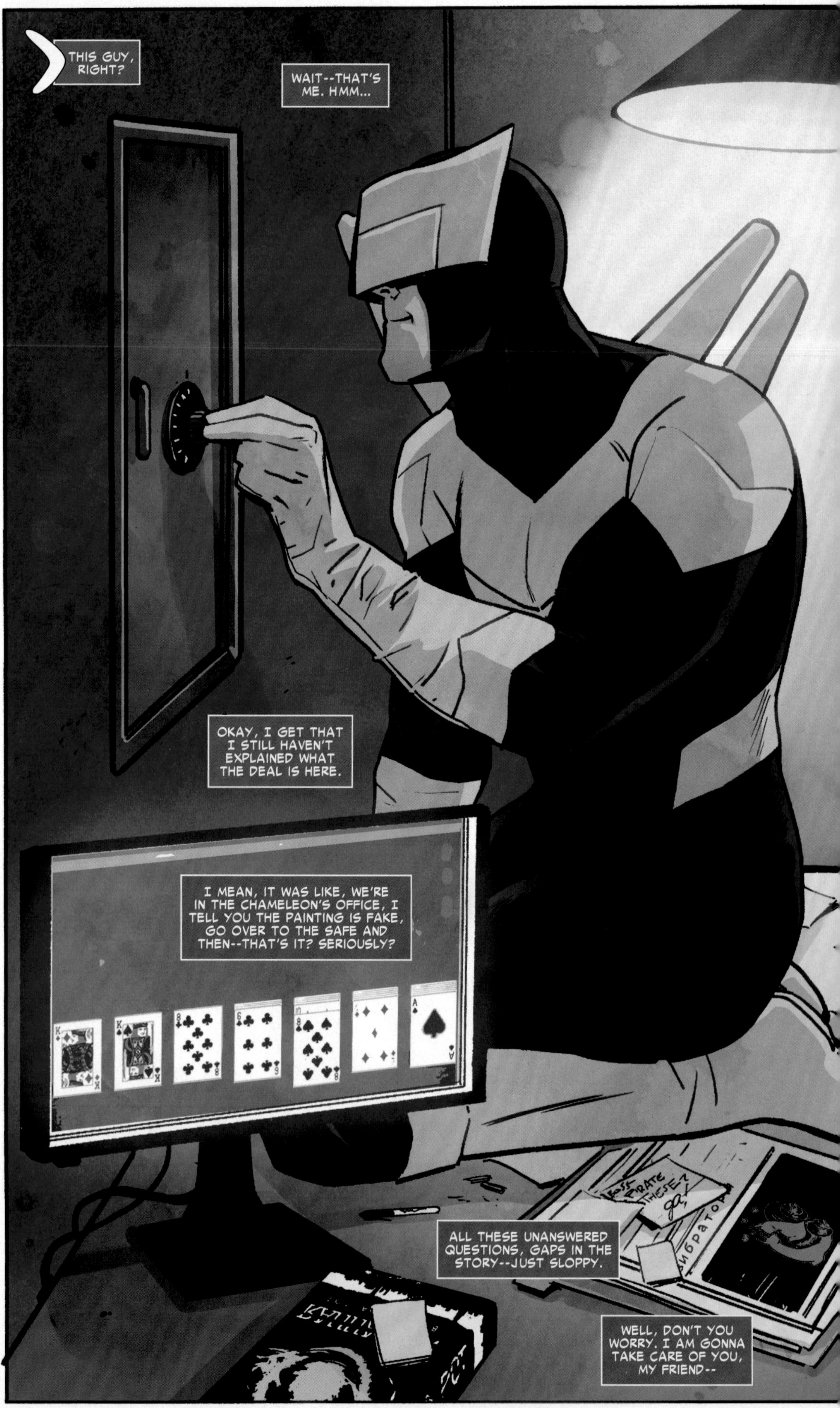
THIS GUY, RIGHT?
WAIT--THAT'S ME. HMM...
OKAY, I GET THAT I STILL HAVEN'T EXPLAINED WHAT THE DEAL IS HERE.
I MEAN, IT WAS LIKE, WE'RE IN THE CHAMELEON'S OFFICE, I TELL YOU THE PAINTING IS FAKE, GO OVER TO THE SAFE AND THEN--THAT'S IT? SERIOUSLY?
ALL THESE UNANSWERED QUESTIONS, GAPS IN THE STORY--JUST SLOPPY.
WELL, DON'T YOU WORRY. I AM GONNA TAKE CARE OF YOU, MY FRIEND--

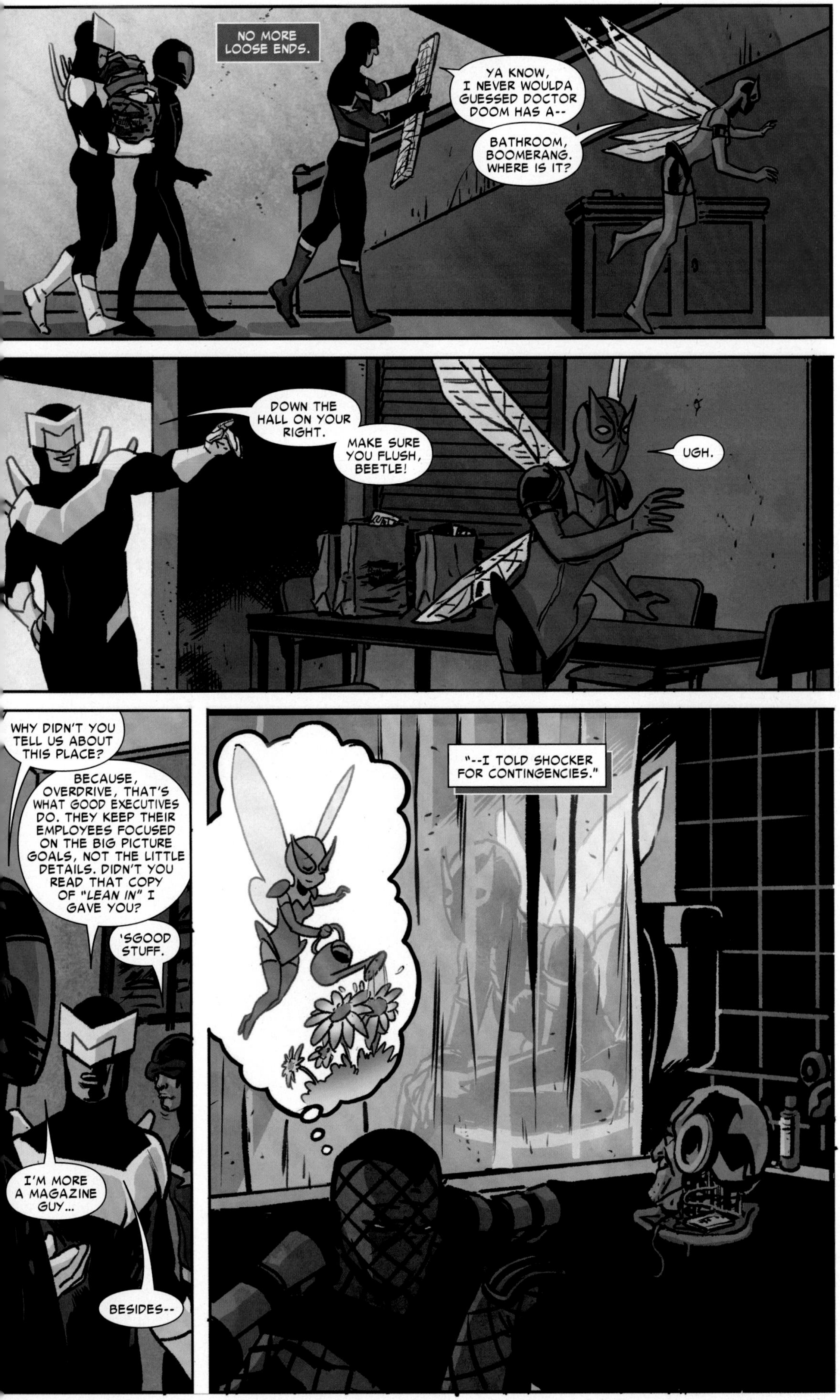
NO MORE LOOSE ENDS.
YA KNOW, I NEVER WOULDA GUESSED DOCTOR DOOM HAS A--
BATHROOM, BOOMERANG. WHERE IS IT?
DOWN THE HALL ON YOUR RIGHT.
MAKE SURE YOU FLUSH, BEETLE!
UGH.
WHY DIDN'T YOU TELL US ABOUT THIS PLACE?
BECAUSE, OVERDRIVE, THAT'S WHAT GOOD EXECUTIVES DO. THEY KEEP THEIR EMPLOYEES FOCUSED ON THE BIG PICTURE GOALS, NOT THE LITTLE DETAILS. DIDN'T YOU READ THAT COPY OF "LEAN IN" I GAVE YOU?
'SGOOD STUFF.
I'M MORE A MAGAZINE GUY...
BESIDES--
"--I TOLD SHOCKER FOR CONTINGENCIES."

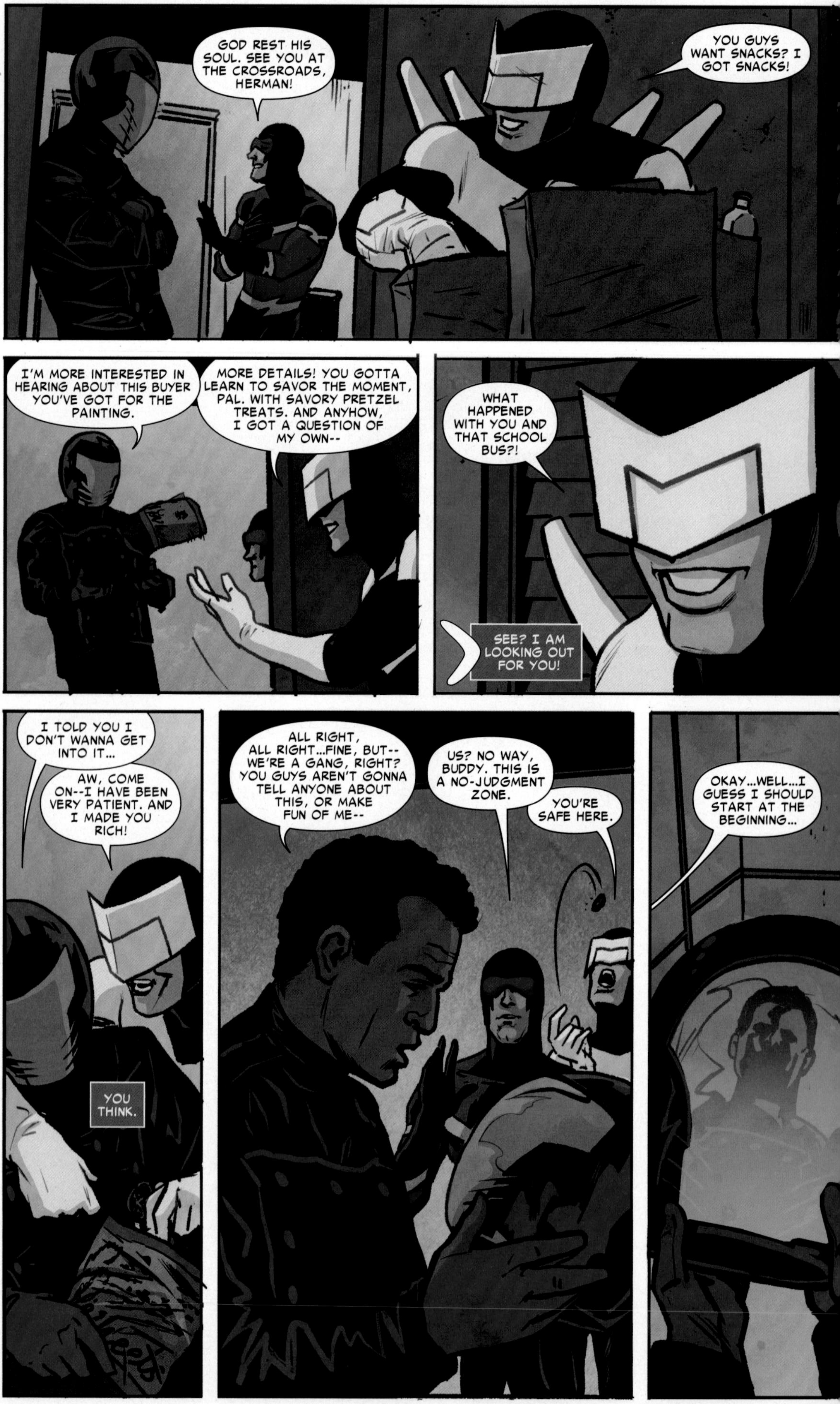
GOD REST HIS SOUL. SEE YOU AT THE CROSSROADS, HERMAN!
YOU GUYS WANT SNACKS? I GOT SNACKS!
I'M MORE INTERESTED IN HEARING ABOUT THIS BUYER YOU'VE GOT FOR THE PAINTING.
MORE DETAILS! YOU GOTTA LEARN TO SAVOR THE MOMENT, PAL. WITH SAVORY PRETZEL TREATS. AND ANYHOW, I GOT A QUESTION OF MY OWN--
WHAT HAPPENED WITH YOU AND THAT SCHOOL BUS?!
SEE? I AM LOOKING OUT FOR YOU!
I TOLD YOU I DON'T WANNA GET INTO IT...
AW, COME ON--I HAVE BEEN VERY PATIENT. AND I MADE YOU RICH!
YOU THINK.
ALL RIGHT, ALL RIGHT...FINE, BUT--WE'RE A GANG, RIGHT? YOU GUYS AREN'T GONNA TELL ANYONE ABOUT THIS, OR MAKE FUN OF ME--
US? NO WAY, BUDDY. THIS IS A NO-JUDGMENT ZONE.
YOU'RE SAFE HERE.
OKAY...WELL...I GUESS I SHOULD START AT THE BEGINNING...

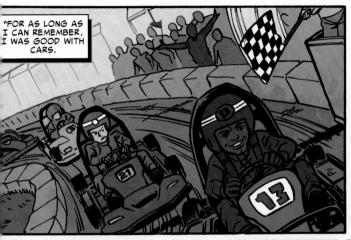

"FOR AS LONG AS I CAN REMEMBER, I WAS GOOD WITH CARS.
"MY OLD MAN WAS A MECHANIC, AND HE DREAMED OF ME GROWING UP TO BECOME A RACE CAR DRIVER. ME, ON THE OTHER HAND--
"I DREAMED OF BEING A *SUPER HERO!*
"I WAS A FAN OF ALL OF THEM--THE AVENGERS, THE FANTASTIC FOUR...
"BUT NONE OF THEM COMPARED TO MY NUMBER ONE GUY--THE AMAZING SPIDER-MAN!
SPIDEY BOOK
HERO OR MENACE?
DAILY BUGLE
"I WANTED TO BE JUST LIKE THOSE GUYS--FIGHTING CRIME, SAVING THE WORLD--ONLY PROBLEM WAS--
"NO POWERS, RIGHT?
"I TRIED EVERYTHING--
"SPIDER-BITES...
"MAIL ORDER MYSTERY SERUMS...
"NOTHING WORKED.
"EVEN TRIED BLASTING MYSELF WITH GAMMA RAYS--
BZAP
DANGER
"PUT ME IN THE BURN WARD FOR THREE MONTHS.

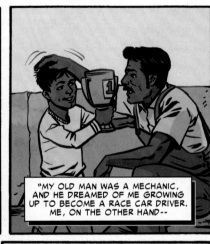

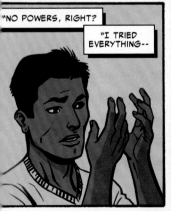

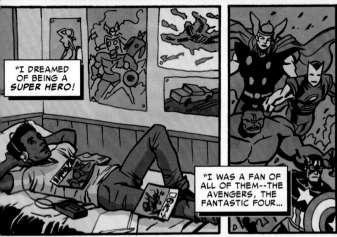

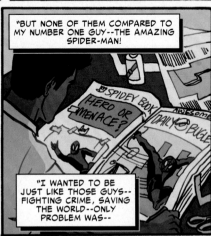

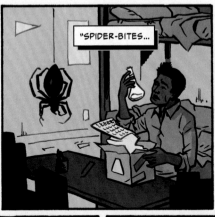

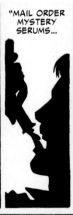

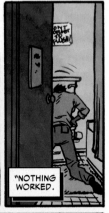

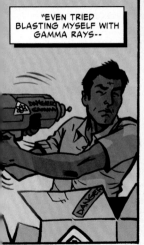

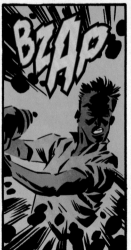

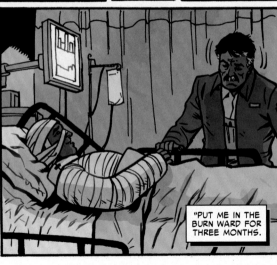

"EVENTUALLY, I THOUGHT I COULD AT LEAST BE ONE OF THOSE NON-POWERED COSTUMED GUYS, YOU KNOW, LIKE HAWKEYE? FIGURED IF I TRAINED HARD ENOUGH--

"BUT TURNS OUT I'M A LOVER, NOT A FIGHTER.

"SO, IN THE END, I WOUND UP EXACTLY WHERE POPS ALWAYS WANTED ME--

"ON THE CIRCUIT, RACING FOR HUNDRED DOLLAR PRIZES.

"AND I WAS ACTUALLY PRETTY GOOD AT IT, WON MY SHARE--

"'TIL A PILEUP PUT ME BACK IN THE BURN WARD FOR ANOTHER THREE MONTHS.

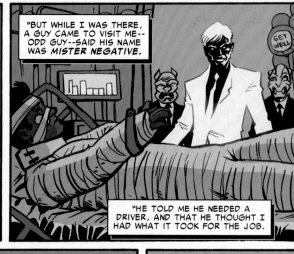
"BUT WHILE I WAS THERE, A GUY CAME TO VISIT ME-- ODD GUY--SAID HIS NAME WAS *MISTER NEGATIVE*.

"HE TOLD ME HE NEEDED A DRIVER, AND THAT HE THOUGHT I HAD WHAT IT TOOK FOR THE JOB.

"WHEN I POINTED OUT THE WHOLE FULL BODY CAST THING, HE TOLD ME WHY THIS WAS NO ORDINARY GIG.

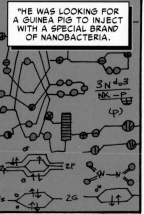
"HE WAS LOOKING FOR A GUINEA PIG TO INJECT WITH A SPECIAL BRAND OF NANOBACTERIA.

"THE NANITES WOULD ALLOW ME TO SUPERCHARGE ANY VEHICLE AT MY DISPOSAL, TAKE IT FROM ZERO TO 180 IN A SECOND.

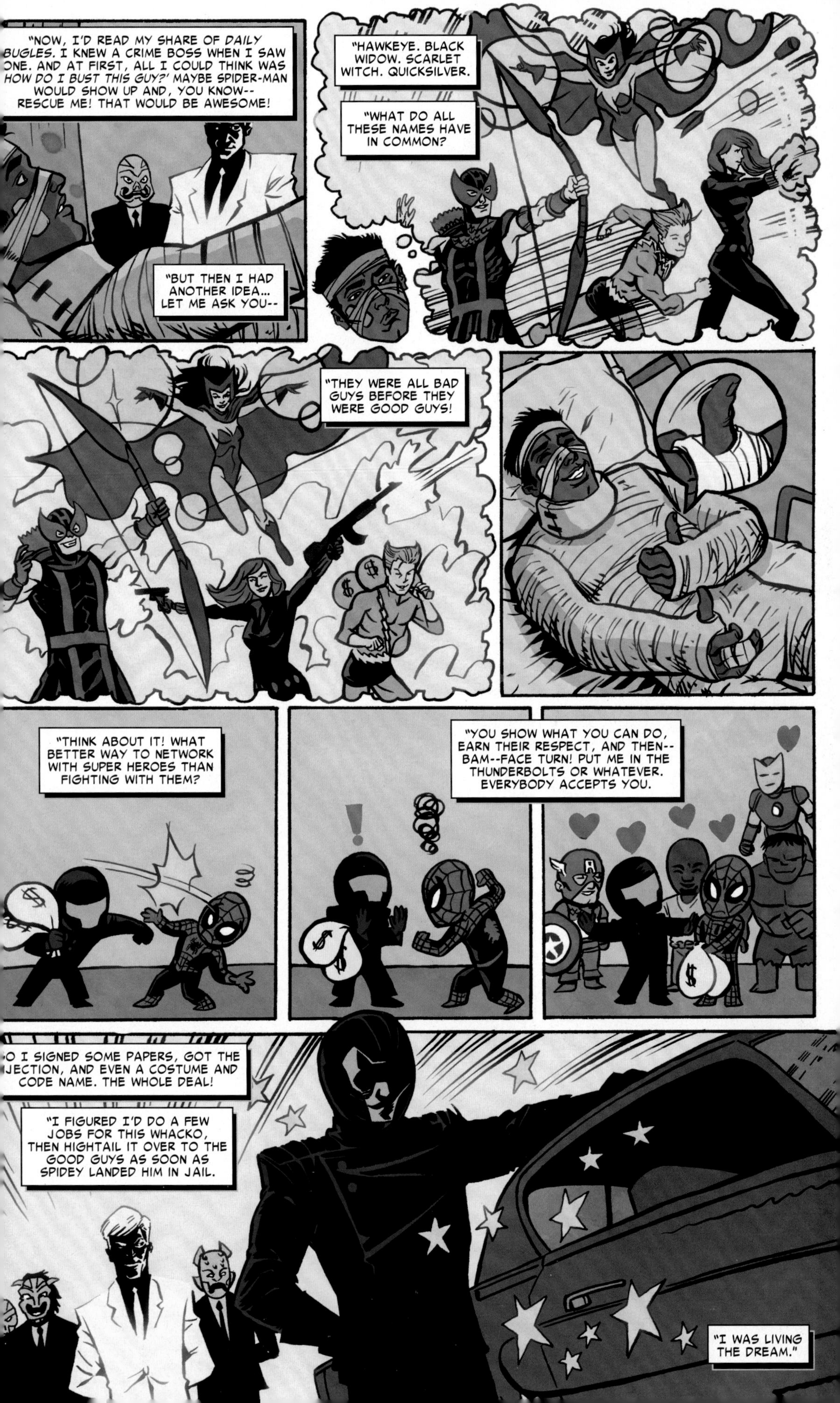
"NOW, I'D READ MY SHARE OF *DAILY BUGLES*. I KNEW A CRIME BOSS WHEN I SAW ONE. AND AT FIRST, ALL I COULD THINK WAS *HOW DO I BUST THIS GUY?'* MAYBE SPIDER-MAN WOULD SHOW UP AND, YOU KNOW-- RESCUE ME! THAT WOULD BE AWESOME!
"BUT THEN I HAD ANOTHER IDEA... LET ME ASK YOU--
"HAWKEYE. BLACK WIDOW. SCARLET WITCH. QUICKSILVER.
"WHAT DO ALL THESE NAMES HAVE IN COMMON?
"THEY WERE ALL BAD GUYS BEFORE THEY WERE GOOD GUYS!
"THINK ABOUT IT! WHAT BETTER WAY TO NETWORK WITH SUPER HEROES THAN FIGHTING WITH THEM?
"YOU SHOW WHAT YOU CAN DO, EARN THEIR RESPECT, AND THEN-- BAM--FACE TURN! PUT ME IN THE THUNDERBOLTS OR WHATEVER. EVERYBODY ACCEPTS YOU.
O I SIGNED SOME PAPERS, GOT THE JECTION, AND EVEN A COSTUME AND CODE NAME. THE WHOLE DEAL!
"I FIGURED I'D DO A FEW JOBS FOR THIS WHACKO, THEN HIGHTAIL IT OVER TO THE GOOD GUYS AS SOON AS SPIDEY LANDED HIM IN JAIL.
"I WAS LIVING THE DREAM."

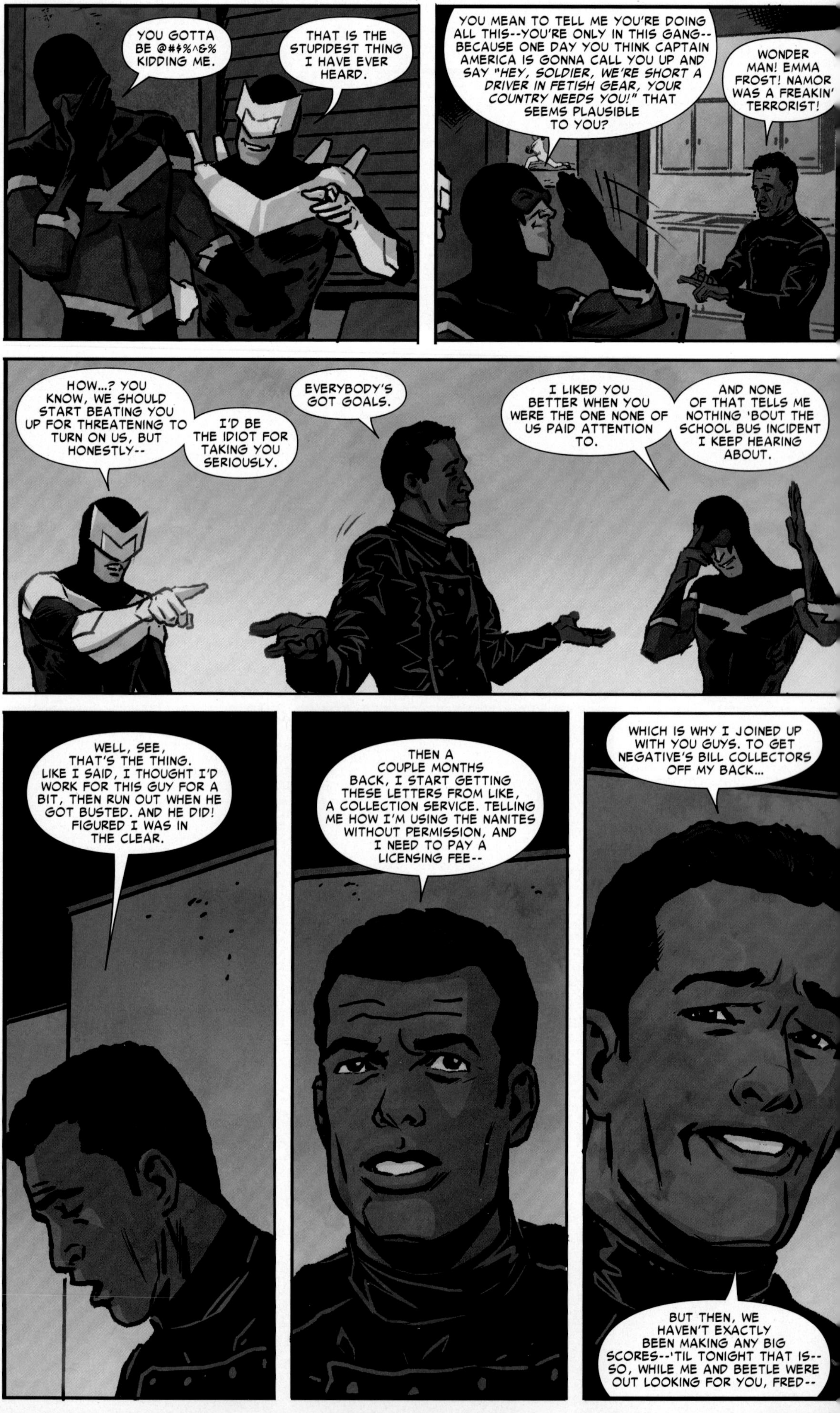
YOU GOTTA BE @#$%^&% KIDDING ME.
THAT IS THE STUPIDEST THING I HAVE EVER HEARD.
YOU MEAN TO TELL ME YOU'RE DOING ALL THIS--YOU'RE ONLY IN THIS GANG--BECAUSE ONE DAY YOU THINK CAPTAIN AMERICA IS GONNA CALL YOU UP AND SAY "HEY, SOLDIER, WE'RE SHORT A DRIVER IN FETISH GEAR, YOUR COUNTRY NEEDS YOU!" THAT SEEMS PLAUSIBLE TO YOU?
WONDER MAN! EMMA FROST! NAMOR WAS A FREAKIN' TERRORIST!
HOW...? YOU KNOW, WE SHOULD START BEATING YOU UP FOR THREATENING TO TURN ON US, BUT HONESTLY--
I'D BE THE IDIOT FOR TAKING YOU SERIOUSLY.
EVERYBODY'S GOT GOALS.
I LIKED YOU BETTER WHEN YOU WERE THE ONE NONE OF US PAID ATTENTION TO.
AND NONE OF THAT TELLS ME NOTHING 'BOUT THE SCHOOL BUS INCIDENT I KEEP HEARING ABOUT.
WELL, SEE, THAT'S THE THING. LIKE I SAID, I THOUGHT I'D WORK FOR THIS GUY FOR A BIT, THEN RUN OUT WHEN HE GOT BUSTED. AND HE DID! FIGURED I WAS IN THE CLEAR.
THEN A COUPLE MONTHS BACK, I START GETTING THESE LETTERS FROM LIKE, A COLLECTION SERVICE. TELLING ME HOW I'M USING THE NANITES WITHOUT PERMISSION, AND I NEED TO PAY A LICENSING FEE--
WHICH IS WHY I JOINED UP WITH YOU GUYS. TO GET NEGATIVE'S BILL COLLECTORS OFF MY BACK...
BUT THEN, WE HAVEN'T EXACTLY BEEN MAKING ANY BIG SCORES--'TIL TONIGHT THAT IS--SO, WHILE ME AND BEETLE WERE OUT LOOKING FOR YOU, FRED--

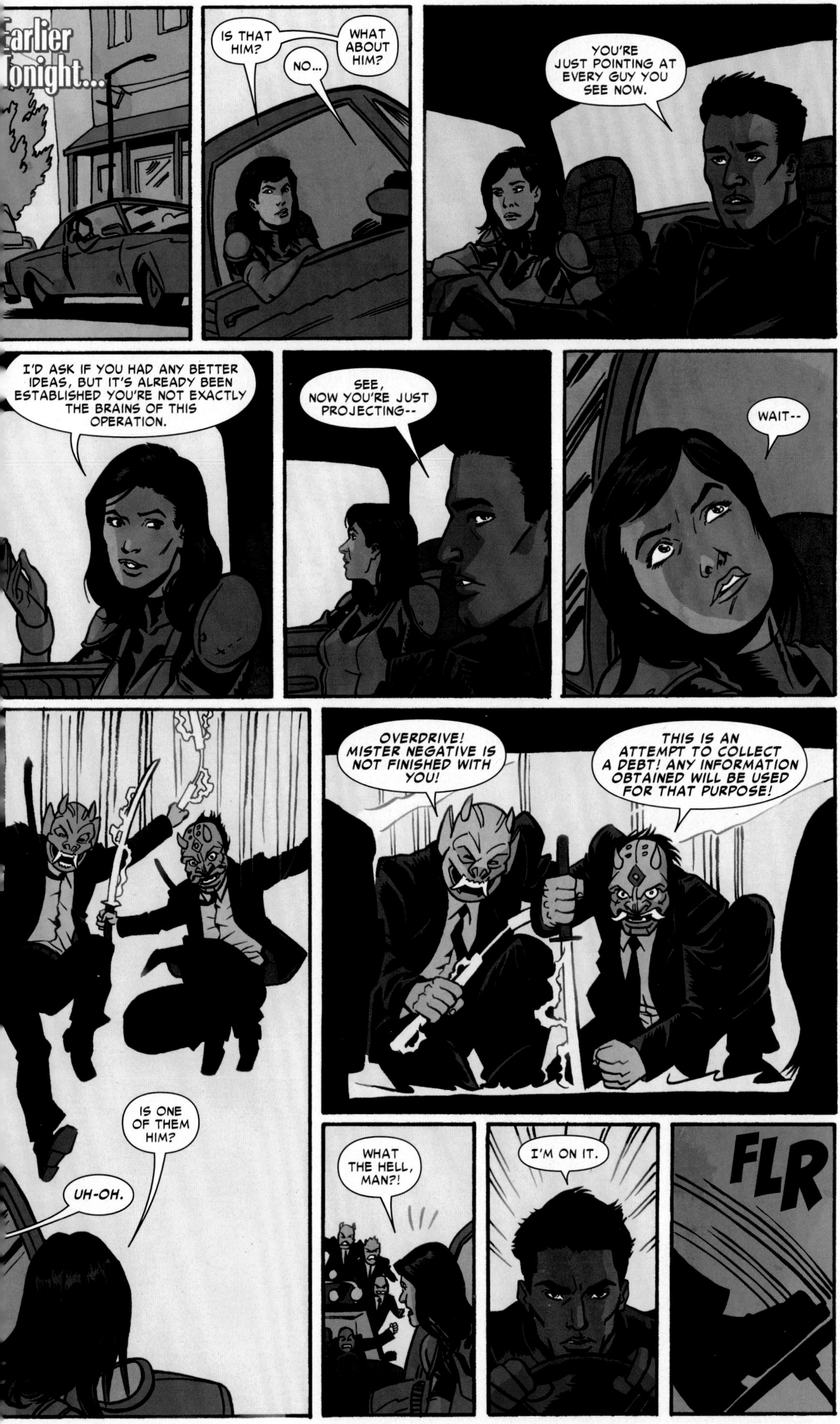
Earlier Tonight...
IS THAT HIM?
WHAT ABOUT HIM?
NO...
YOU'RE JUST POINTING AT EVERY GUY YOU SEE NOW.
I'D ASK IF YOU HAD ANY BETTER IDEAS, BUT IT'S ALREADY BEEN ESTABLISHED YOU'RE NOT EXACTLY THE BRAINS OF THIS OPERATION.
SEE, NOW YOU'RE JUST PROJECTING--
WAIT--
IS ONE OF THEM HIM?
UH-OH.
OVERDRIVE! MISTER NEGATIVE IS NOT FINISHED WITH YOU!
THIS IS AN ATTEMPT TO COLLECT A DEBT! ANY INFORMATION OBTAINED WILL BE USED FOR THAT PURPOSE!
WHAT THE HELL, MAN?!
I'M ON IT.
FLR

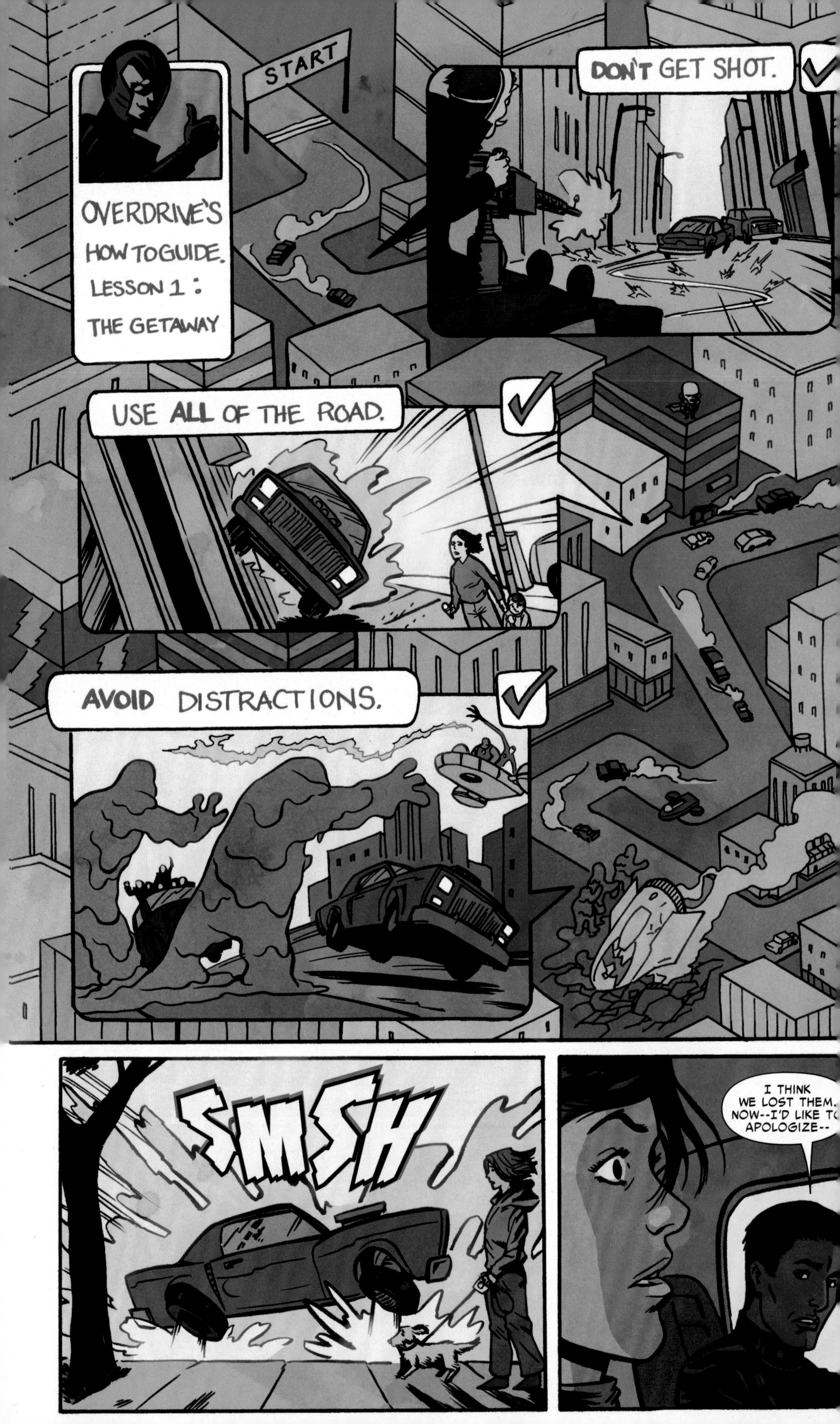

START
OVERDRIVE'S HOW TO GUIDE. LESSON 1: THE GETAWAY
DON'T GET SHOT.
USE ALL OF THE ROAD.
AVOID DISTRACTIONS.
SMSH
I THINK WE LOST THEM. NOW--I'D LIKE TO APOLOGIZE--

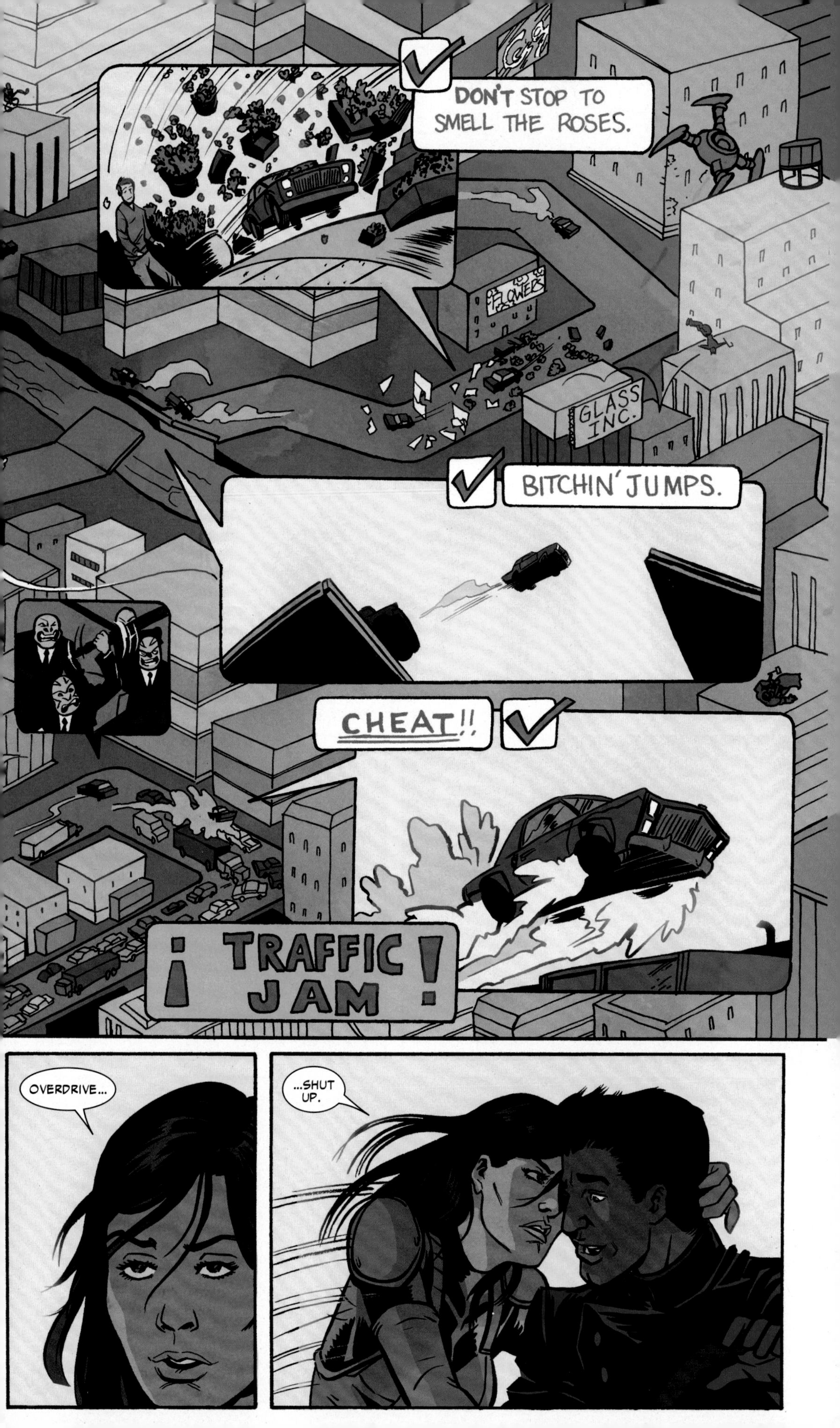
DON'T STOP TO SMELL THE ROSES.
FLOWERS
GLASS INC.
BITCHIN' JUMPS.
CHEAT!!
¡ TRAFFIC JAM !
OVERDRIVE...
...SHUT UP.

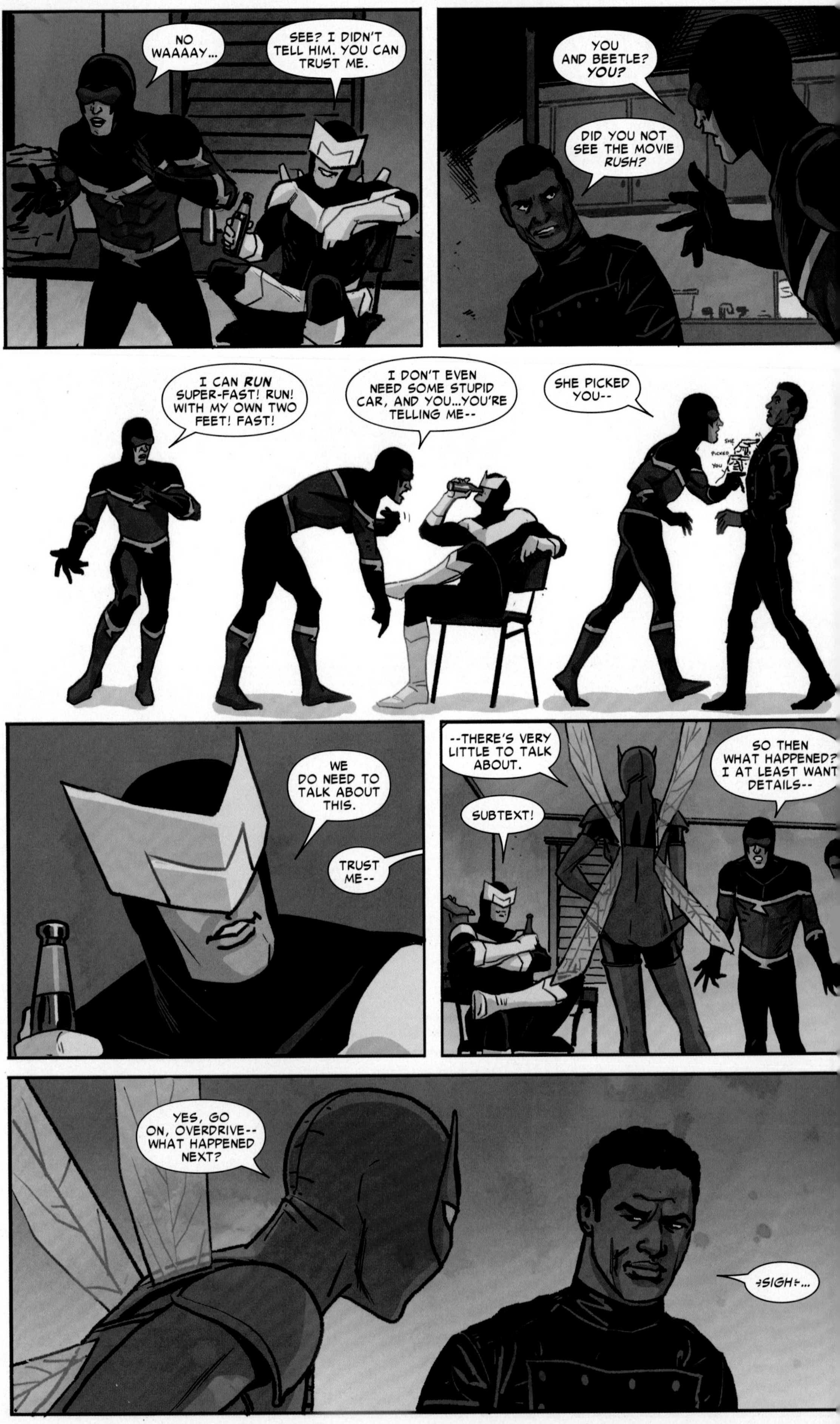
NO WAAAAY...
SEE? I DIDN'T TELL HIM. YOU CAN TRUST ME.
YOU AND BEETLE? *YOU?*
DID YOU NOT SEE THE MOVIE *RUSH?*
I CAN **RUN** SUPER-FAST! RUN! WITH MY OWN TWO FEET! FAST!
I DON'T EVEN NEED SOME STUPID CAR, AND YOU...YOU'RE TELLING ME--
SHE PICKED YOU--
WE DO NEED TO TALK ABOUT THIS.
TRUST ME--
--THERE'S VERY LITTLE TO TALK ABOUT.
SUBTEXT!
SO THEN WHAT HAPPENED? I AT LEAST WANT DETAILS--
YES, GO ON, OVERDRIVE-- WHAT HAPPENED NEXT?
SIGH...

SO, UH, YOU KNOW, IF YOU WANTED, WE COULD GET DINNER SOMETIME--

I'M VERY BUSY.

WELL, AT LEAST WE LOST THE--

AWDANG.

THEY'RE BACK?!

I'M SORRY! LOOK, I CAN LOSE THEM AGAIN, JUST GOTTA--

WELL--GO ON, THEN! MAKE THE CAR--WHATEVER IT IS YOU DO TO THE CAR! MAKE IT PURPLE AND FAST!

I CAN'T!

RUNCHCHCHBRNCHPUKPKCHKTTKPKTPHKTCKT...

WHAT DO YOU MEAN, YOU CAN'T?

OKAY, LOOK, I DON'T REALLY KNOW HOW NANO-BACTERIA WORKS, BUT--IT SEEMS LIKE, AFTER I, UM--EXERT MYSELF, I CAN'T--YOU KNOW--

I JUST NEED A FEW MINUTES, I SWEAR!

ARE YOU SERIOUS?!

TO HELL WITH THIS!

RUN!

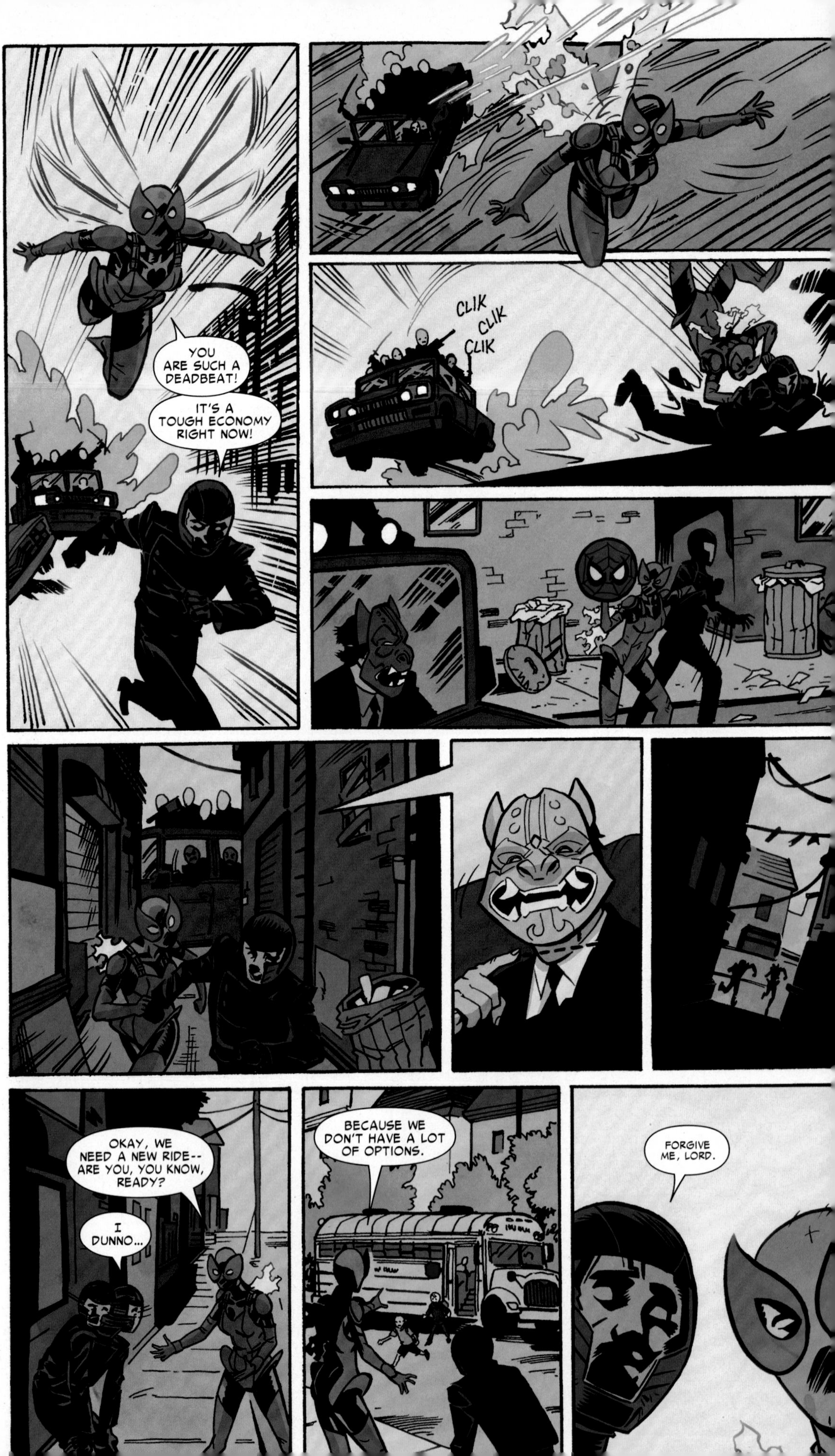
YOU ARE SUCH A DEADBEAT!
IT'S A TOUGH ECONOMY RIGHT NOW!
CLIK
CLIK
CLIK
OKAY, WE NEED A NEW RIDE-- ARE YOU, YOU KNOW, READY?
I DUNNO...
BECAUSE WE DON'T HAVE A LOT OF OPTIONS.
FORGIVE ME, LORD.

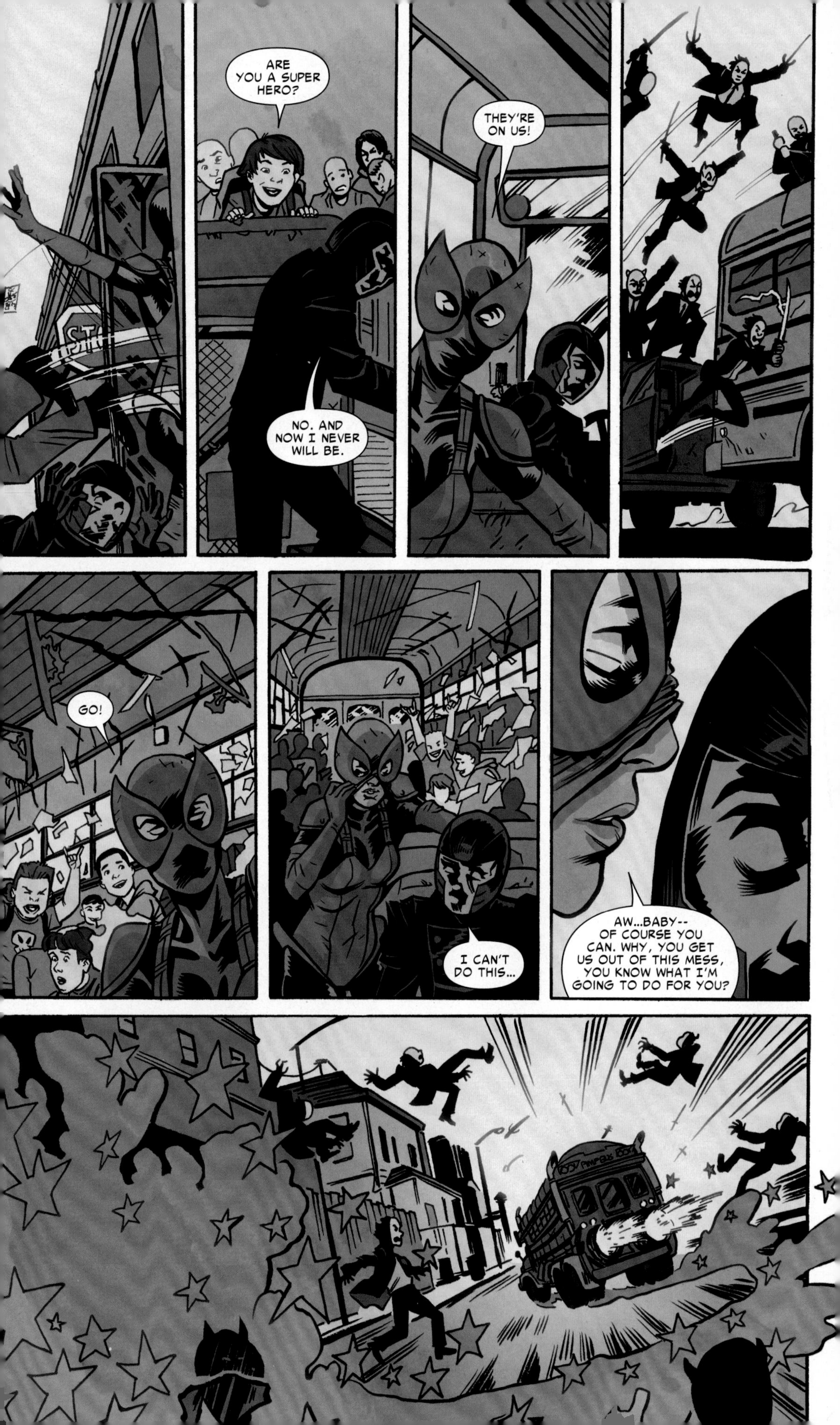
ARE YOU A SUPER HERO?
NO. AND NOW I NEVER WILL BE.
THEY'RE ON US!
GO!
I CAN'T DO THIS...
AW...BABY-- OF COURSE YOU CAN. WHY, YOU GET US OUT OF THIS MESS, YOU KNOW WHAT I'M GOING TO DO FOR YOU?

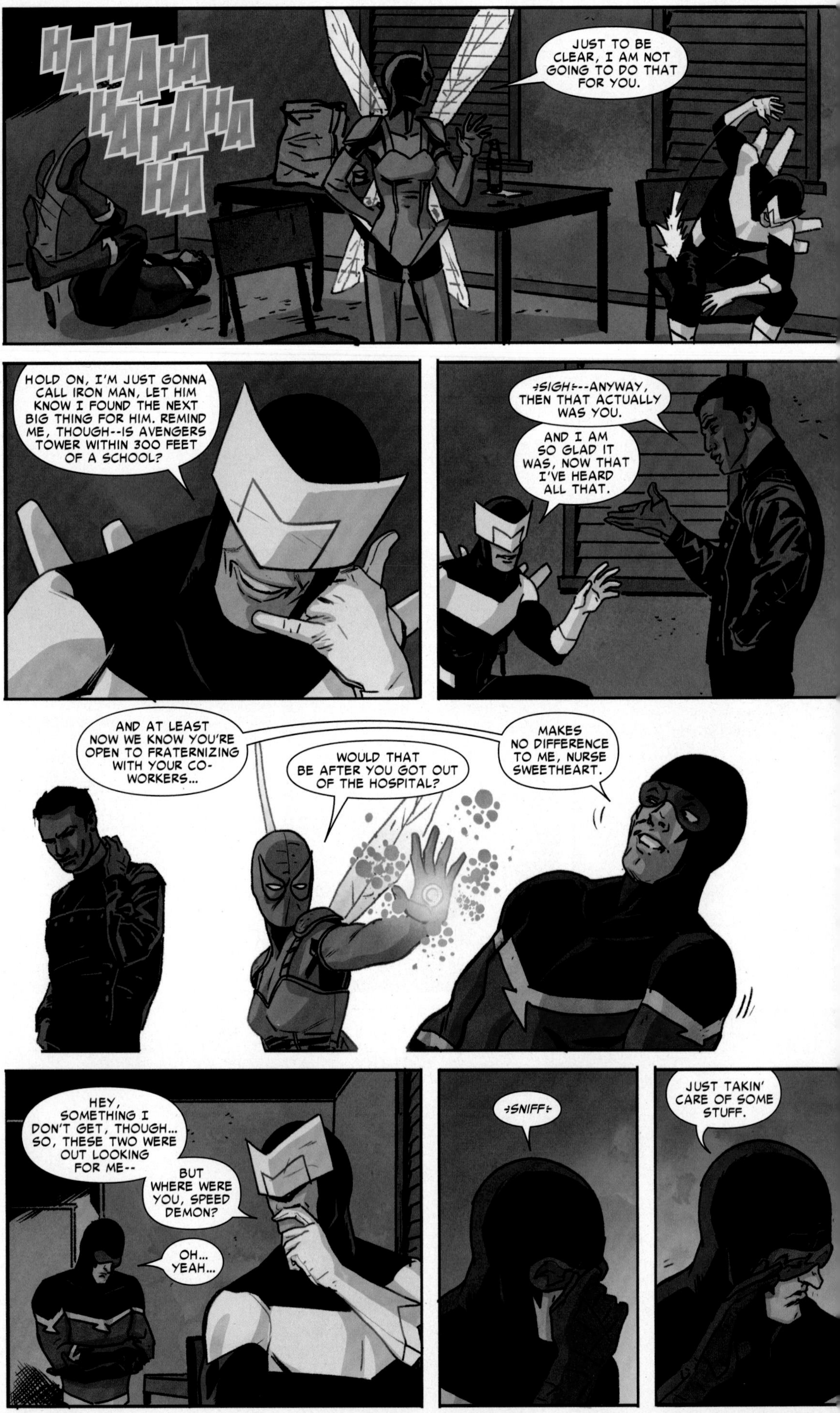
HAHAHA HAHAHAHA HA
JUST TO BE CLEAR, I AM NOT GOING TO DO THAT FOR YOU.
HOLD ON, I'M JUST GONNA CALL IRON MAN, LET HIM KNOW I FOUND THE NEXT BIG THING FOR HIM. REMIND ME, THOUGH--IS AVENGERS TOWER WITHIN 300 FEET OF A SCHOOL?
⇣SIGH⇣--ANYWAY, THEN THAT ACTUALLY WAS YOU.
AND I AM SO GLAD IT WAS, NOW THAT I'VE HEARD ALL THAT.
AND AT LEAST NOW WE KNOW YOU'RE OPEN TO FRATERNIZING WITH YOUR CO-WORKERS...
WOULD THAT BE AFTER YOU GOT OUT OF THE HOSPITAL?
MAKES NO DIFFERENCE TO ME, NURSE SWEETHEART.
HEY, SOMETHING I DON'T GET, THOUGH... SO, THESE TWO WERE OUT LOOKING FOR ME--
BUT WHERE WERE YOU, SPEED DEMON?
OH... YEAH...
⇣SNIFF⇣
JUST TAKIN' CARE OF SOME STUFF.

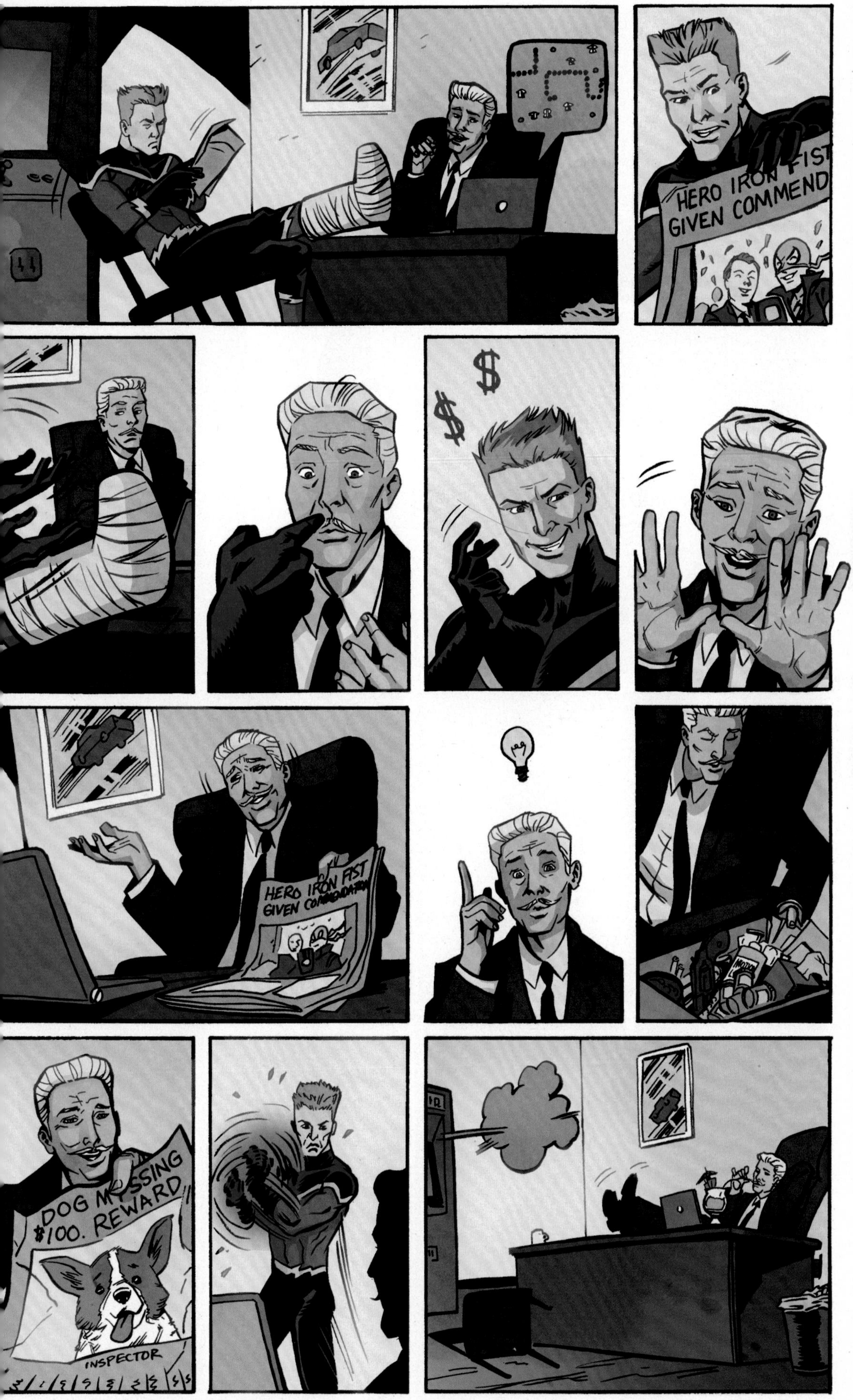
HERO IRON FIST
GIVEN COMMEND
$
$
HERO IRON FIST
GIVEN
DOG MISSING
$100. REWARD
INSPECTOR

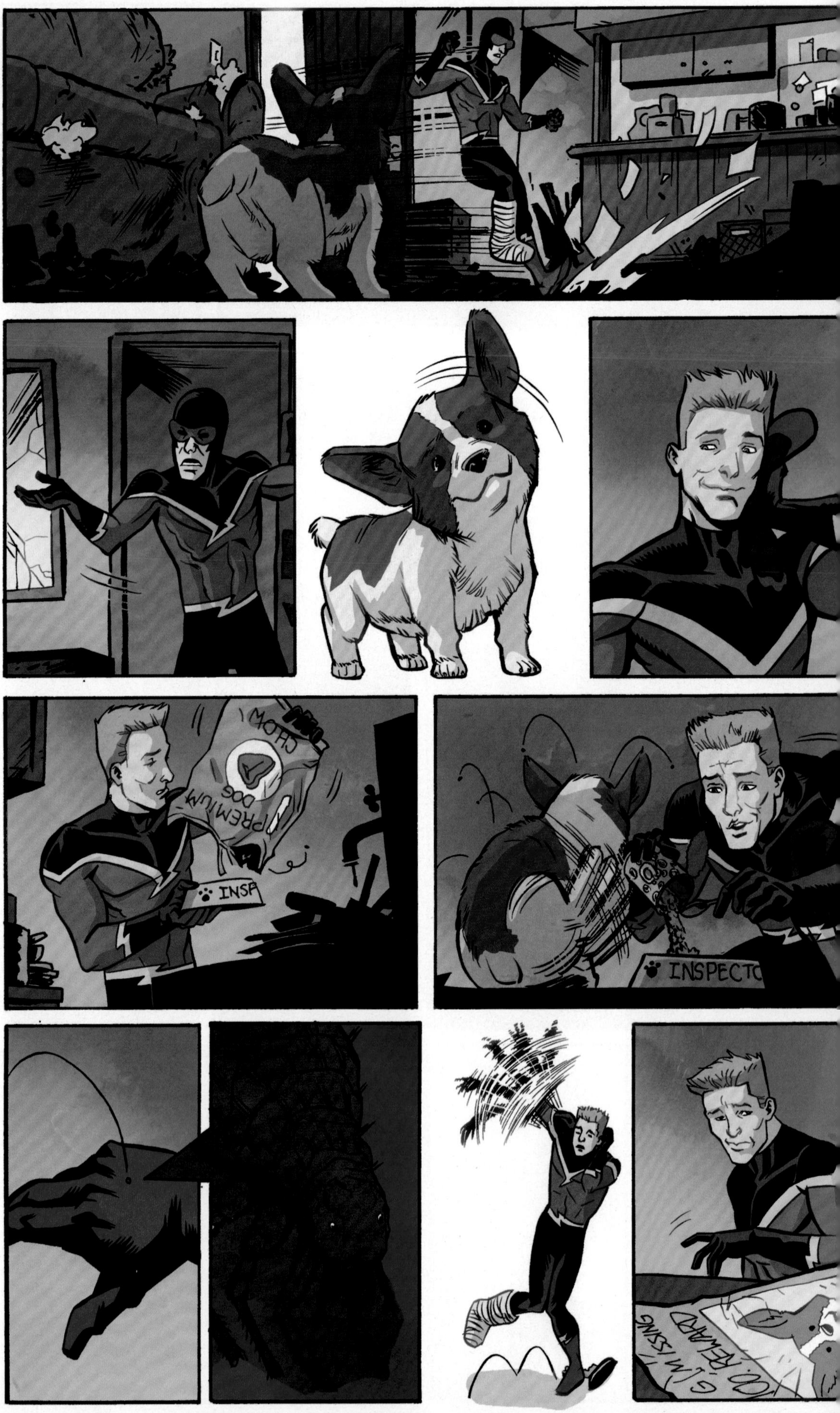
CHOW
PREMIUM
DOG
INSP
INSPECTO

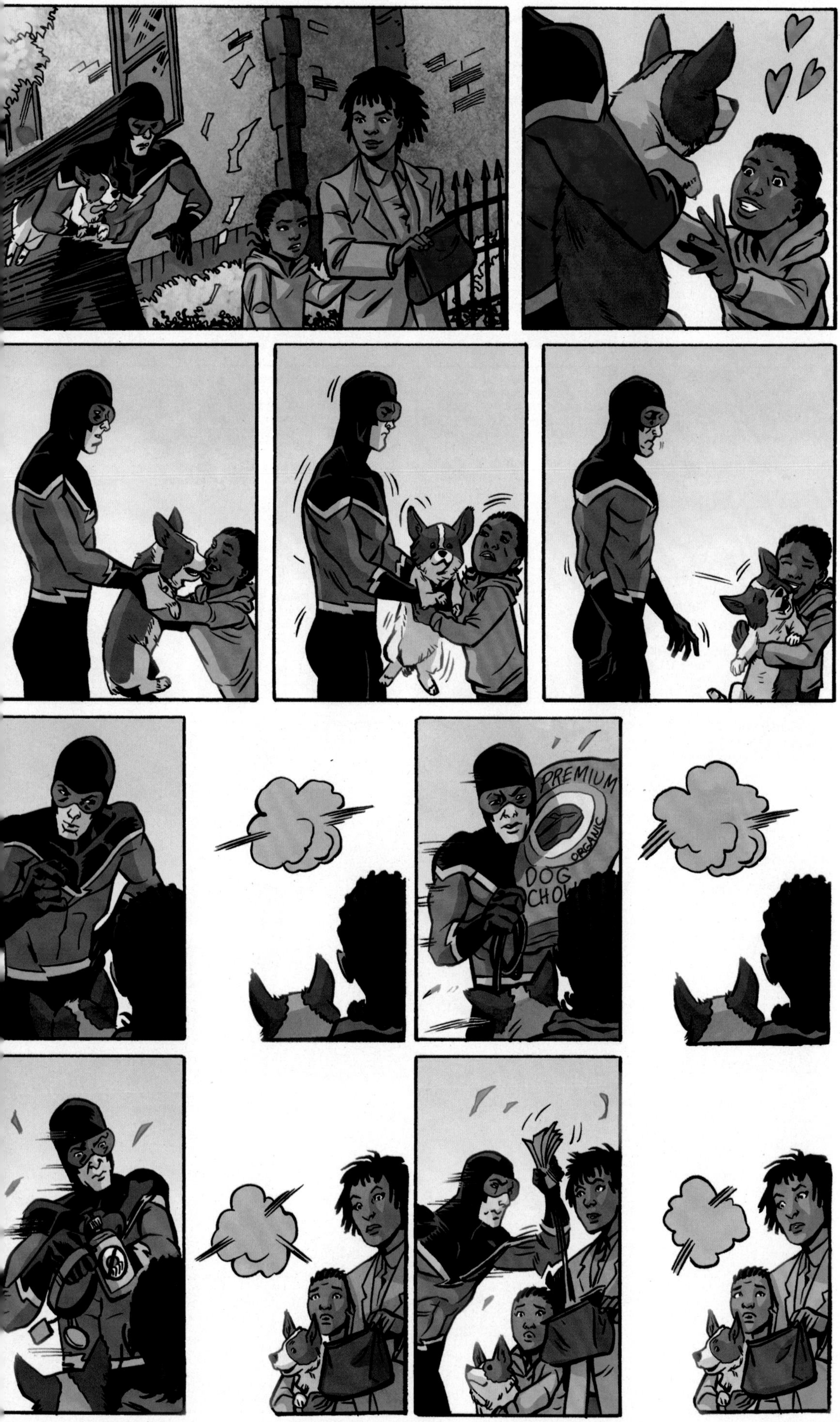
PREMIUM
ORGANIC
DOG CHOW

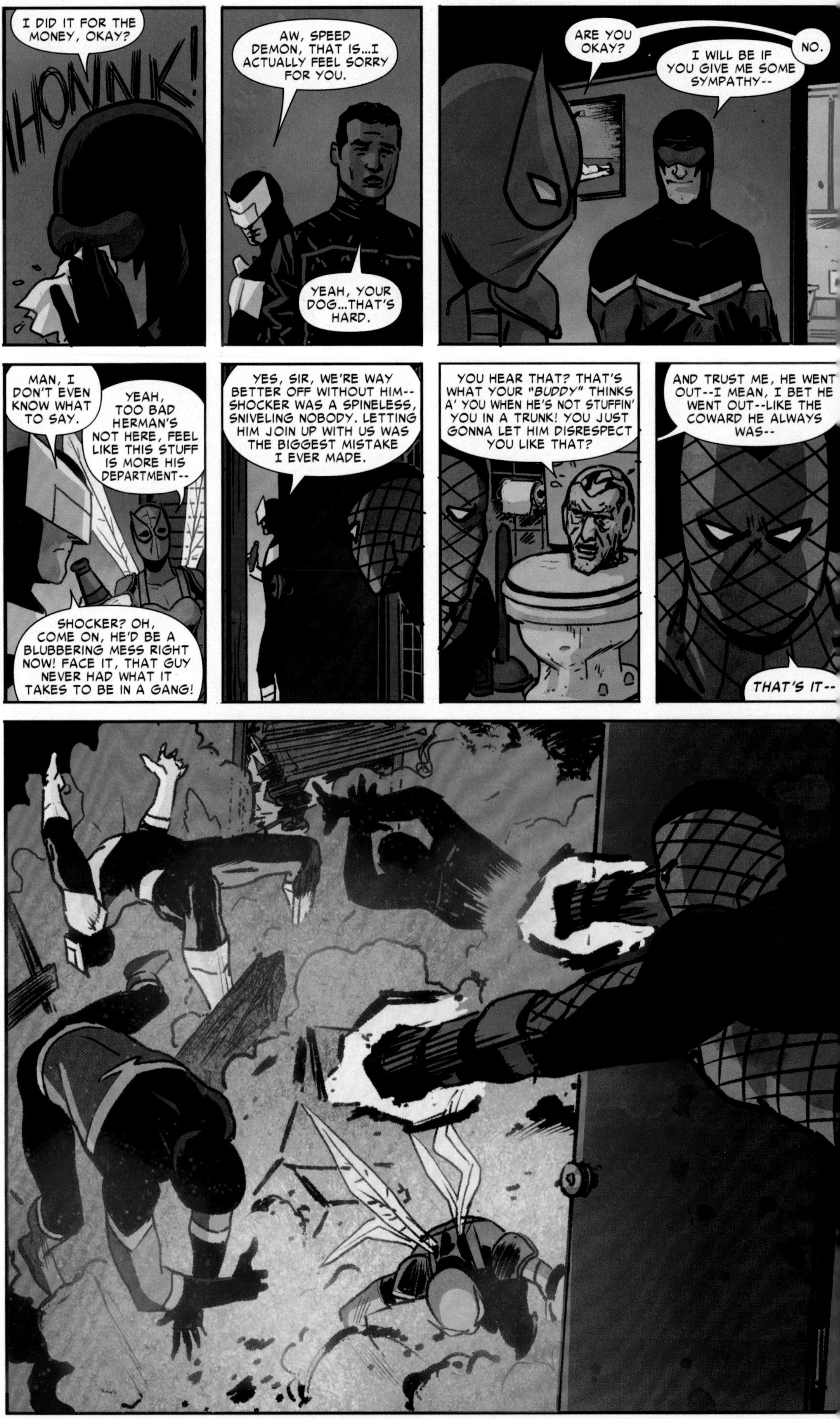
I DID IT FOR THE MONEY, OKAY?
HONNK!
AW, SPEED DEMON, THAT IS...I ACTUALLY FEEL SORRY FOR YOU.
YEAH, YOUR DOG...THAT'S HARD.
ARE YOU OKAY?
NO.
I WILL BE IF YOU GIVE ME SOME SYMPATHY--
MAN, I DON'T EVEN KNOW WHAT TO SAY.
YEAH, TOO BAD HERMAN'S NOT HERE, FEEL LIKE THIS STUFF IS MORE HIS DEPARTMENT--
SHOCKER? OH, COME ON, HE'D BE A BLUBBERING MESS RIGHT NOW! FACE IT, THAT GUY NEVER HAD WHAT IT TAKES TO BE IN A GANG!
YES, SIR, WE'RE WAY BETTER OFF WITHOUT HIM--SHOCKER WAS A SPINELESS, SNIVELING NOBODY. LETTING HIM JOIN UP WITH US WAS THE BIGGEST MISTAKE I EVER MADE.
YOU HEAR THAT? THAT'S WHAT YOUR "BUDDY" THINKS A' YOU WHEN HE'S NOT STUFFIN' YOU IN A TRUNK! YOU JUST GONNA LET HIM DISRESPECT YOU LIKE THAT?
AND TRUST ME, HE WENT OUT--I MEAN, I BET HE WENT OUT--LIKE THE COWARD HE ALWAYS WAS--
THAT'S IT--

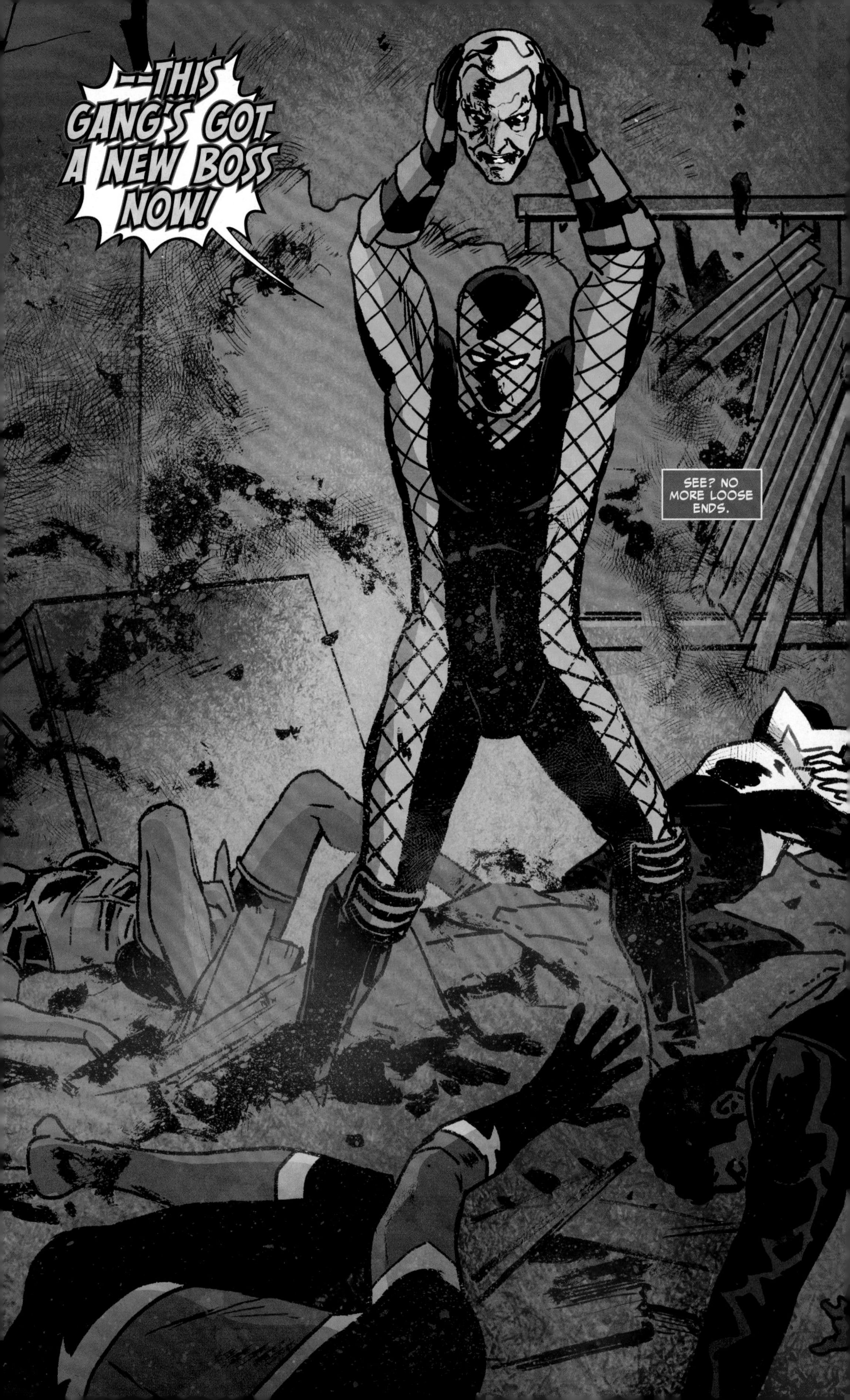
--THIS GANG'S GOT A NEW BOSS NOW!
SEE? NO MORE LOOSE ENDS.

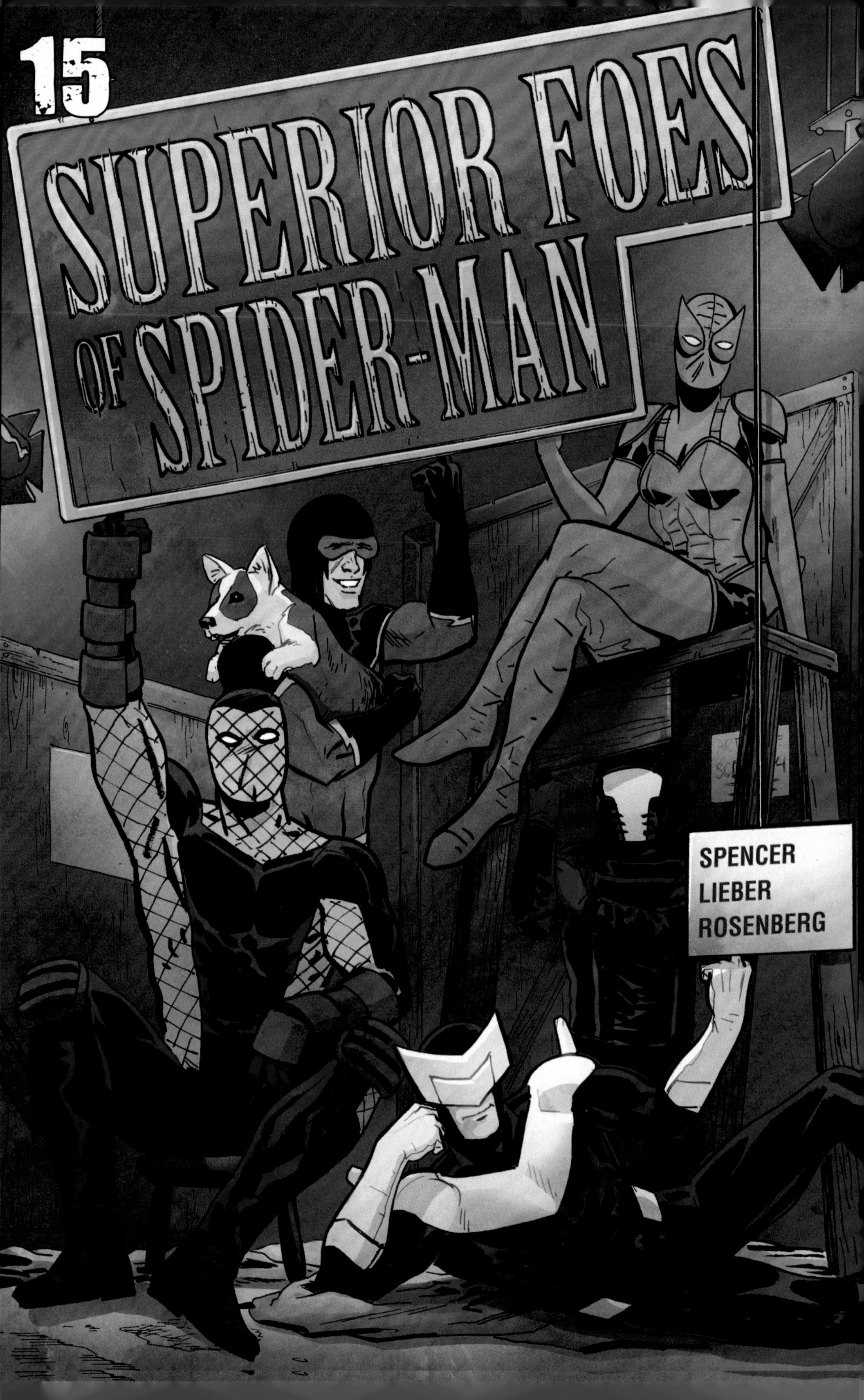
15
SUPERIOR FOES OF SPIDER-MAN
SPENCER
LIEBER
ROSENBERG

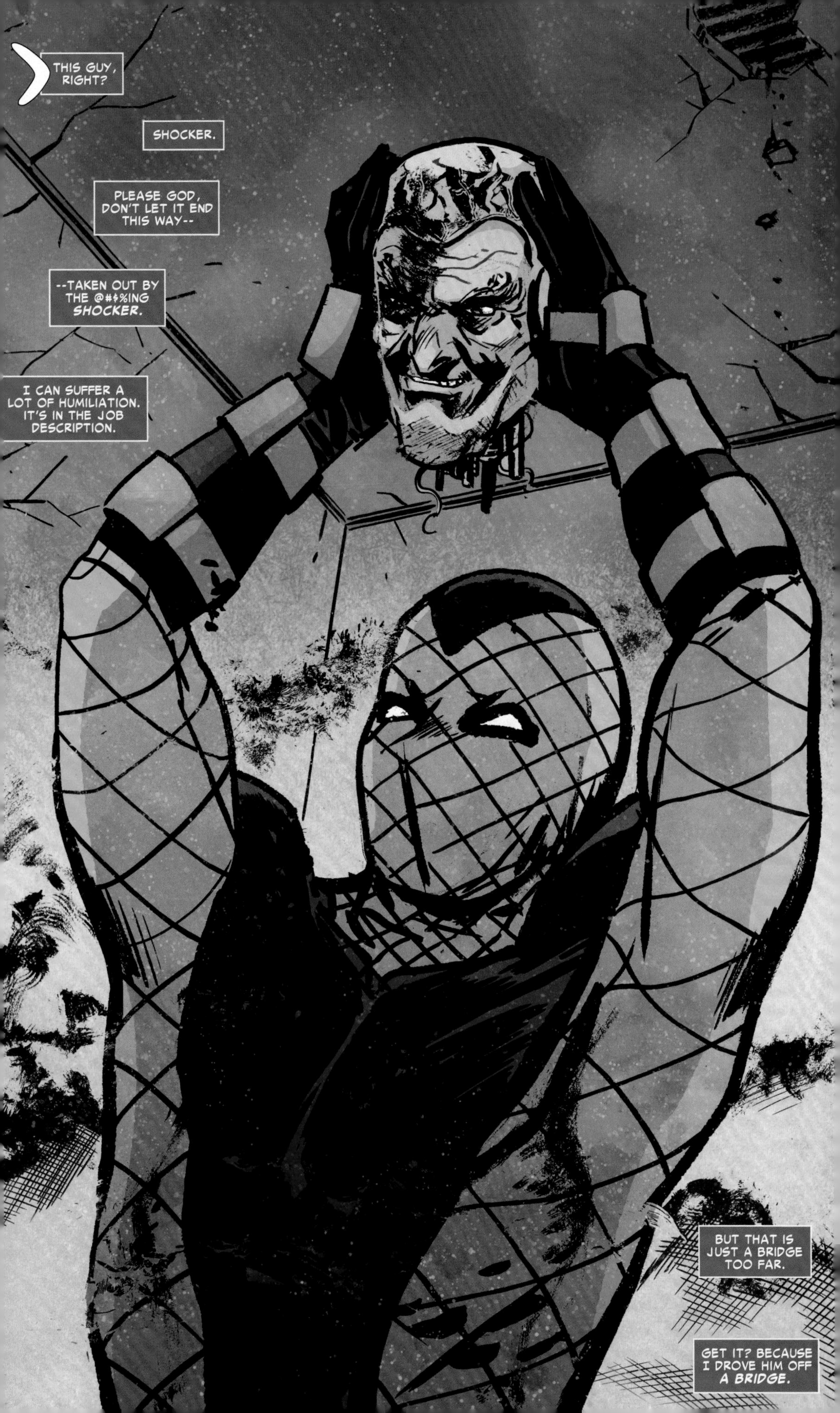
THIS GUY, RIGHT?
SHOCKER.
PLEASE GOD, DON'T LET IT END THIS WAY--
--TAKEN OUT BY THE @#$%ING *SHOCKER*.
I CAN SUFFER A LOT OF HUMILIATION. IT'S IN THE JOB DESCRIPTION.
BUT THAT IS JUST A BRIDGE TOO FAR.
GET IT? BECAUSE I DROVE HIM OFF *A BRIDGE*.

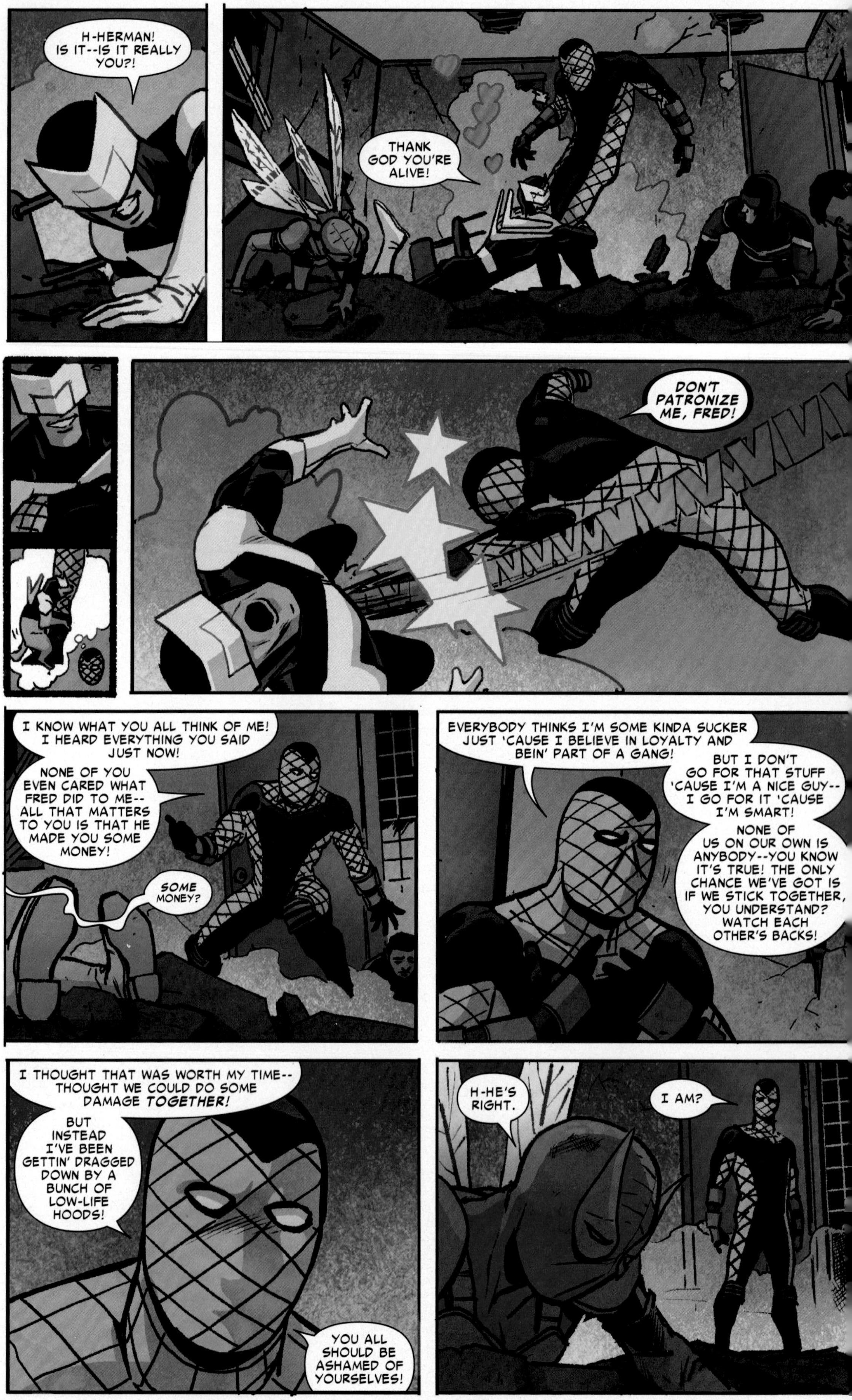
H-HERMAN! IS IT--IS IT REALLY YOU?!
THANK GOD YOU'RE ALIVE!
DON'T PATRONIZE ME, FRED!
I KNOW WHAT YOU ALL THINK OF ME! I HEARD EVERYTHING YOU SAID JUST NOW!
NONE OF YOU EVEN CARED WHAT FRED DID TO ME--ALL THAT MATTERS TO YOU IS THAT HE MADE YOU SOME MONEY!
SOME MONEY?
EVERYBODY THINKS I'M SOME KINDA SUCKER JUST 'CAUSE I BELIEVE IN LOYALTY AND BEIN' PART OF A GANG!
BUT I DON'T GO FOR THAT STUFF 'CAUSE I'M A NICE GUY--I GO FOR IT 'CAUSE I'M SMART!
NONE OF US ON OUR OWN IS ANYBODY--YOU KNOW IT'S TRUE! THE ONLY CHANCE WE'VE GOT IS IF WE STICK TOGETHER, YOU UNDERSTAND? WATCH EACH OTHER'S BACKS!
I THOUGHT THAT WAS WORTH MY TIME--THOUGHT WE COULD DO SOME DAMAGE *TOGETHER!*
BUT INSTEAD I'VE BEEN GETTIN' DRAGGED DOWN BY A BUNCH OF LOW-LIFE HOODS!
YOU ALL SHOULD BE ASHAMED OF YOURSELVES!
H-HE'S RIGHT.
I AM?

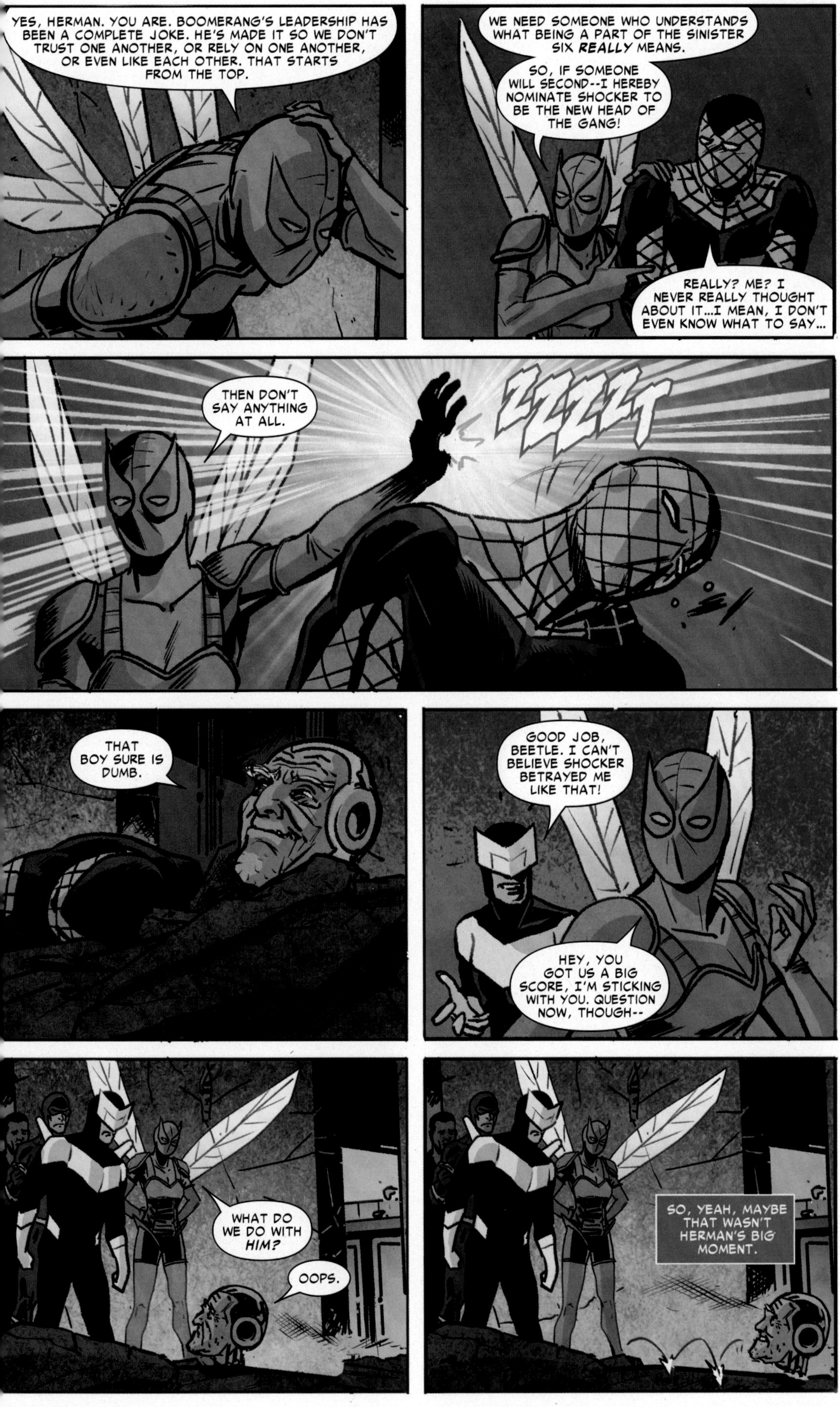
YES, HERMAN. YOU ARE. BOOMERANG'S LEADERSHIP HAS BEEN A COMPLETE JOKE. HE'S MADE IT SO WE DON'T TRUST ONE ANOTHER, OR RELY ON ONE ANOTHER, OR EVEN LIKE EACH OTHER. THAT STARTS FROM THE TOP.
WE NEED SOMEONE WHO UNDERSTANDS WHAT BEING A PART OF THE SINISTER SIX *REALLY* MEANS.
SO, IF SOMEONE WILL SECOND--I HEREBY NOMINATE SHOCKER TO BE THE NEW HEAD OF THE GANG!
REALLY? ME? I NEVER REALLY THOUGHT ABOUT IT...I MEAN, I DON'T EVEN KNOW WHAT TO SAY...
THEN DON'T SAY ANYTHING AT ALL.
ZZZZZT
THAT BOY SURE IS DUMB.
GOOD JOB, BEETLE. I CAN'T BELIEVE SHOCKER BETRAYED ME LIKE THAT!
HEY, YOU GOT US A BIG SCORE, I'M STICKING WITH YOU. QUESTION NOW, THOUGH--
WHAT DO WE DO WITH *HIM?*
OOPS.
SO, YEAH, MAYBE THAT WASN'T HERMAN'S BIG MOMENT.

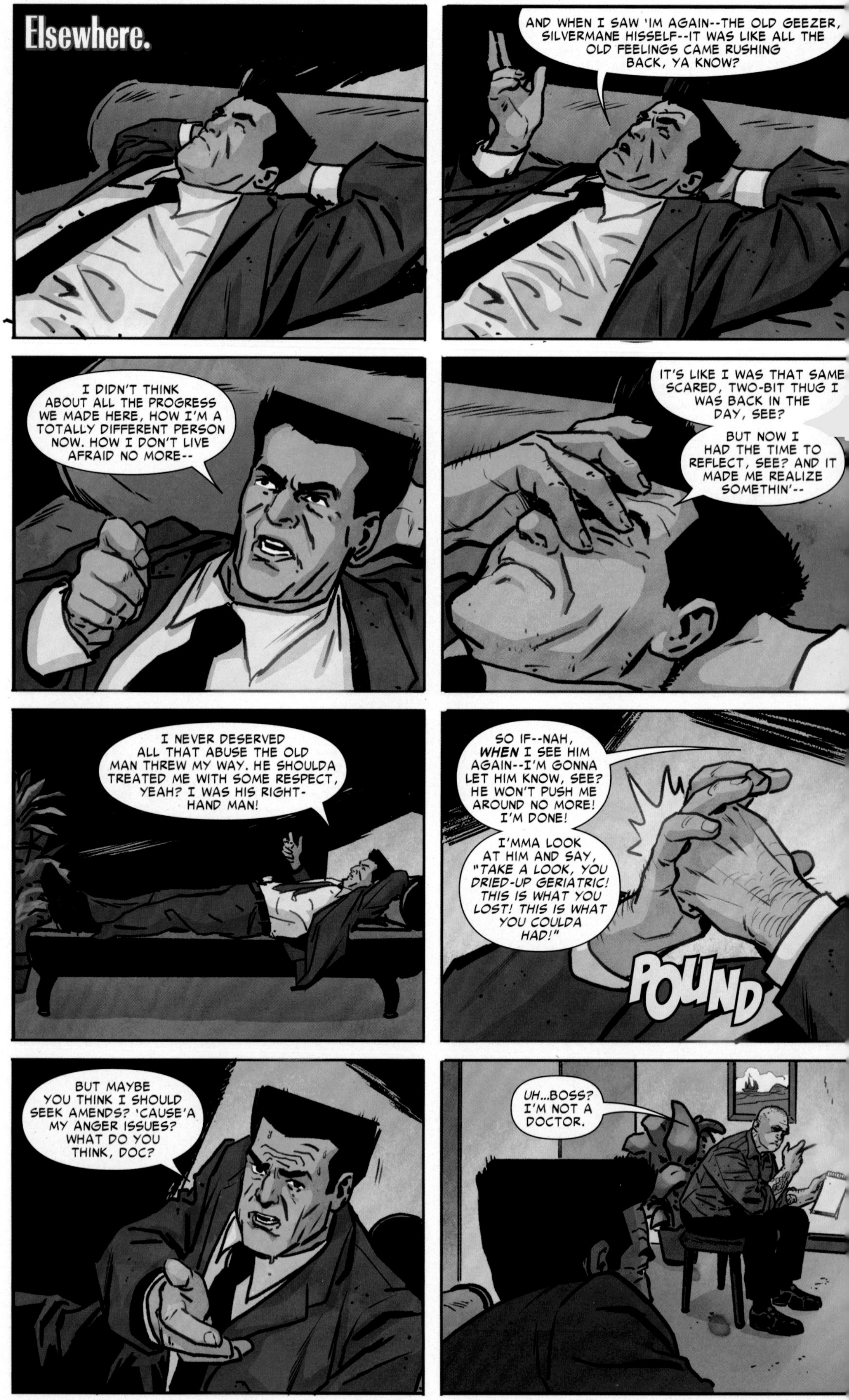
Elsewhere.
AND WHEN I SAW 'IM AGAIN--THE OLD GEEZER, SILVERMANE HISSELF--IT WAS LIKE ALL THE OLD FEELINGS CAME RUSHING BACK, YA KNOW?
I DIDN'T THINK ABOUT ALL THE PROGRESS WE MADE HERE, HOW I'M A TOTALLY DIFFERENT PERSON NOW. HOW I DON'T LIVE AFRAID NO MORE--
IT'S LIKE I WAS THAT SAME SCARED, TWO-BIT THUG I WAS BACK IN THE DAY, SEE?
BUT NOW I HAD THE TIME TO REFLECT, SEE? AND IT MADE ME REALIZE SOMETHIN'--
I NEVER DESERVED ALL THAT ABUSE THE OLD MAN THREW MY WAY. HE SHOULDA TREATED ME WITH SOME RESPECT, YEAH? I WAS HIS RIGHT-HAND MAN!
SO IF--NAH, ***WHEN*** I SEE HIM AGAIN--I'M GONNA LET HIM KNOW, SEE? HE WON'T PUSH ME AROUND NO MORE! I'M DONE!
I'MMA LOOK AT HIM AND SAY, *"TAKE A LOOK, YOU DRIED-UP GERIATRIC! THIS IS WHAT YOU LOST! THIS IS WHAT YOU COULDA HAD!"*
POUND
BUT MAYBE YOU THINK I SHOULD SEEK AMENDS? 'CAUSE'A MY ANGER ISSUES? WHAT DO YOU THINK, DOC?
UH...BOSS? I'M NOT A DOCTOR.

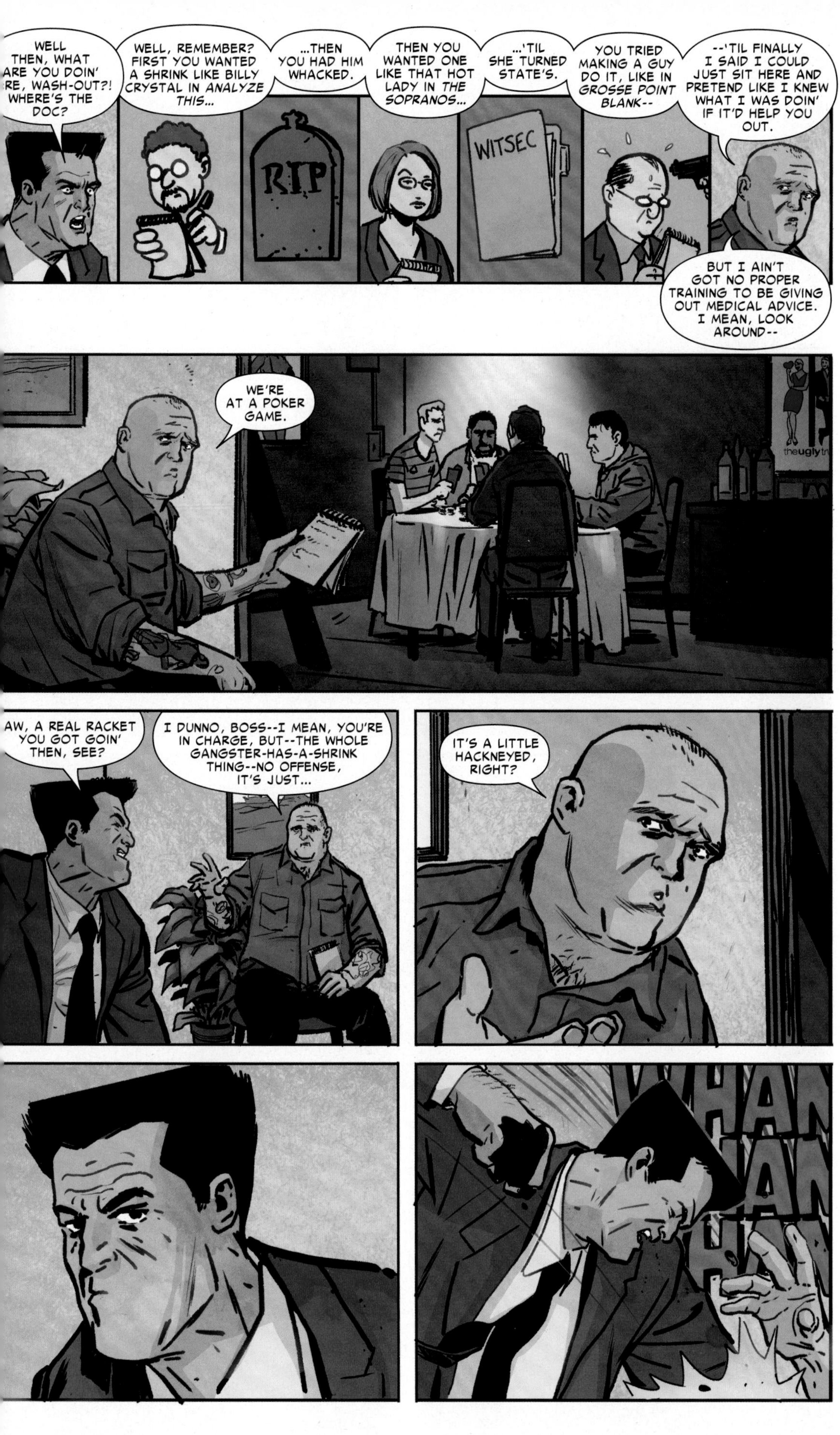
WELL THEN, WHAT ARE YOU DOIN' 'RE, WASH-OUT?! WHERE'S THE DOC?
WELL, REMEMBER? FIRST YOU WANTED A SHRINK LIKE BILLY CRYSTAL IN *ANALYZE THIS*...
RIP
...THEN YOU HAD HIM WHACKED.
THEN YOU WANTED ONE LIKE THAT HOT LADY IN *THE SOPRANOS*...
...'TIL SHE TURNED STATE'S.
WITSEC
YOU TRIED MAKING A GUY DO IT, LIKE IN *GROSSE POINT BLANK*--
--'TIL FINALLY I SAID I COULD JUST SIT HERE AND PRETEND LIKE I KNEW WHAT I WAS DOIN' IF IT'D HELP YOU OUT.
BUT I AIN'T GOT NO PROPER TRAINING TO BE GIVING OUT MEDICAL ADVICE. I MEAN, LOOK AROUND--
WE'RE AT A POKER GAME.
AW, A REAL RACKET YOU GOT GOIN' THEN, SEE?
I DUNNO, BOSS--I MEAN, YOU'RE IN CHARGE, BUT--THE WHOLE GANGSTER-HAS-A-SHRINK THING--NO OFFENSE, IT'S JUST...
IT'S A LITTLE HACKNEYED, RIGHT?

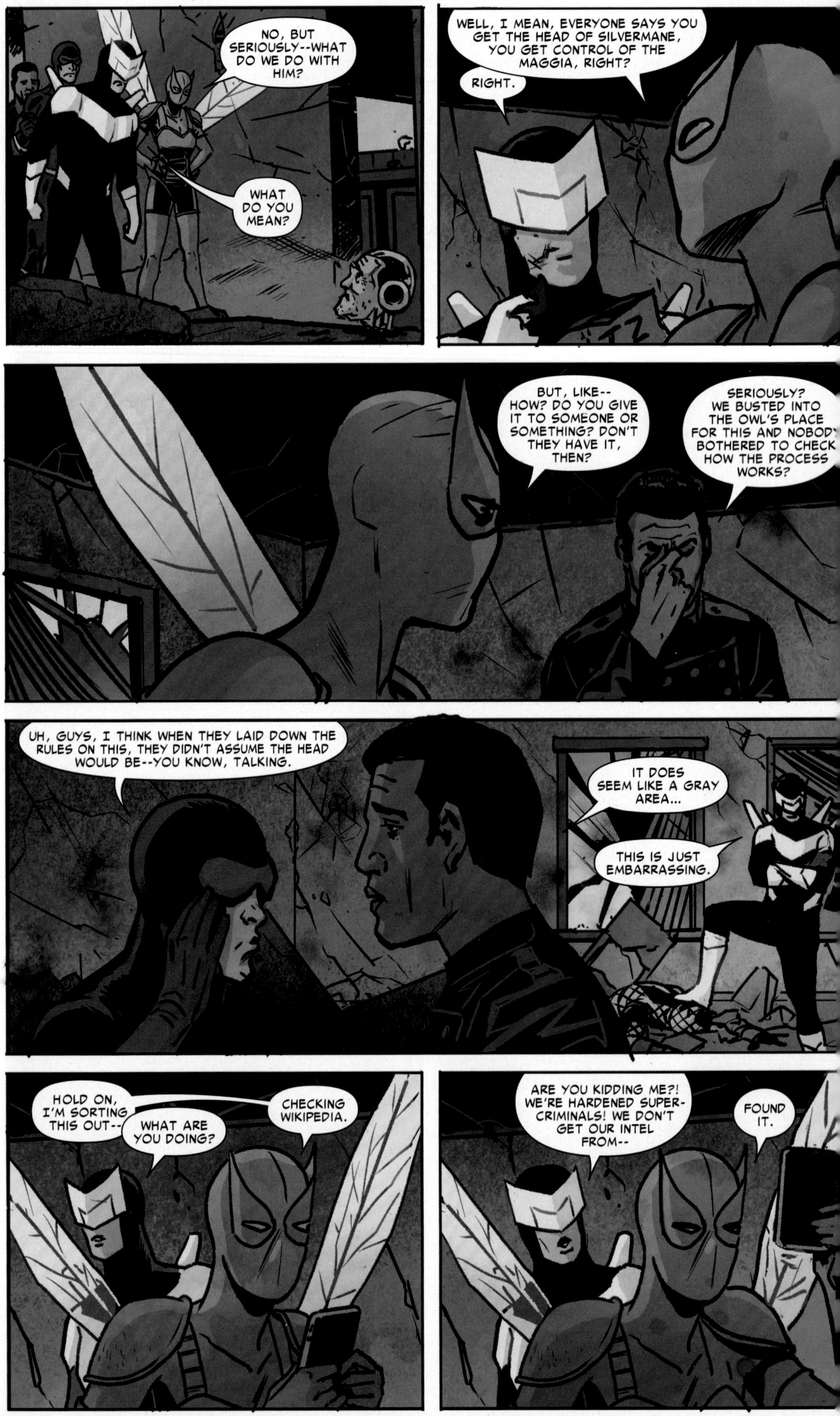
NO, BUT SERIOUSLY--WHAT DO WE DO WITH HIM?
WHAT DO YOU MEAN?
WELL, I MEAN, EVERYONE SAYS YOU GET THE HEAD OF SILVERMANE, YOU GET CONTROL OF THE MAGGIA, RIGHT?
RIGHT.
BUT, LIKE--HOW? DO YOU GIVE IT TO SOMEONE OR SOMETHING? DON'T THEY HAVE IT, THEN?
SERIOUSLY? WE BUSTED INTO THE OWL'S PLACE FOR THIS AND NOBODY BOTHERED TO CHECK HOW THE PROCESS WORKS?
UH, GUYS, I THINK WHEN THEY LAID DOWN THE RULES ON THIS, THEY DIDN'T ASSUME THE HEAD WOULD BE--YOU KNOW, TALKING.
IT DOES SEEM LIKE A GRAY AREA...
THIS IS JUST EMBARRASSING.
HOLD ON, I'M SORTING THIS OUT--
WHAT ARE YOU DOING?
CHECKING WIKIPEDIA.
ARE YOU KIDDING ME?! WE'RE HARDENED SUPER-CRIMINALS! WE DON'T GET OUR INTEL FROM--
FOUND IT.

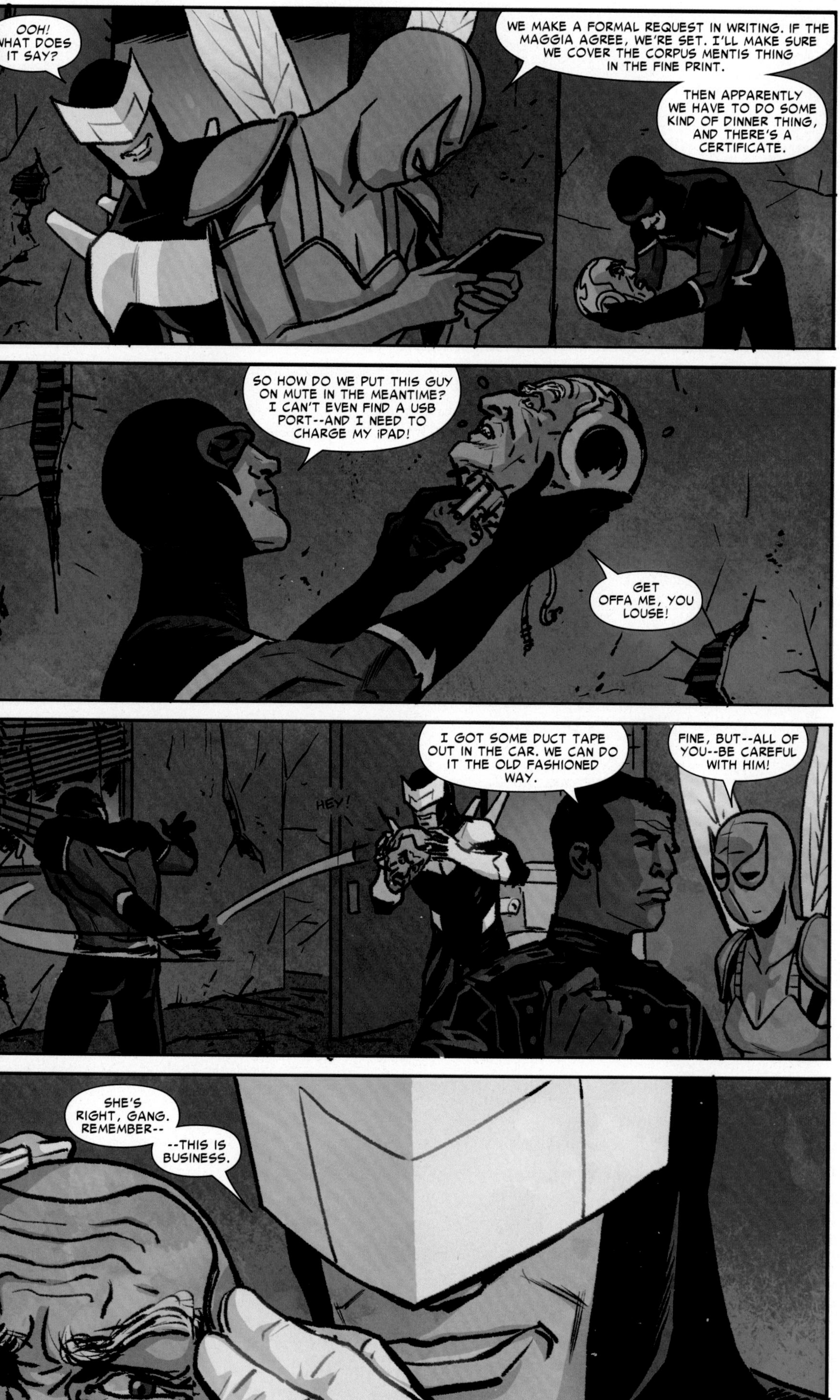
OOH! WHAT DOES IT SAY?
WE MAKE A FORMAL REQUEST IN WRITING. IF THE MAGGIA AGREE, WE'RE SET. I'LL MAKE SURE WE COVER THE CORPUS MENTIS THING IN THE FINE PRINT.
THEN APPARENTLY WE HAVE TO DO SOME KIND OF DINNER THING, AND THERE'S A CERTIFICATE.
SO HOW DO WE PUT THIS GUY ON MUTE IN THE MEANTIME? I CAN'T EVEN FIND A USB PORT--AND I NEED TO CHARGE MY iPAD!
GET OFFA ME, YOU LOUSE!
I GOT SOME DUCT TAPE OUT IN THE CAR. WE CAN DO IT THE OLD FASHIONED WAY.
HEY!
FINE, BUT--ALL OF YOU--BE CAREFUL WITH HIM!
SHE'S RIGHT, GANG. REMEMBER--
--THIS IS BUSINESS.

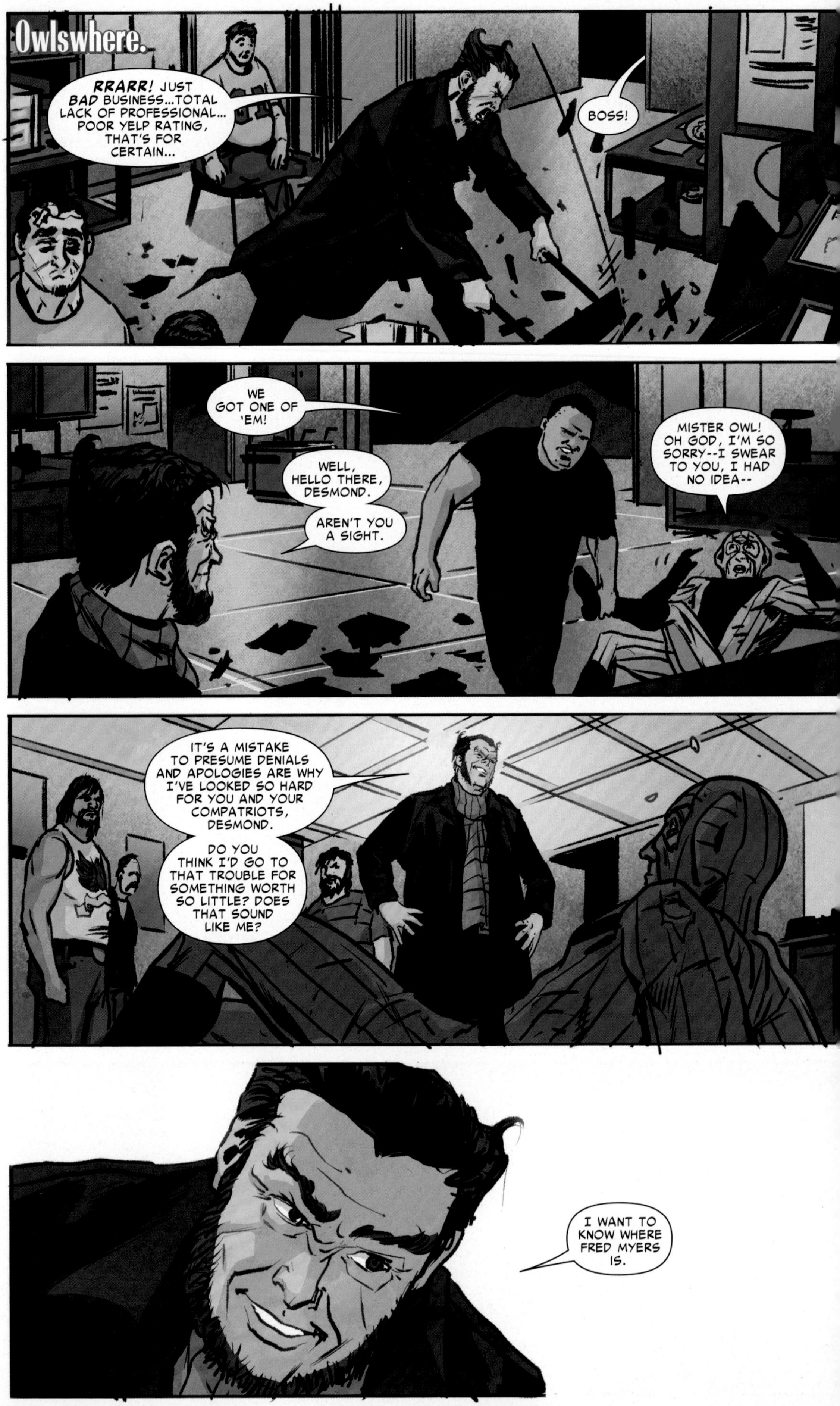
Owlswhere.
RRARR! JUST BAD BUSINESS...TOTAL LACK OF PROFESSIONAL... POOR YELP RATING, THAT'S FOR CERTAIN...
BOSS!
WE GOT ONE OF 'EM!
WELL, HELLO THERE, DESMOND.
AREN'T YOU A SIGHT.
MISTER OWL! OH GOD, I'M SO SORRY--I SWEAR TO YOU, I HAD NO IDEA--
IT'S A MISTAKE TO PRESUME DENIALS AND APOLOGIES ARE WHY I'VE LOOKED SO HARD FOR YOU AND YOUR COMPATRIOTS, DESMOND.
DO YOU THINK I'D GO TO THAT TROUBLE FOR SOMETHING WORTH SO LITTLE? DOES THAT SOUND LIKE ME?
I WANT TO KNOW WHERE FRED MYERS IS.

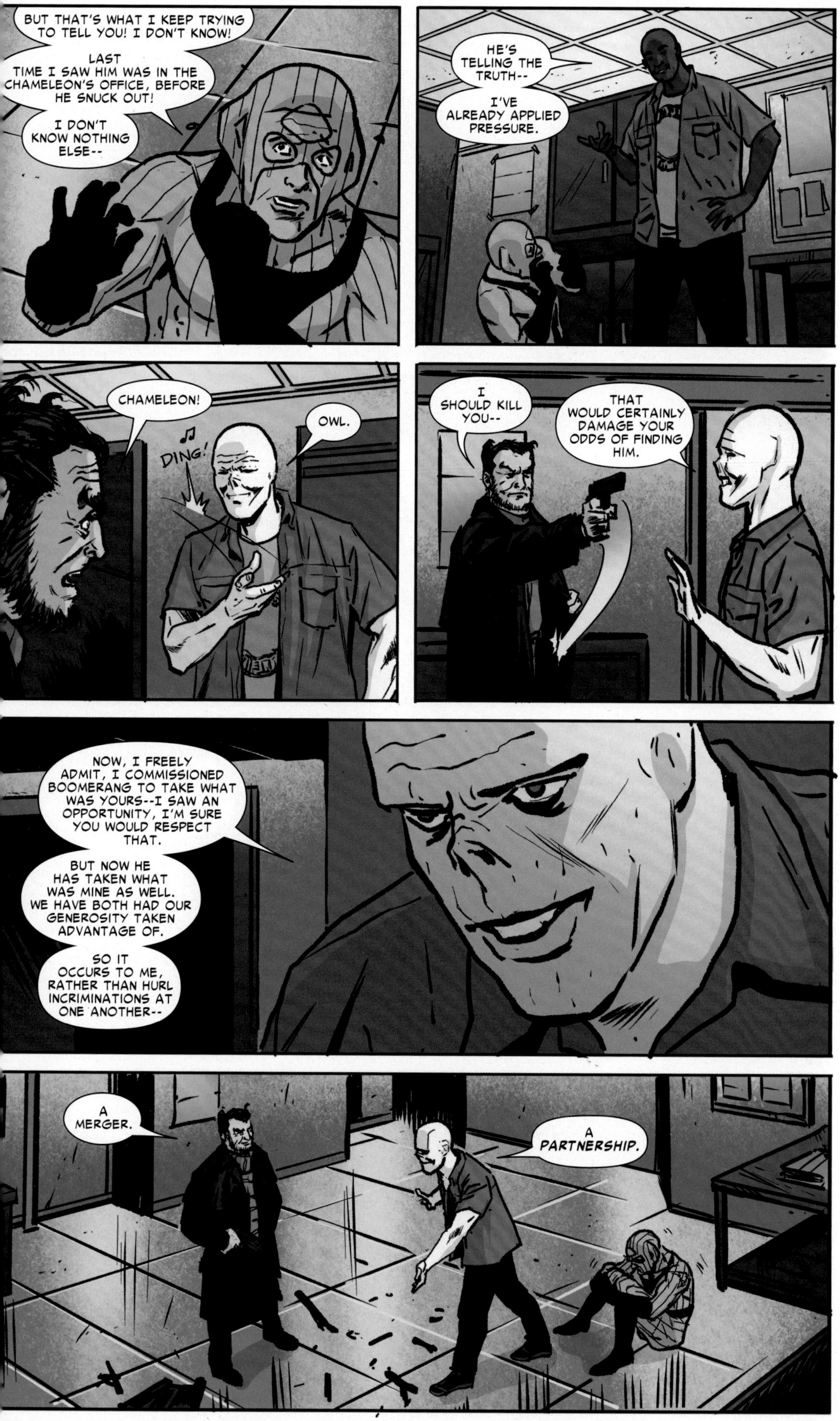
BUT THAT'S WHAT I KEEP TRYING TO TELL YOU! I DON'T KNOW!
LAST TIME I SAW HIM WAS IN THE CHAMELEON'S OFFICE, BEFORE HE SNUCK OUT!
I DON'T KNOW NOTHING ELSE--
HE'S TELLING THE TRUTH--
I'VE ALREADY APPLIED PRESSURE.
CHAMELEON!
DING!
OWL.
I SHOULD KILL YOU--
THAT WOULD CERTAINLY DAMAGE YOUR ODDS OF FINDING HIM.
NOW, I FREELY ADMIT, I COMMISSIONED BOOMERANG TO TAKE WHAT WAS YOURS--I SAW AN OPPORTUNITY, I'M SURE YOU WOULD RESPECT THAT.
BUT NOW HE HAS TAKEN WHAT WAS MINE AS WELL. WE HAVE BOTH HAD OUR GENEROSITY TAKEN ADVANTAGE OF.
SO IT OCCURS TO ME, RATHER THAN HURL INCRIMINATIONS AT ONE ANOTHER--
A MERGER.
A *PARTNERSHIP.*

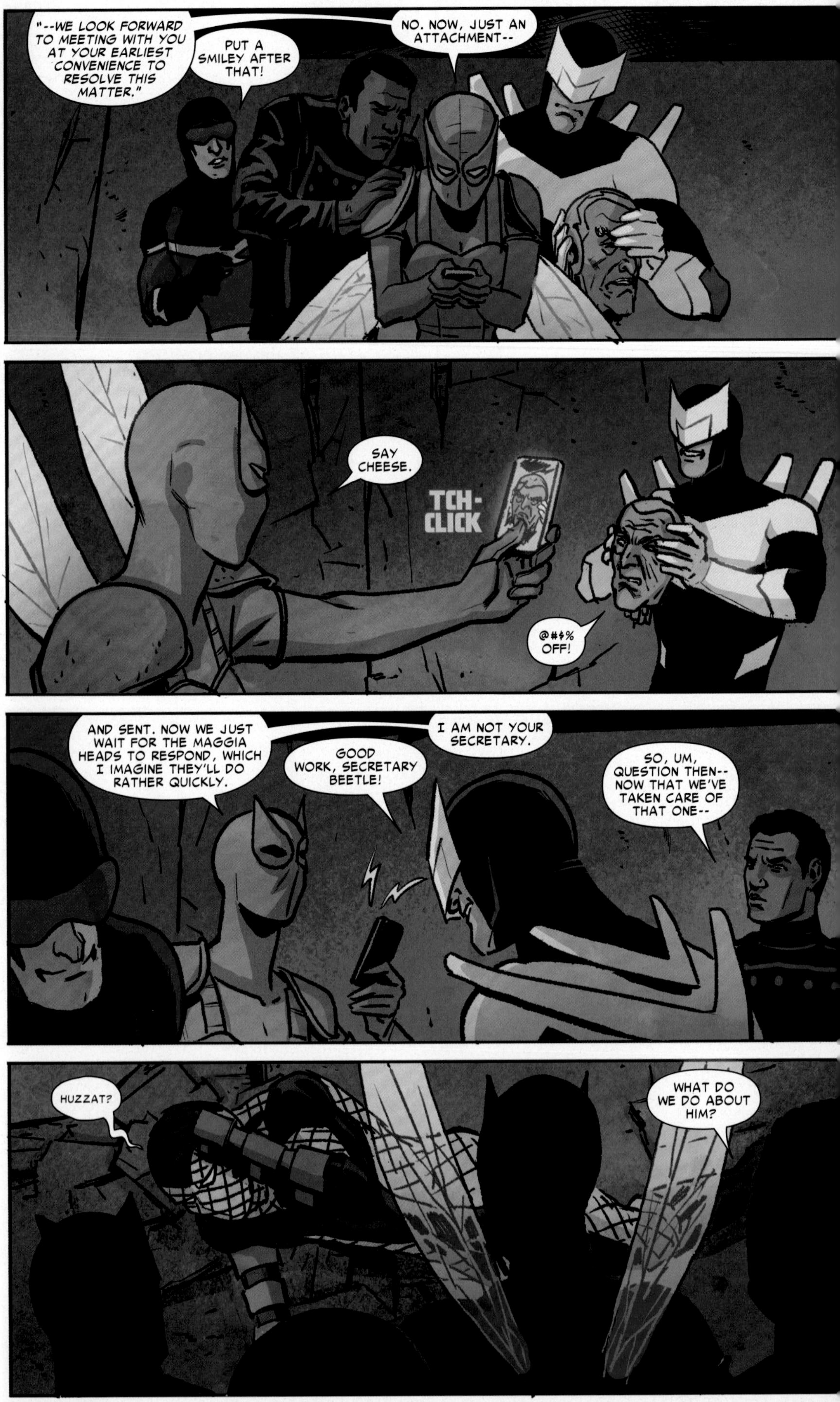
"--WE LOOK FORWARD TO MEETING WITH YOU AT YOUR EARLIEST CONVENIENCE TO RESOLVE THIS MATTER."
PUT A SMILEY AFTER THAT!
NO. NOW, JUST AN ATTACHMENT--
SAY CHEESE.
TCH-CLICK
@#$% OFF!
AND SENT. NOW WE JUST WAIT FOR THE MAGGIA HEADS TO RESPOND, WHICH I IMAGINE THEY'LL DO RATHER QUICKLY.
GOOD WORK, SECRETARY BEETLE!
I AM NOT YOUR SECRETARY.
SO, UM, QUESTION THEN--NOW THAT WE'VE TAKEN CARE OF THAT ONE--
HUZZAT?
WHAT DO WE DO ABOUT HIM?

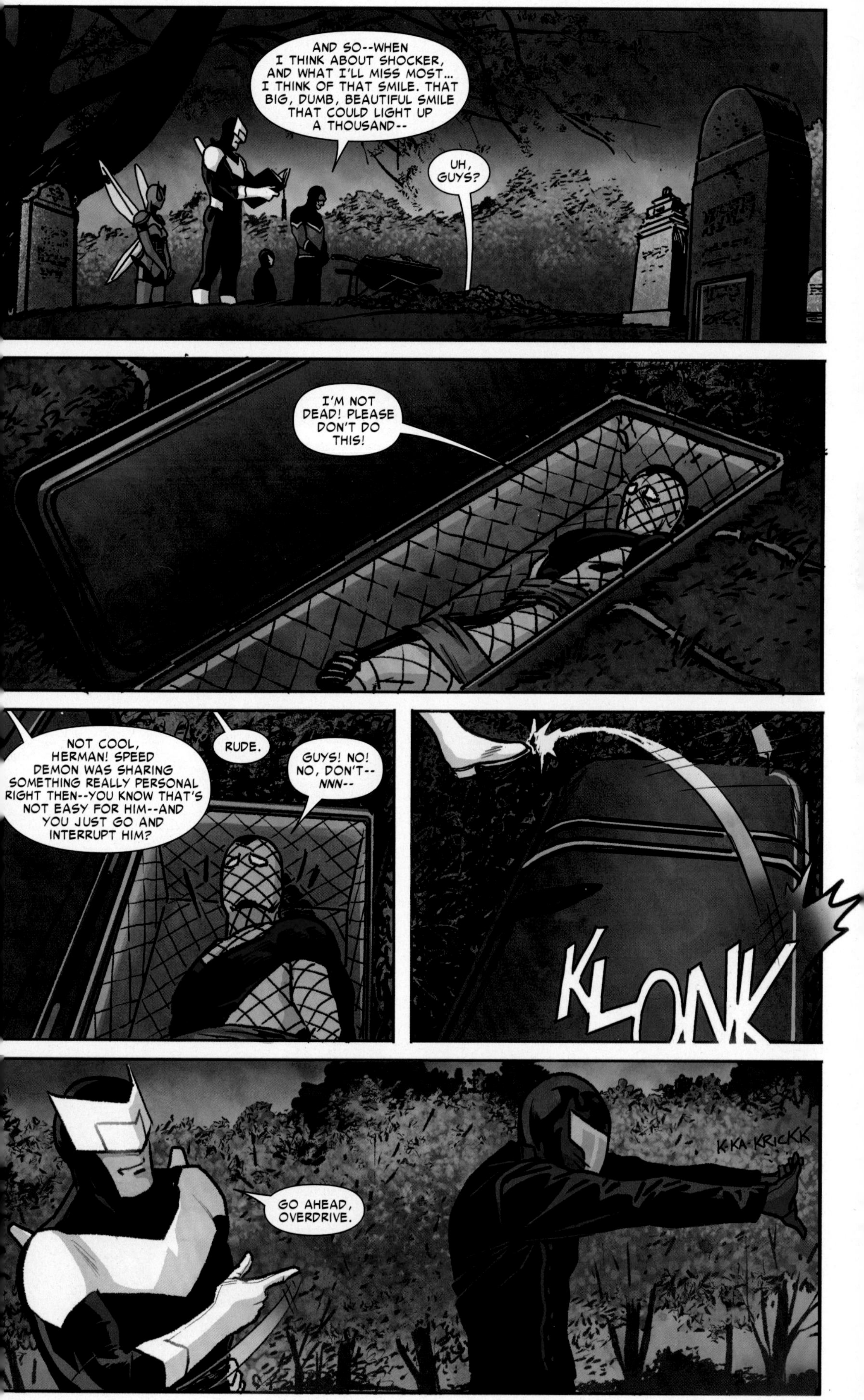
AND SO--WHEN I THINK ABOUT SHOCKER, AND WHAT I'LL MISS MOST... I THINK OF THAT SMILE. THAT BIG, DUMB, BEAUTIFUL SMILE THAT COULD LIGHT UP A THOUSAND--
UH, GUYS?
I'M NOT DEAD! PLEASE DON'T DO THIS!
NOT COOL, HERMAN! SPEED DEMON WAS SHARING SOMETHING REALLY PERSONAL RIGHT THEN--YOU KNOW THAT'S NOT EASY FOR HIM--AND YOU JUST GO AND INTERRUPT HIM?
RUDE.
GUYS! NO! NO, DON'T-- NNN--
KLONK
K-KA-KRICKK
GO AHEAD, OVERDRIVE.

BACKHOE!

NOW THE HEALING CAN BEGIN.

MAGGIA JUST EMAILED BACK. WE'RE SET FOR TOMORROW NIGHT, RIVERSIDE DOCKS.

WOO-HOO! THIS CALLS FOR A CELEBRATION! DRINKS ARE ON ME!

FRED, YOU DON'T THINK THAT'S A LITTLE IN POOR TASTE? WE DID JUST BURY OUR BEST PAL.

NO, JAMES, I DON'T THINK IT IS. BECAUSE YOU AND I BOTH KNOW, ABOVE ALL--

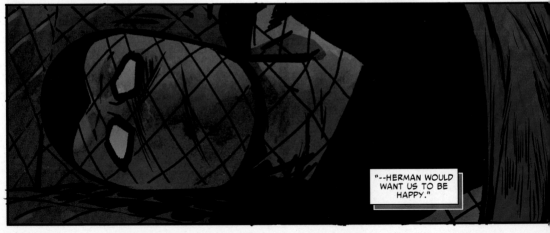

"--HERMAN WOULD WANT US TO BE HAPPY."

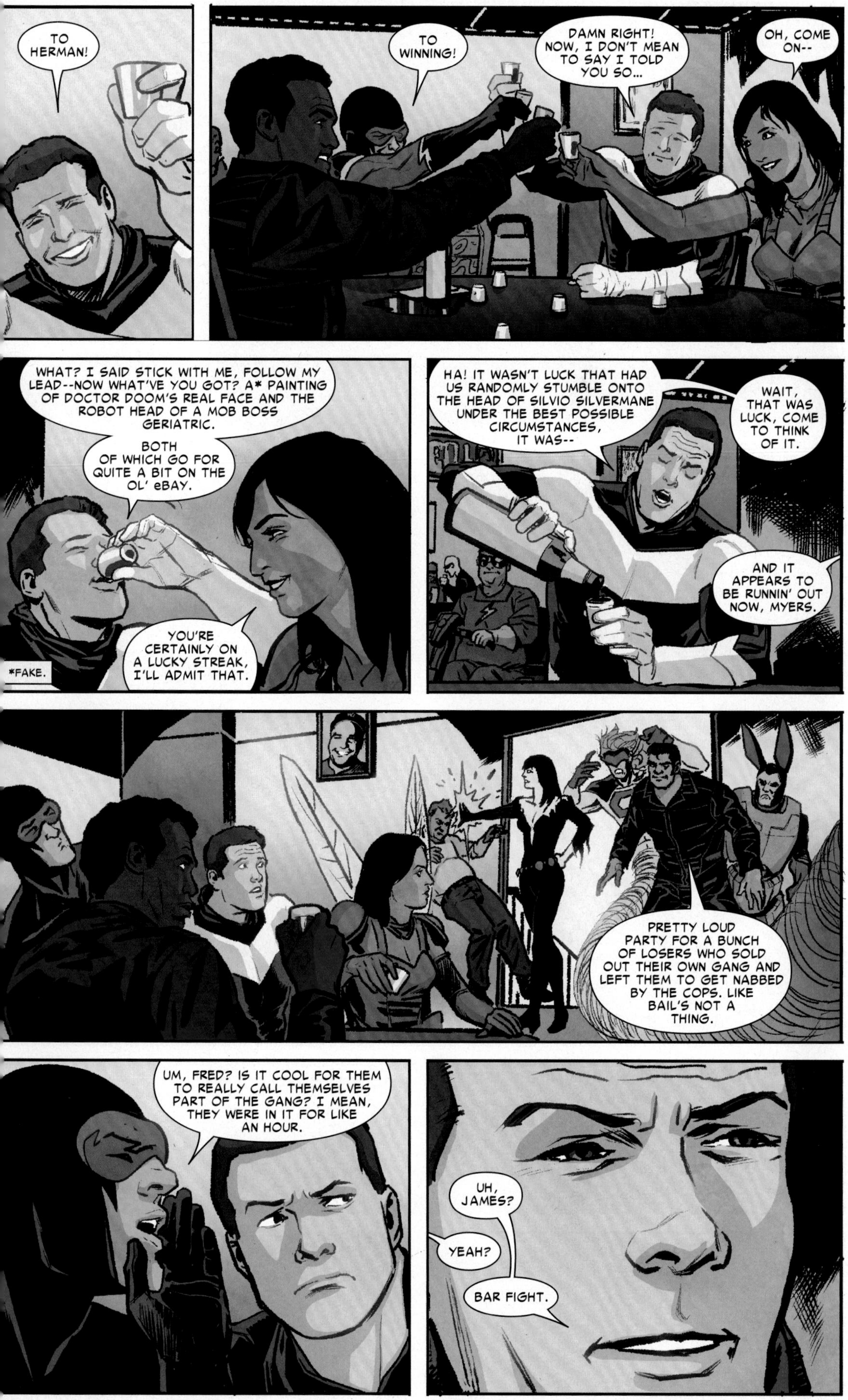
TO HERMAN!
TO WINNING!
DAMN RIGHT! NOW, I DON'T MEAN TO SAY I TOLD YOU SO...
OH, COME ON--
WHAT? I SAID STICK WITH ME, FOLLOW MY LEAD--NOW WHAT'VE YOU GOT? A* PAINTING OF DOCTOR DOOM'S REAL FACE AND THE ROBOT HEAD OF A MOB BOSS GERIATRIC.
BOTH OF WHICH GO FOR QUITE A BIT ON THE OL' eBAY.
YOU'RE CERTAINLY ON A LUCKY STREAK, I'LL ADMIT THAT.
*FAKE.
HA! IT WASN'T LUCK THAT HAD US RANDOMLY STUMBLE ONTO THE HEAD OF SILVIO SILVERMANE UNDER THE BEST POSSIBLE CIRCUMSTANCES, IT WAS--
WAIT, THAT WAS LUCK, COME TO THINK OF IT.
AND IT APPEARS TO BE RUNNIN' OUT NOW, MYERS.
PRETTY LOUD PARTY FOR A BUNCH OF LOSERS WHO SOLD OUT THEIR OWN GANG AND LEFT THEM TO GET NABBED BY THE COPS. LIKE BAIL'S NOT A THING.
UM, FRED? IS IT COOL FOR THEM TO REALLY CALL THEMSELVES PART OF THE GANG? I MEAN, THEY WERE IN IT FOR LIKE AN HOUR.
UH, JAMES?
YEAH?
BAR FIGHT.

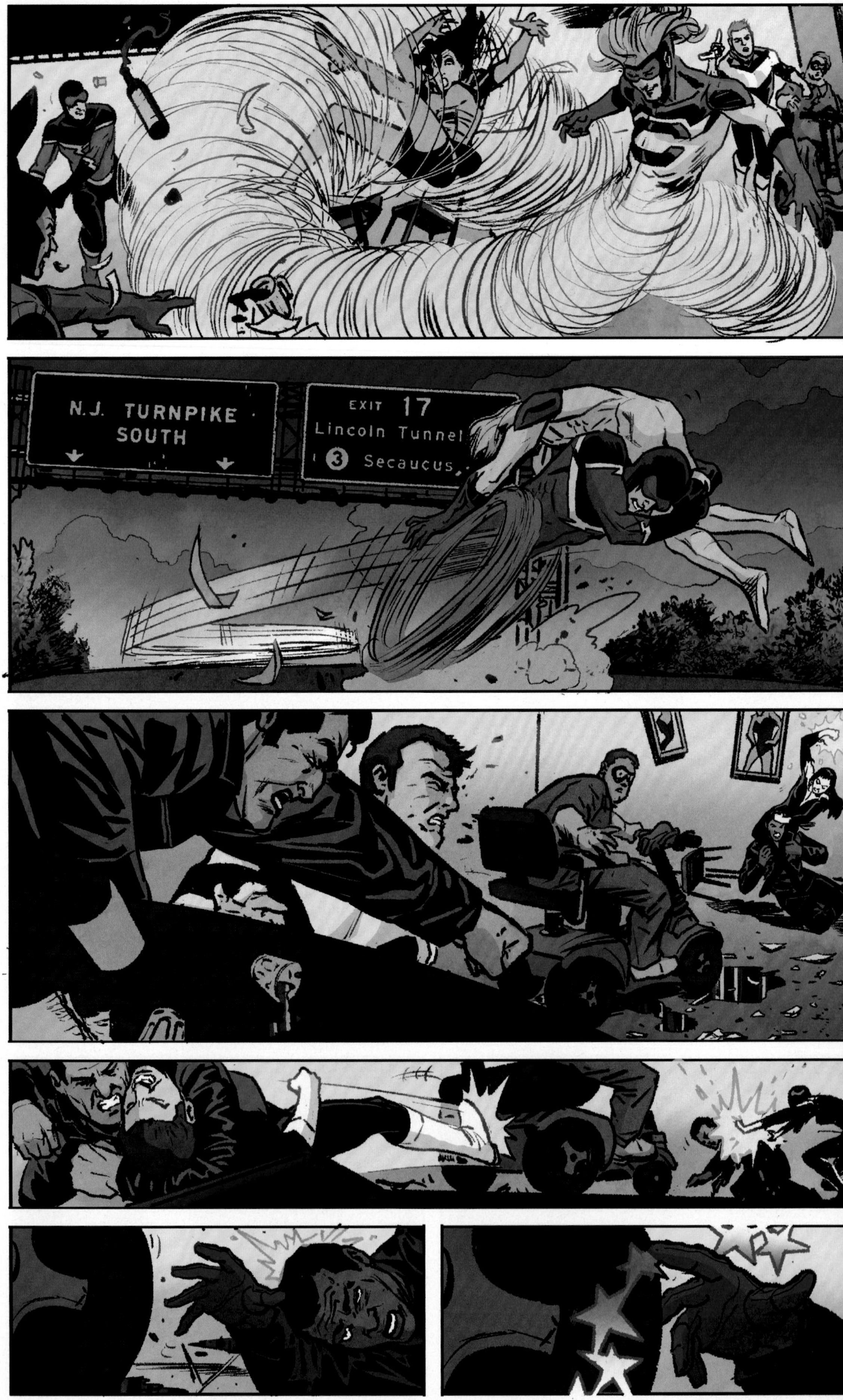
N.J. TURNPIKE
SOUTH
EXIT 17
Lincoln Tunnel
3 Secaucus

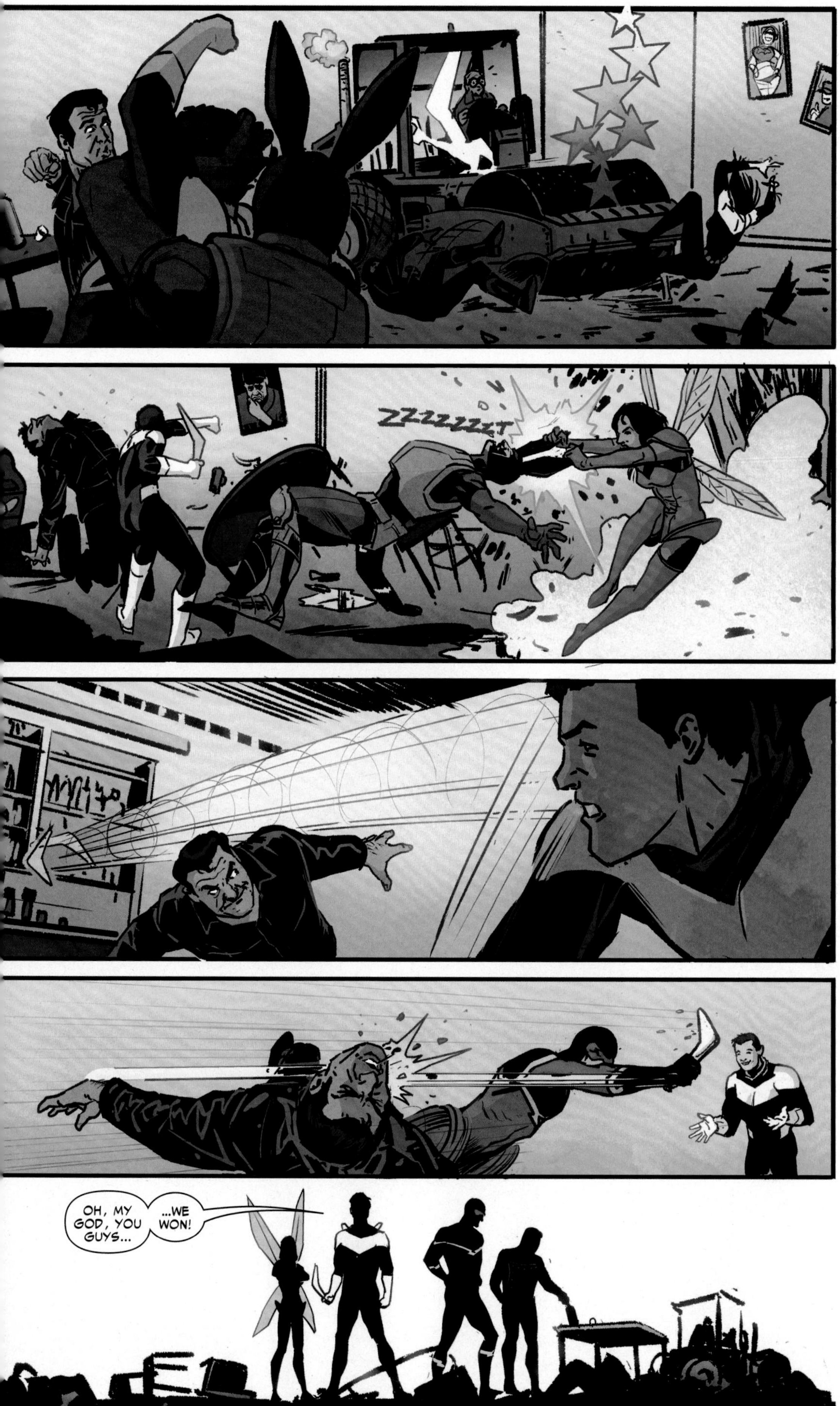
ZZZZZZZT
OH, MY GOD, YOU GUYS...
...WE WON!

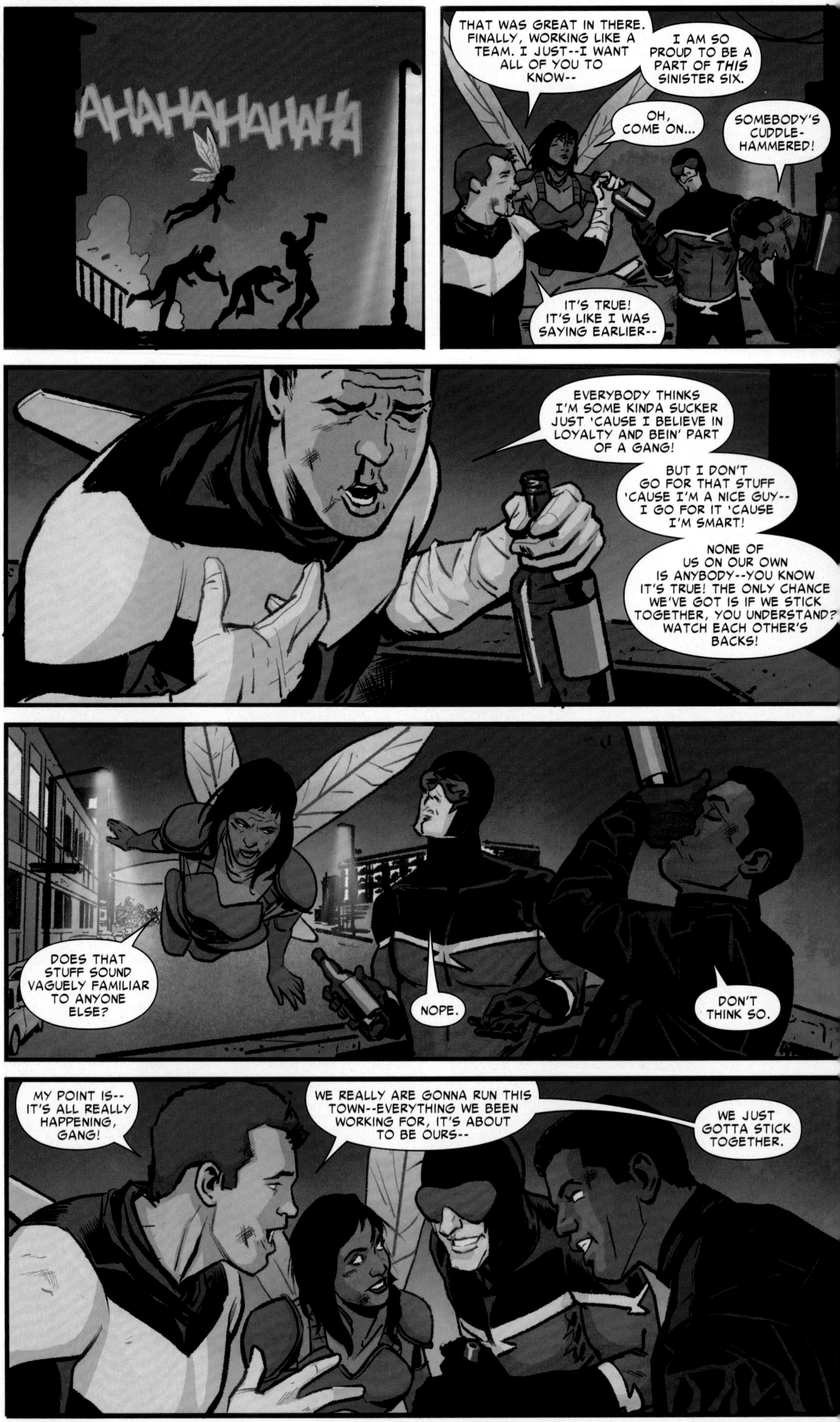
AHAHAHAHAHA
THAT WAS GREAT IN THERE. FINALLY, WORKING LIKE A TEAM. I JUST--I WANT ALL OF YOU TO KNOW--
I AM SO PROUD TO BE A PART OF *THIS* SINISTER SIX.
OH, COME ON...
SOMEBODY'S CUDDLE-HAMMERED!
IT'S TRUE! IT'S LIKE I WAS SAYING EARLIER--
EVERYBODY THINKS I'M SOME KINDA SUCKER JUST 'CAUSE I BELIEVE IN LOYALTY AND BEIN' PART OF A GANG!
BUT I DON'T GO FOR THAT STUFF 'CAUSE I'M A NICE GUY-- I GO FOR IT 'CAUSE I'M SMART!
NONE OF US ON OUR OWN IS ANYBODY--YOU KNOW IT'S TRUE! THE ONLY CHANCE WE'VE GOT IS IF WE STICK TOGETHER, YOU UNDERSTAND? WATCH EACH OTHER'S BACKS!
DOES THAT STUFF SOUND VAGUELY FAMILIAR TO ANYONE ELSE?
NOPE.
DON'T THINK SO.
MY POINT IS-- IT'S ALL REALLY HAPPENING, GANG!
WE REALLY ARE GONNA RUN THIS TOWN--EVERYTHING WE BEEN WORKING FOR, IT'S ABOUT TO BE OURS--
WE JUST GOTTA STICK TOGETHER.

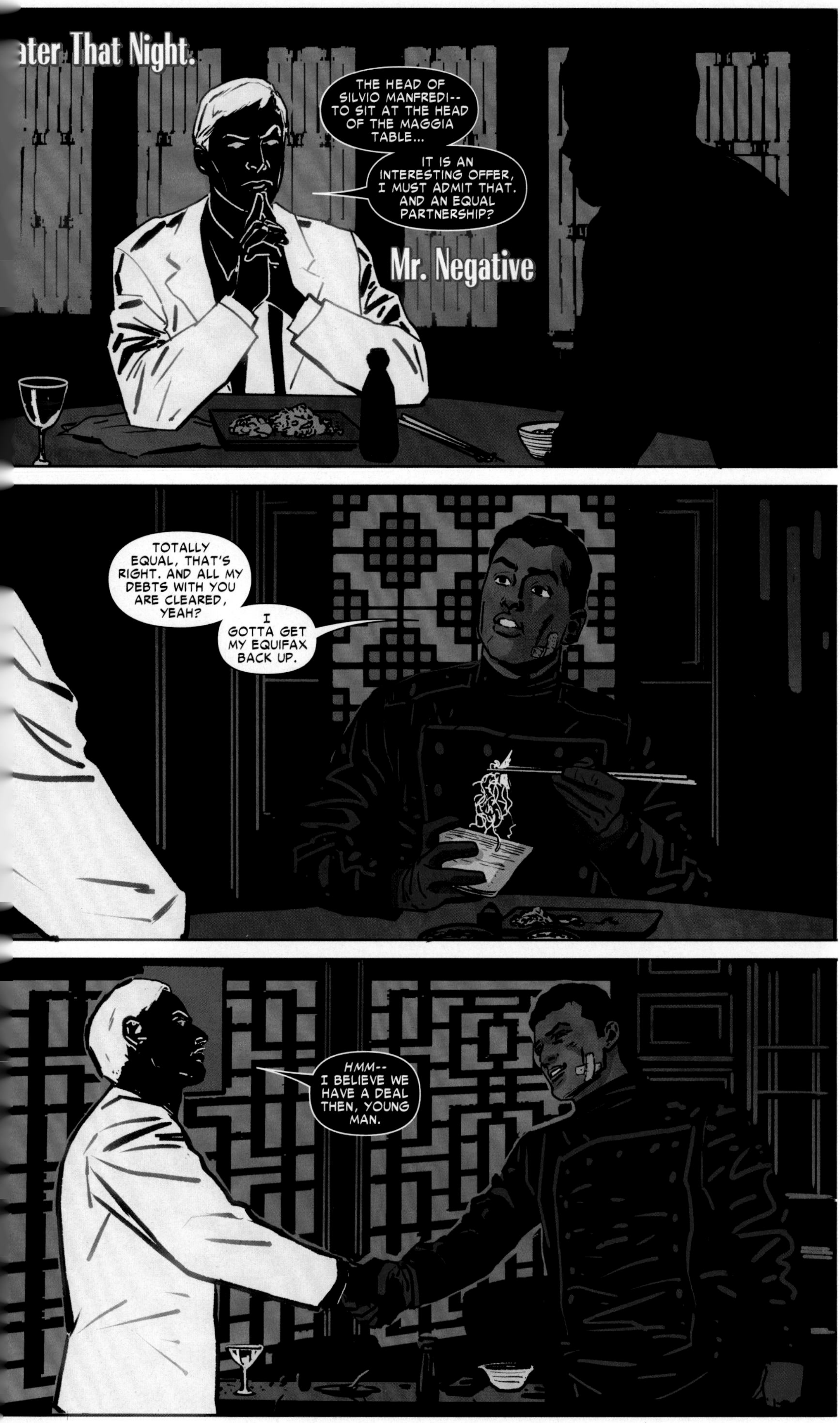
ater That Night.
THE HEAD OF SILVIO MANFREDI-- TO SIT AT THE HEAD OF THE MAGGIA TABLE...
IT IS AN INTERESTING OFFER, I MUST ADMIT THAT. AND AN EQUAL PARTNERSHIP?
Mr. Negative
TOTALLY EQUAL, THAT'S RIGHT. AND ALL MY DEBTS WITH YOU ARE CLEARED, YEAH?
I GOTTA GET MY EQUIFAX BACK UP.
HMM-- I BELIEVE WE HAVE A DEAL THEN, YOUNG MAN.

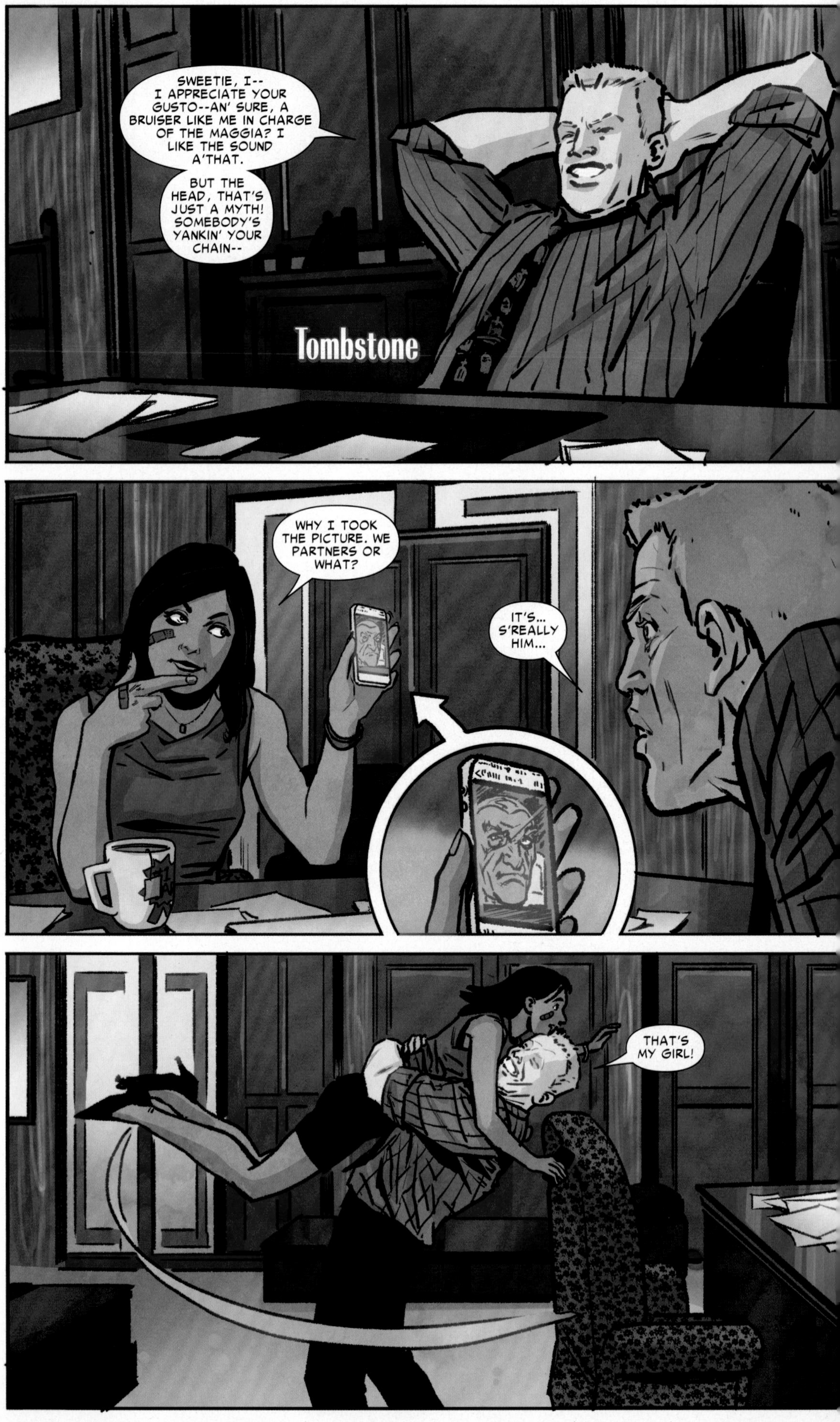
SWEETIE, I-- I APPRECIATE YOUR GUSTO--AN' SURE, A BRUISER LIKE ME IN CHARGE OF THE MAGGIA? I LIKE THE SOUND A'THAT.
BUT THE HEAD, THAT'S JUST A MYTH! SOMEBODY'S YANKIN' YOUR CHAIN--
Tombstone
WHY I TOOK THE PICTURE. WE PARTNERS OR WHAT?
IT'S... S'REALLY HIM...
THAT'S MY GIRL!

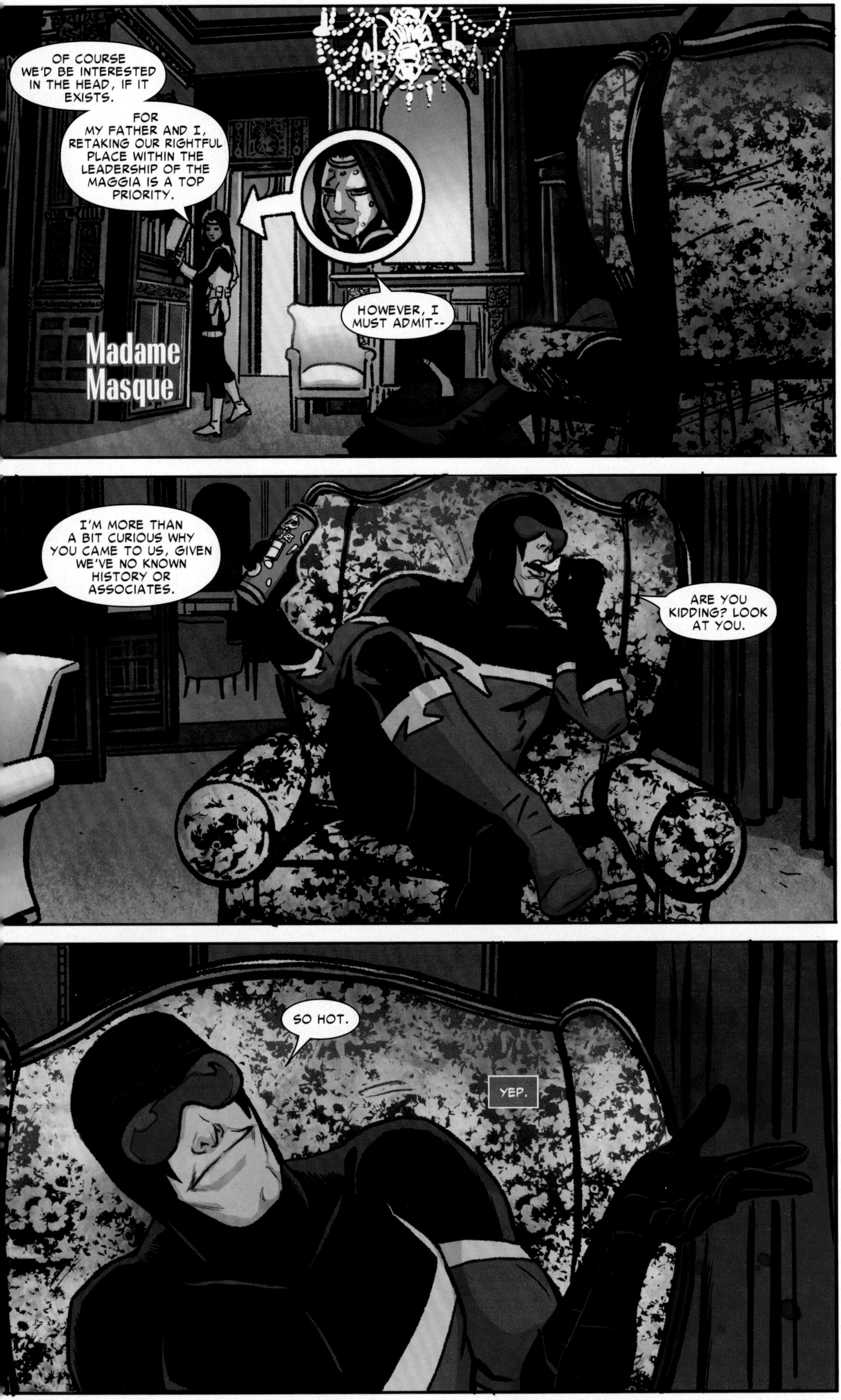
OF COURSE WE'D BE INTERESTED IN THE HEAD, IF IT EXISTS.
FOR MY FATHER AND I, RETAKING OUR RIGHTFUL PLACE WITHIN THE LEADERSHIP OF THE MAGGIA IS A TOP PRIORITY.
Madame Masque
HOWEVER, I MUST ADMIT--
I'M MORE THAN A BIT CURIOUS WHY YOU CAME TO US, GIVEN WE'VE NO KNOWN HISTORY OR ASSOCIATES.
ARE YOU KIDDING? LOOK AT YOU.
SO HOT.
YEP.

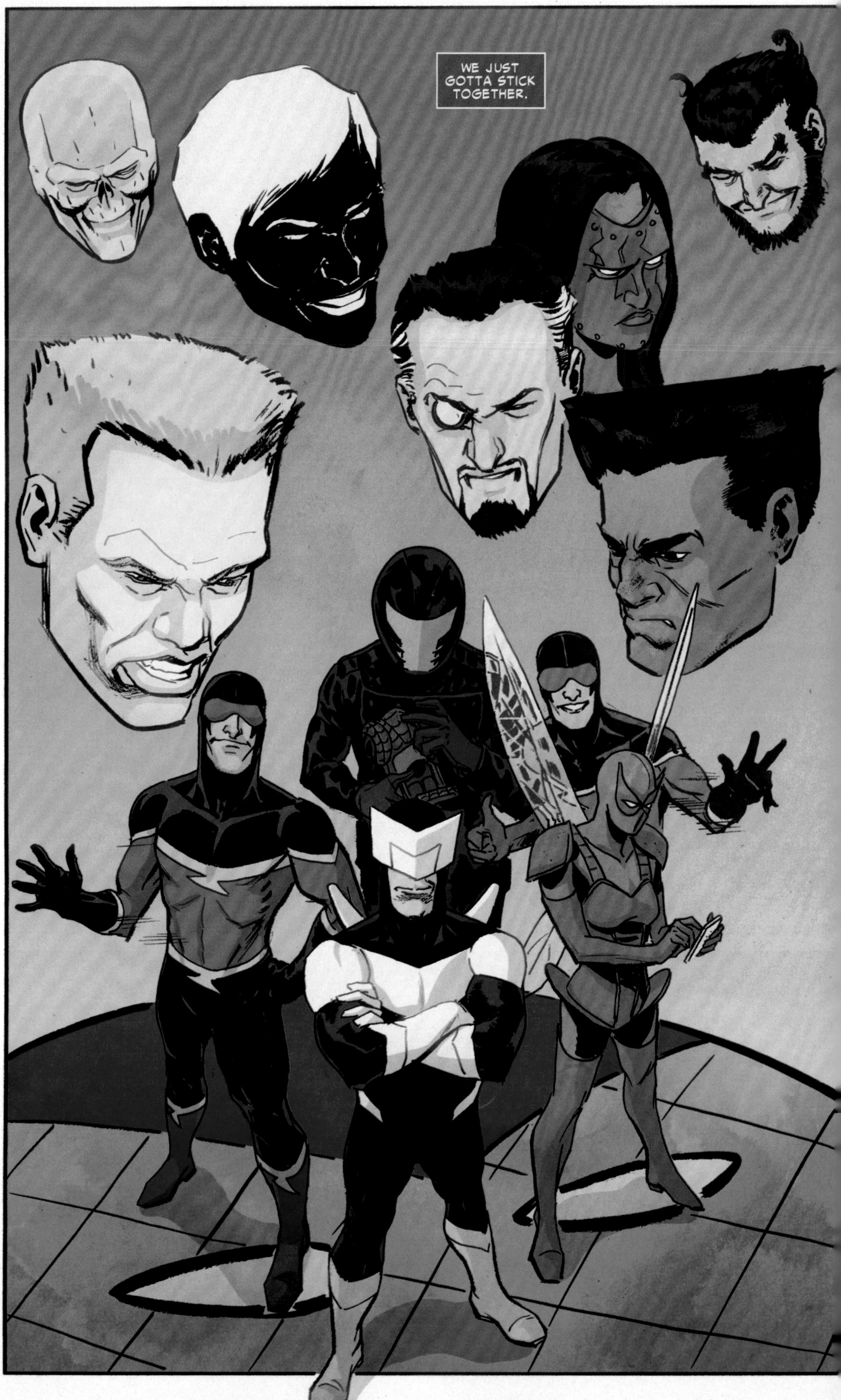
WE JUST GOTTA STICK TOGETHER.

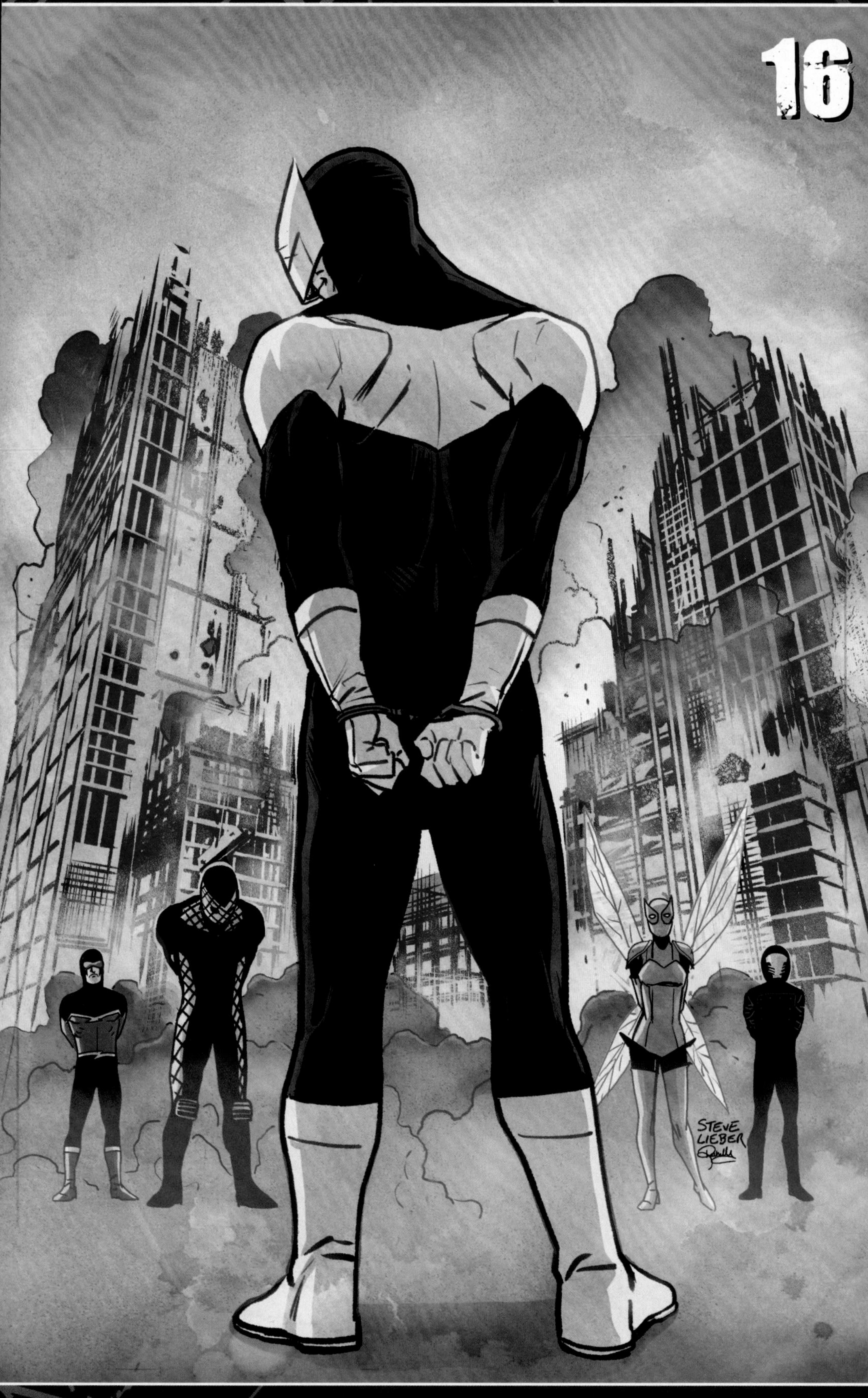
16
STEVE LIEBER

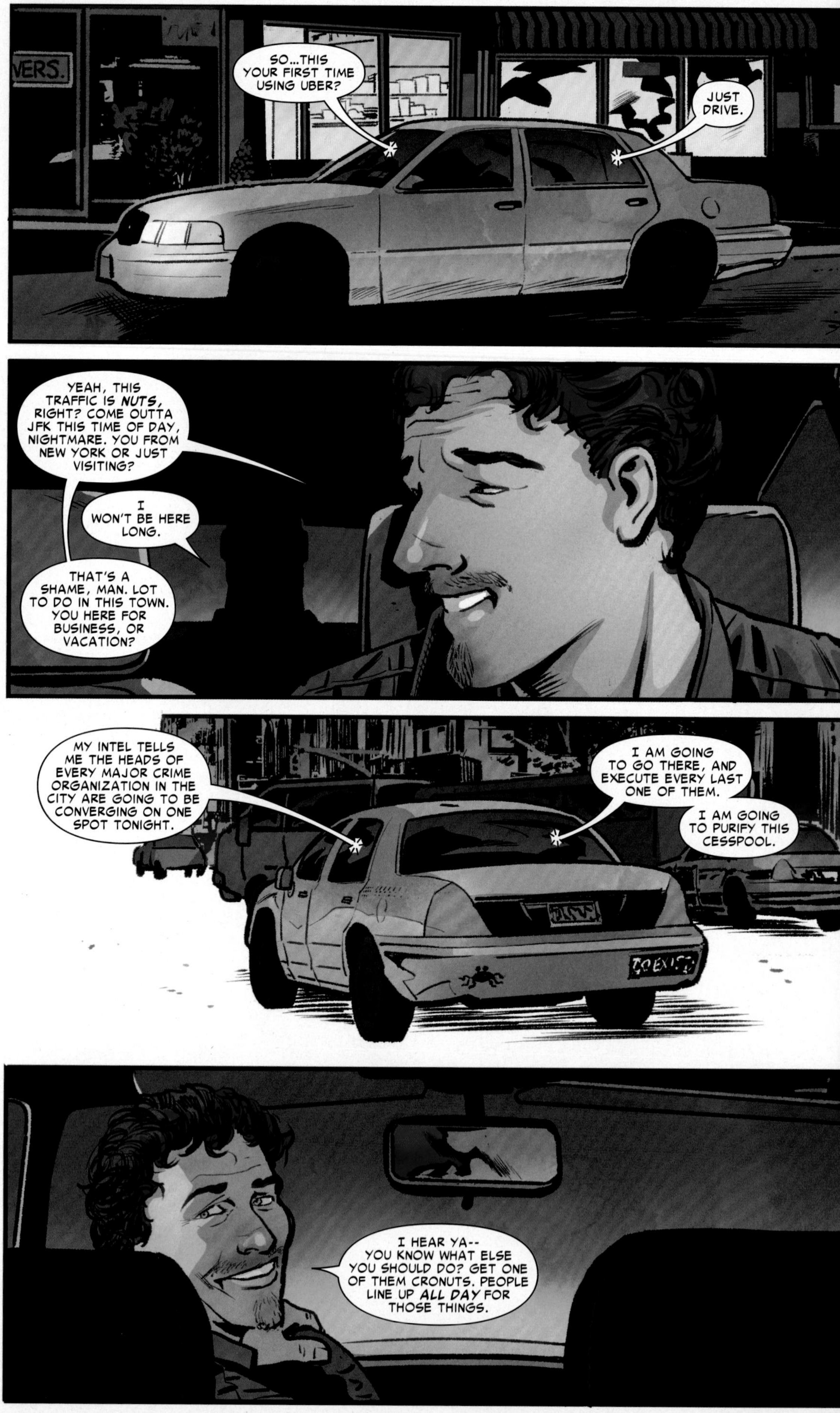
VERS.
SO...THIS YOUR FIRST TIME USING UBER?
JUST DRIVE.
YEAH, THIS TRAFFIC IS NUTS, RIGHT? COME OUTTA JFK THIS TIME OF DAY, NIGHTMARE. YOU FROM NEW YORK OR JUST VISITING?
I WON'T BE HERE LONG.
THAT'S A SHAME, MAN. LOT TO DO IN THIS TOWN. YOU HERE FOR BUSINESS, OR VACATION?
MY INTEL TELLS ME THE HEADS OF EVERY MAJOR CRIME ORGANIZATION IN THE CITY ARE GOING TO BE CONVERGING ON ONE SPOT TONIGHT.
I AM GOING TO GO THERE, AND EXECUTE EVERY LAST ONE OF THEM.
I AM GOING TO PURIFY THIS CESSPOOL.
I HEAR YA-- YOU KNOW WHAT ELSE YOU SHOULD DO? GET ONE OF THEM CRONUTS. PEOPLE LINE UP ALL DAY FOR THOSE THINGS.

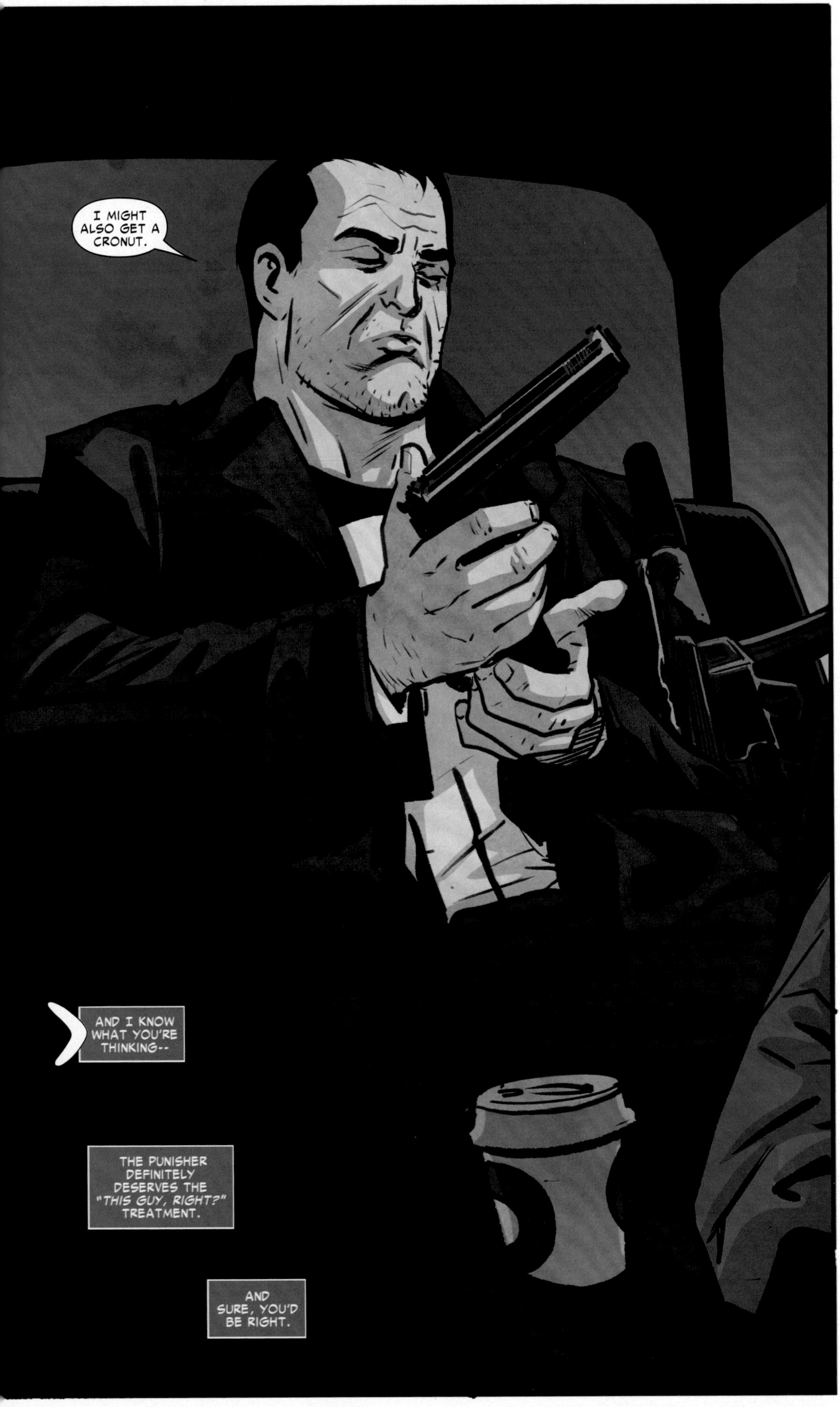
I MIGHT ALSO GET A CRONUT.
AND I KNOW WHAT YOU'RE THINKING--
THE PUNISHER DEFINITELY DESERVES THE "*THIS GUY, RIGHT?*" TREATMENT.
AND SURE, YOU'D BE RIGHT.

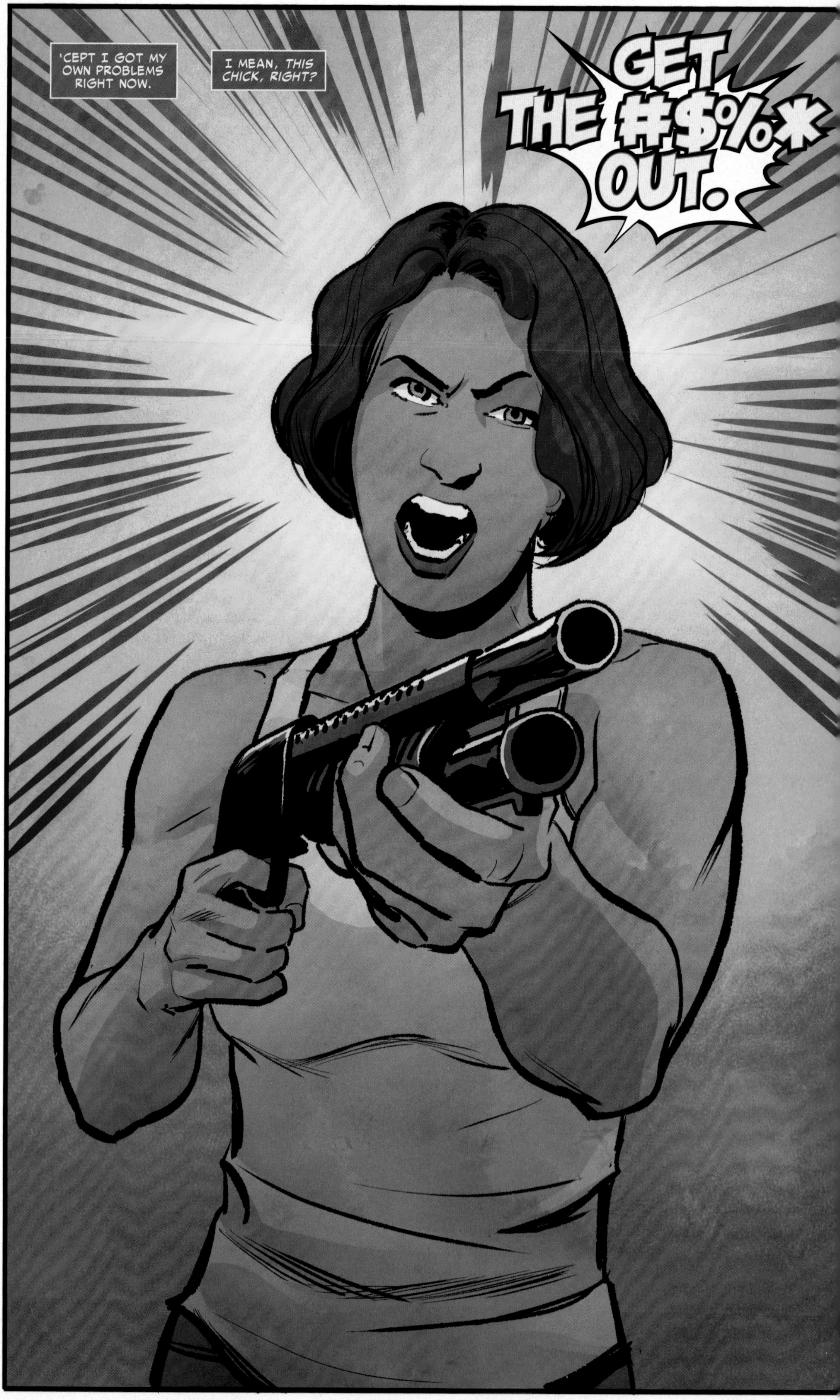
'CEPT I GOT MY OWN PROBLEMS RIGHT NOW.
I MEAN, THIS CHICK, RIGHT?
GET THE #$%* OUT.

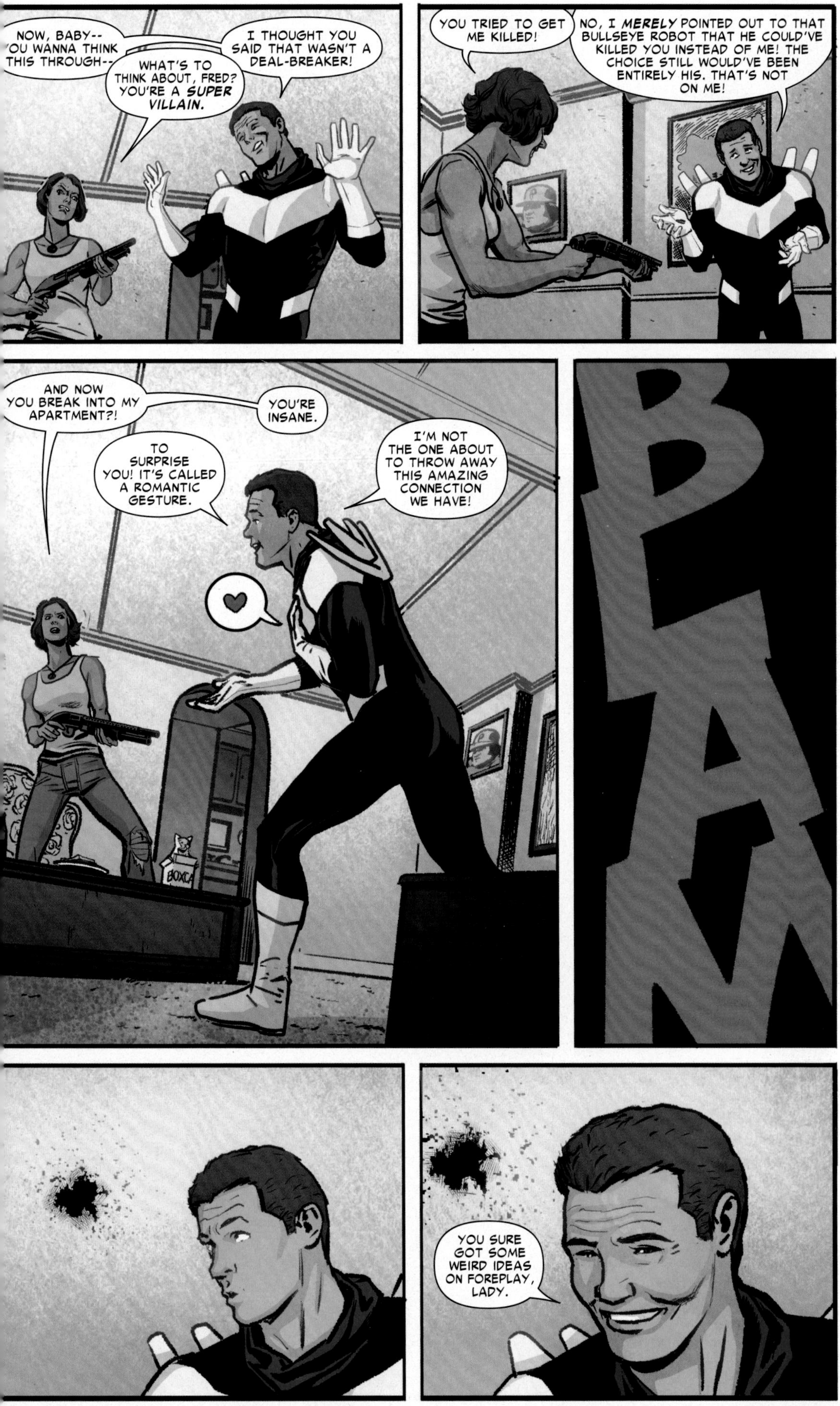

NOW, BABY-- 'OU WANNA THINK THIS THROUGH--
I THOUGHT YOU SAID THAT WASN'T A DEAL-BREAKER!
WHAT'S TO THINK ABOUT, FRED? YOU'RE A *SUPER VILLAIN.*
YOU TRIED TO GET ME KILLED!
NO, I *MERELY* POINTED OUT TO THAT BULLSEYE ROBOT THAT HE COULD'VE KILLED YOU INSTEAD OF ME! THE CHOICE STILL WOULD'VE BEEN ENTIRELY HIS. THAT'S NOT ON ME!
AND NOW YOU BREAK INTO MY APARTMENT?!
YOU'RE INSANE.
TO SURPRISE YOU! IT'S CALLED A ROMANTIC GESTURE.
I'M NOT THE ONE ABOUT TO THROW AWAY THIS AMAZING CONNECTION WE HAVE!
BOXCA
BAM
YOU SURE GOT SOME WEIRD IDEAS ON FOREPLAY, LADY.

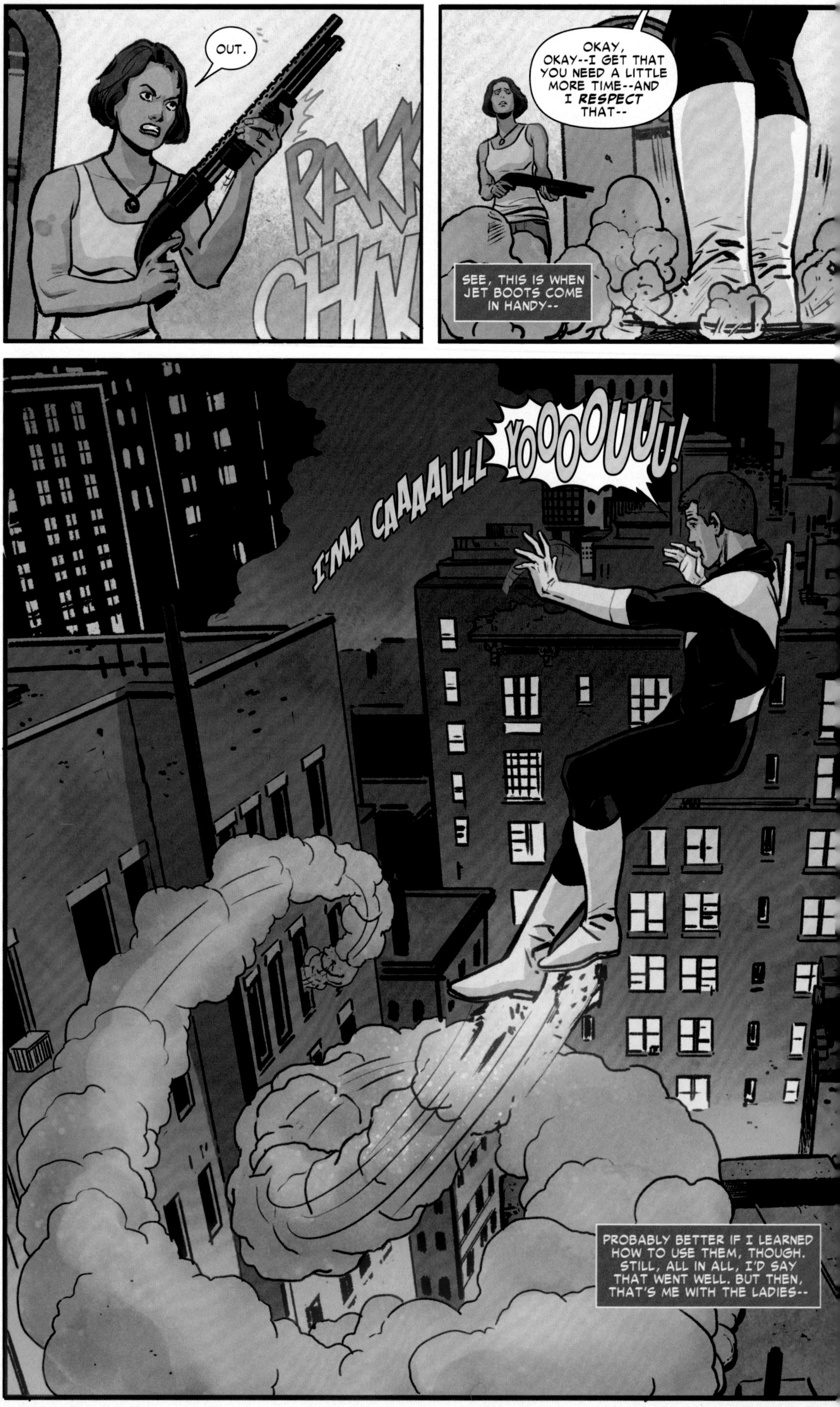
OUT.
RAKK CHK
OKAY, OKAY--I GET THAT YOU NEED A LITTLE MORE TIME--AND I RESPECT THAT--
SEE, THIS IS WHEN JET BOOTS COME IN HANDY--
I'MA CAAAALLLL YOOOOUUUU!
PROBABLY BETTER IF I LEARNED HOW TO USE THEM, THOUGH. STILL, ALL IN ALL, I'D SAY THAT WENT WELL. BUT THEN, THAT'S ME WITH THE LADIES--

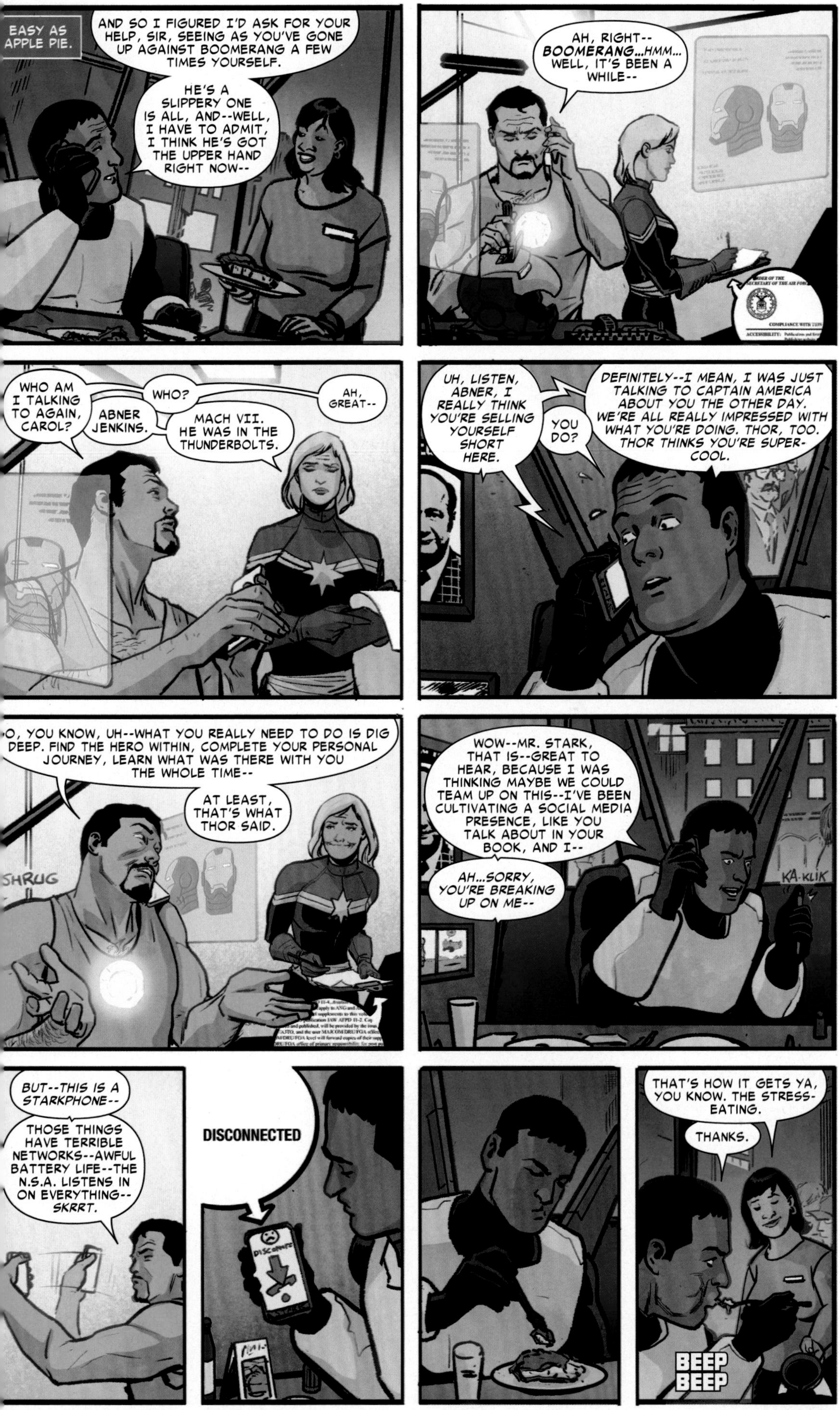

EASY AS APPLE PIE.
AND SO I FIGURED I'D ASK FOR YOUR HELP, SIR, SEEING AS YOU'VE GONE UP AGAINST BOOMERANG A FEW TIMES YOURSELF.
HE'S A SLIPPERY ONE IS ALL, AND--WELL, I HAVE TO ADMIT, I THINK HE'S GOT THE UPPER HAND RIGHT NOW--
AH, RIGHT-- BOOMERANG...HMM... WELL, IT'S BEEN A WHILE--
WHO AM I TALKING TO AGAIN, CAROL?
WHO?
AH, GREAT--
ABNER JENKINS.
MACH VII. HE WAS IN THE THUNDERBOLTS.
UH, LISTEN, ABNER, I REALLY THINK YOU'RE SELLING YOURSELF SHORT HERE.
YOU DO?
DEFINITELY--I MEAN, I WAS JUST TALKING TO CAPTAIN AMERICA ABOUT YOU THE OTHER DAY. WE'RE ALL REALLY IMPRESSED WITH WHAT YOU'RE DOING. THOR, TOO. THOR THINKS YOU'RE SUPER-COOL.
O, YOU KNOW, UH--WHAT YOU REALLY NEED TO DO IS DIG DEEP. FIND THE HERO WITHIN, COMPLETE YOUR PERSONAL JOURNEY, LEARN WHAT WAS THERE WITH YOU THE WHOLE TIME--
AT LEAST, THAT'S WHAT THOR SAID.
SHRUG
WOW--MR. STARK, THAT IS--GREAT TO HEAR, BECAUSE I WAS THINKING MAYBE WE COULD TEAM UP ON THIS--I'VE BEEN CULTIVATING A SOCIAL MEDIA PRESENCE, LIKE YOU TALK ABOUT IN YOUR BOOK, AND I--
AH...SORRY, YOU'RE BREAKING UP ON ME--
KA-KLIK
BUT--THIS IS A STARKPHONE--
THOSE THINGS HAVE TERRIBLE NETWORKS--AWFUL BATTERY LIFE--THE N.S.A. LISTENS IN ON EVERYTHING--SKRRT.
DISCONNECTED
THAT'S HOW IT GETS YA, YOU KNOW. THE STRESS-EATING.
THANKS.
BEEP BEEP

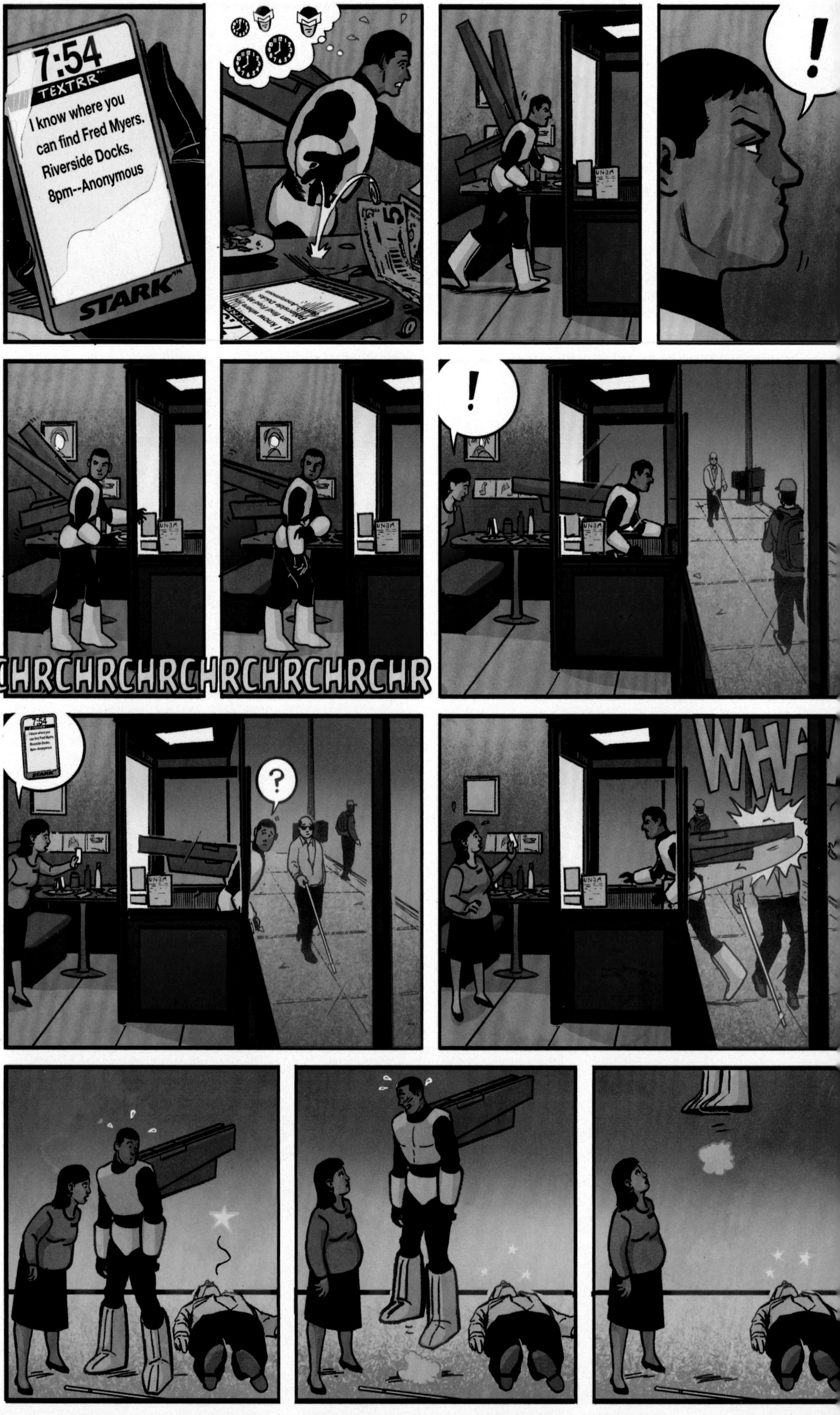
7:54
TEXTRR
I know where you can find Fred Myers. Riverside Docks. 8pm--Anonymous
STARK
!
CHRCHRCHRCHRCHRCHRCHRCHR
!
?
WHA

YOU'RE LATE.

I HAVE A LIFE OUTSIDE OF WORK, YOU KNOW!

WELL, YOU PICKED THE WRONG NIGHT TO PROVE IT-- SEEING AS IT'S THE BIGGEST OF OUR CAREERS.

MAGGIA LEADERSHIP JUST TEXTED TO SAY THEY'LL BE HERE ANY MINUTE TO SEE THE HEAD FOR THEMSELVES.

AND BOY WILL THEY GET A ROCKTACULAR SURPRISE WHEN THEY DO!

I'LL GET YOU FOR THIS @#$!%!

QUIET, STARCHILD.

YOU GUYS ARE GONNA GET US ALL KILLED.

YOU KNOW WHAT KILLS, BEETLE? STRESS.

YOU GOTTA RELAX--I MEAN, LOOK AT US. WE'RE ABOUT TO BECOME ROYALTY IN THIS TOWN. MAGGIA DONS.

DOESN'T THAT WARM YOUR VICIOUS ICE QUEEN HEART JUST A LITTLE?

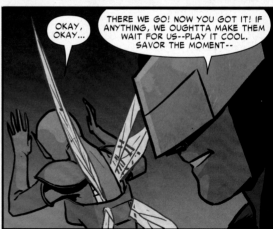

OKAY, OKAY...

THERE WE GO! NOW YOU GOT IT! IF ANYTHING, WE OUGHTTA MAKE THEM WAIT FOR US--PLAY IT COOL. SAVOR THE MOMENT--

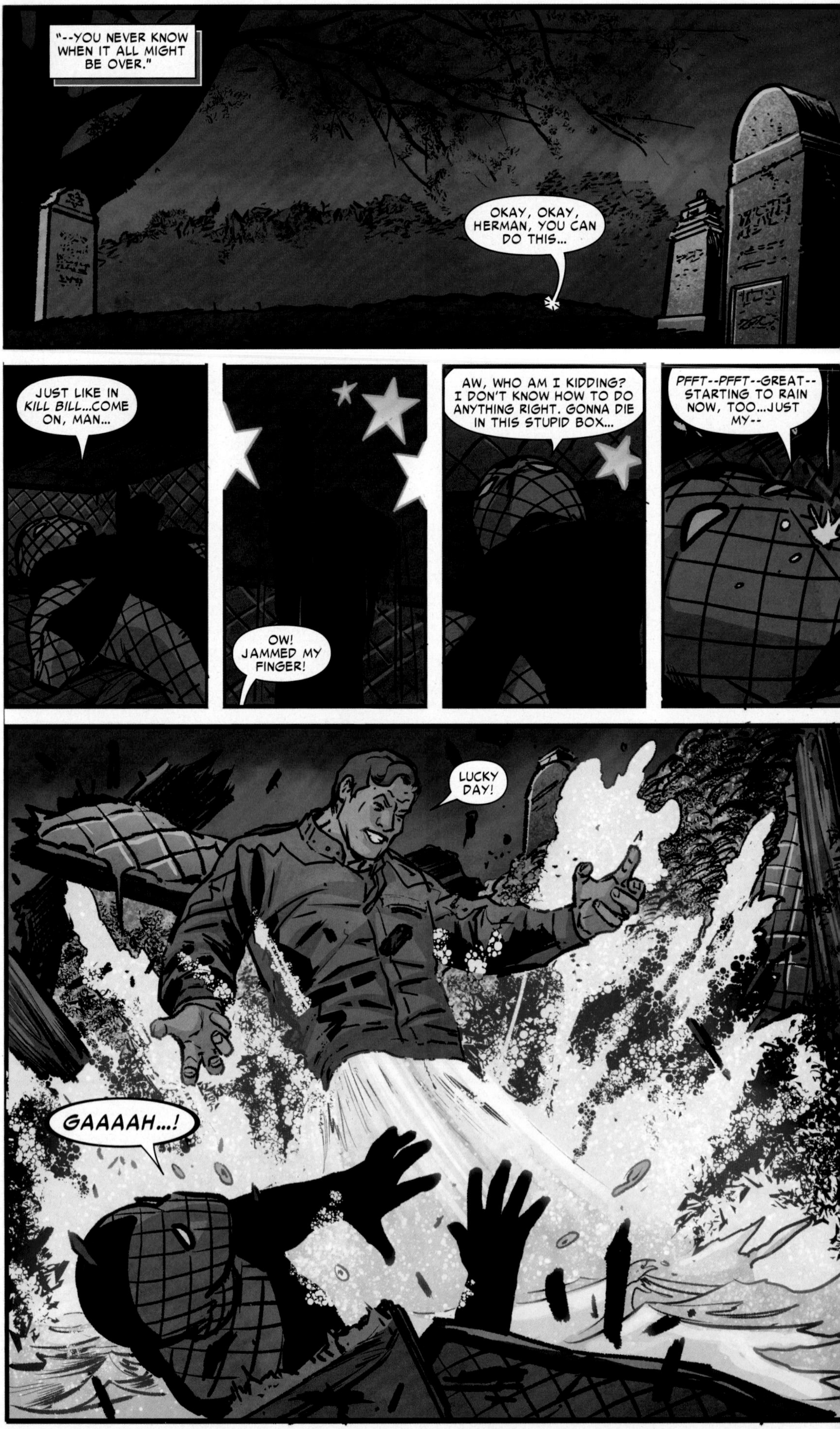
"--YOU NEVER KNOW WHEN IT ALL MIGHT BE OVER."
OKAY, OKAY, HERMAN, YOU CAN DO THIS...
JUST LIKE IN KILL BILL...COME ON, MAN...
OW! JAMMED MY FINGER!
AW, WHO AM I KIDDING? I DON'T KNOW HOW TO DO ANYTHING RIGHT. GONNA DIE IN THIS STUPID BOX...
PFFT--PFFT--GREAT--STARTING TO RAIN NOW, TOO...JUST MY--
LUCKY DAY!
GAAAAH...!

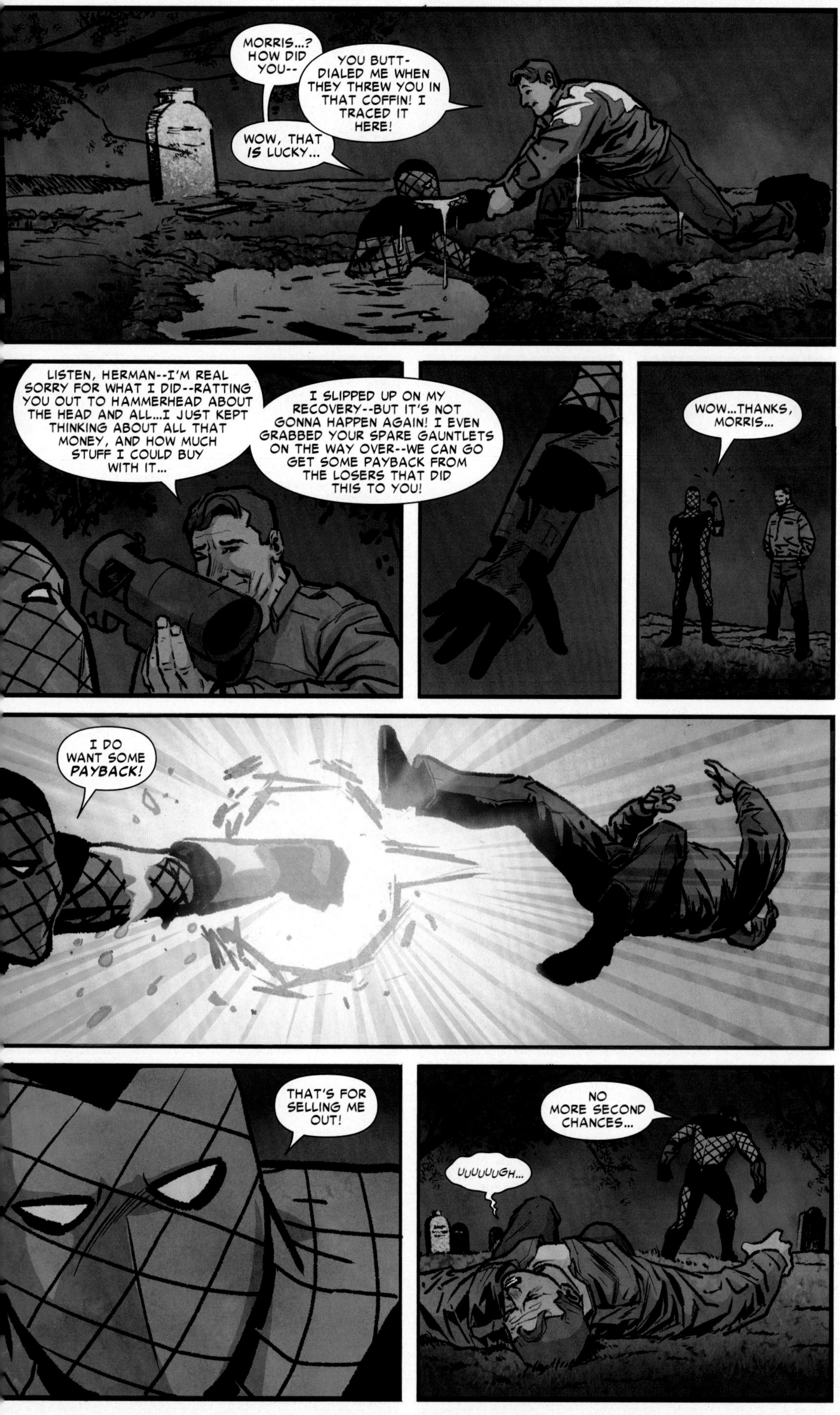
MORRIS...? HOW DID YOU--
YOU BUTT-DIALED ME WHEN THEY THREW YOU IN THAT COFFIN! I TRACED IT HERE!
WOW, THAT IS LUCKY...
LISTEN, HERMAN--I'M REAL SORRY FOR WHAT I DID--RATTING YOU OUT TO HAMMERHEAD ABOUT THE HEAD AND ALL...I JUST KEPT THINKING ABOUT ALL THAT MONEY, AND HOW MUCH STUFF I COULD BUY WITH IT...
I SLIPPED UP ON MY RECOVERY--BUT IT'S NOT GONNA HAPPEN AGAIN! I EVEN GRABBED YOUR SPARE GAUNTLETS ON THE WAY OVER--WE CAN GO GET SOME PAYBACK FROM THE LOSERS THAT DID THIS TO YOU!
WOW...THANKS, MORRIS...
I DO WANT SOME PAYBACK!
THAT'S FOR SELLING ME OUT!
NO MORE SECOND CHANCES...
UUUUUUGH...

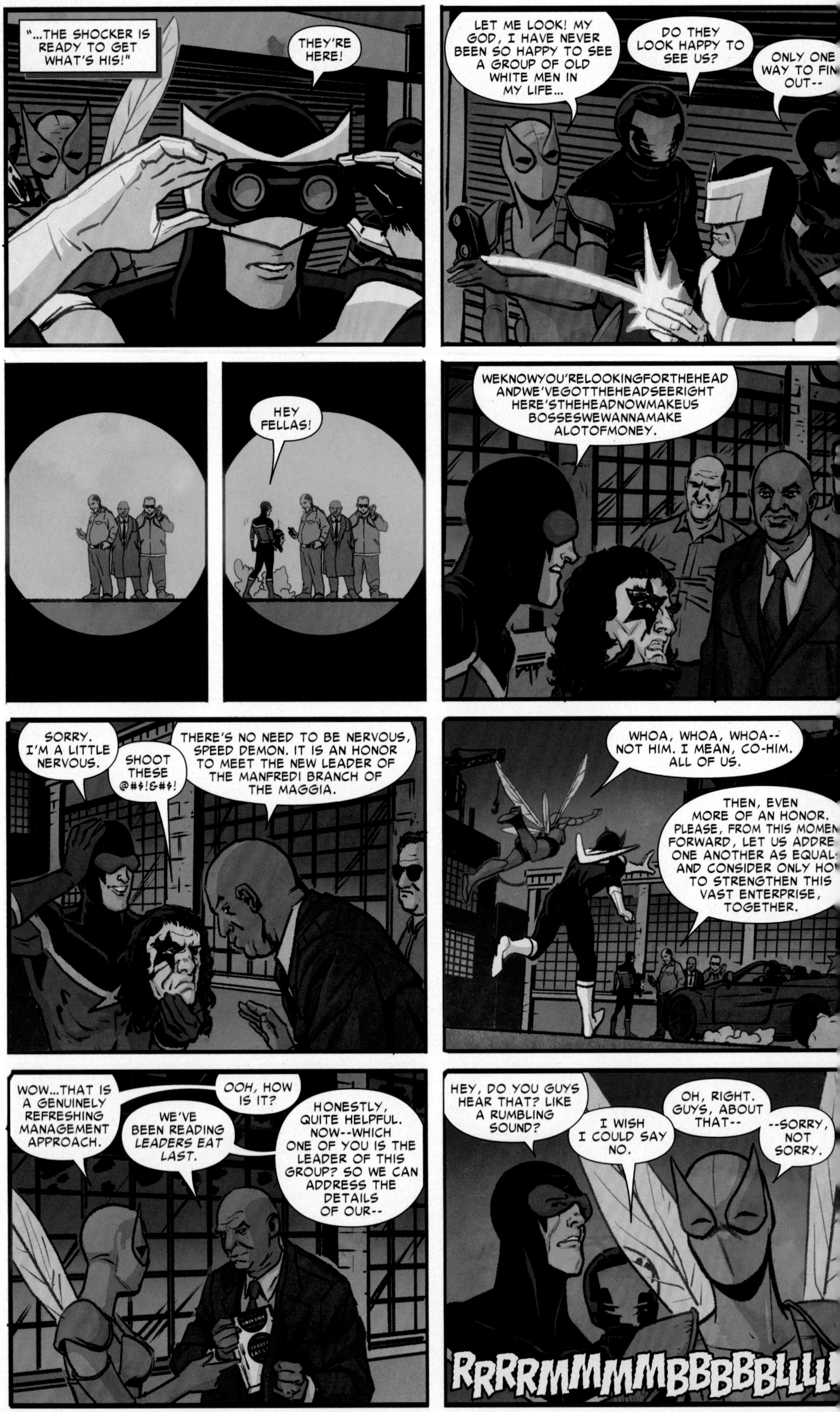
"...THE SHOCKER IS READY TO GET WHAT'S HIS!"
THEY'RE HERE!
LET ME LOOK! MY GOD, I HAVE NEVER BEEN SO HAPPY TO SEE A GROUP OF OLD WHITE MEN IN MY LIFE...
DO THEY LOOK HAPPY TO SEE US?
ONLY ONE WAY TO FIN OUT--
HEY FELLAS!
WEKNOWYOU'RELOOKINGFORTHEHEAD ANDWE'VEGOTTHEHEADSEERIGHT HERE'STHEHEADNOWMAKEUS BOSSESWEWANNAMAKE ALOTOFMONEY.
SORRY. I'M A LITTLE NERVOUS.
SHOOT THESE @#$!&#$!
THERE'S NO NEED TO BE NERVOUS, SPEED DEMON. IT IS AN HONOR TO MEET THE NEW LEADER OF THE MANFREDI BRANCH OF THE MAGGIA.
WHOA, WHOA, WHOA-- NOT HIM. I MEAN, CO-HIM. ALL OF US.
THEN, EVEN MORE OF AN HONOR. PLEASE, FROM THIS MOMEN FORWARD, LET US ADDRE ONE ANOTHER AS EQUAL- AND CONSIDER ONLY HO TO STRENGTHEN THIS VAST ENTERPRISE, TOGETHER.
WOW...THAT IS A GENUINELY REFRESHING MANAGEMENT APPROACH.
WE'VE BEEN READING *LEADERS EAT LAST.*
OOH, HOW IS IT?
HONESTLY, QUITE HELPFUL. NOW--WHICH ONE OF YOU IS THE LEADER OF THIS GROUP? SO WE CAN ADDRESS THE DETAILS OF OUR--
HEY, DO YOU GUYS HEAR THAT? LIKE A RUMBLING SOUND?
I WISH I COULD SAY NO.
OH, RIGHT. GUYS, ABOUT THAT--
--SORRY, NOT SORRY.
RRRRMMMMMBBBBBLLLL

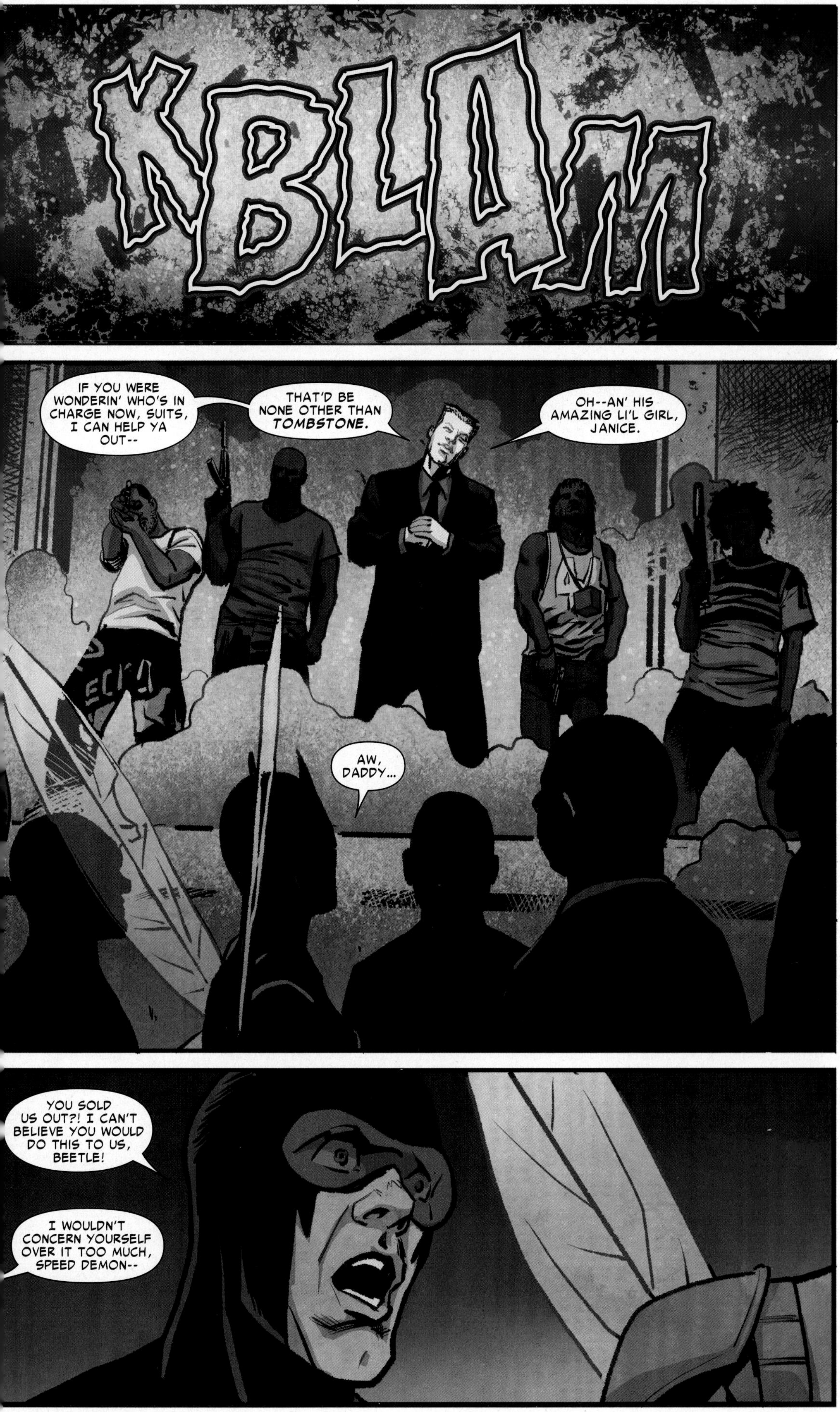
KBLAM
IF YOU WERE WONDERIN' WHO'S IN CHARGE NOW, SUITS, I CAN HELP YA OUT--
THAT'D BE NONE OTHER THAN *TOMBSTONE.*
OH--AN' HIS AMAZING LI'L GIRL, JANICE.
AW, DADDY...
YOU SOLD US OUT?! I CAN'T BELIEVE YOU WOULD DO THIS TO US, BEETLE!
I WOULDN'T CONCERN YOURSELF OVER IT TOO MUCH, SPEED DEMON--

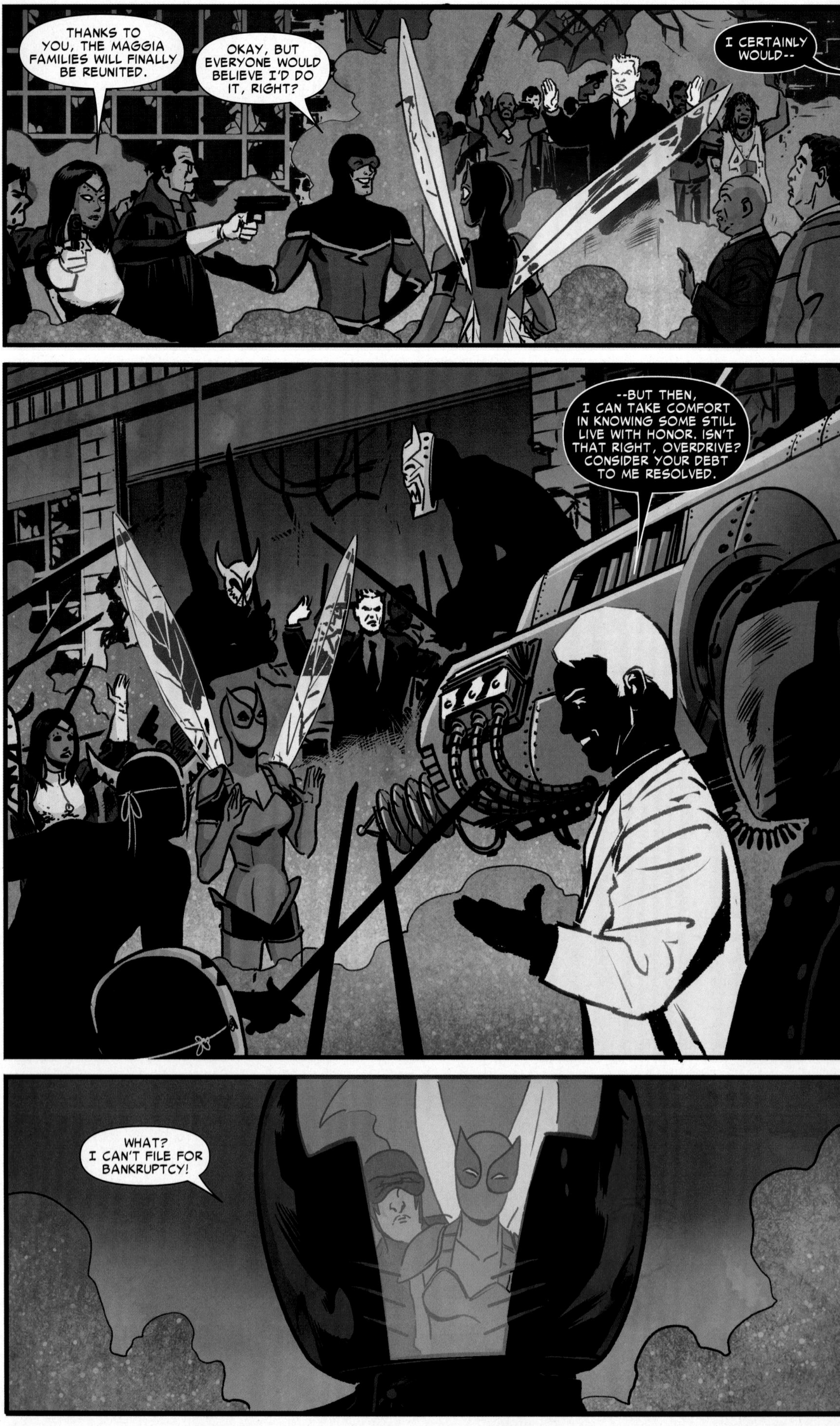
THANKS TO YOU, THE MAGGIA FAMILIES WILL FINALLY BE REUNITED.
OKAY, BUT EVERYONE WOULD BELIEVE I'D DO IT, RIGHT?
I CERTAINLY WOULD--
--BUT THEN, I CAN TAKE COMFORT IN KNOWING SOME STILL LIVE WITH HONOR. ISN'T THAT RIGHT, OVERDRIVE? CONSIDER YOUR DEBT TO ME RESOLVED.
WHAT? I CAN'T FILE FOR BANKRUPTCY!

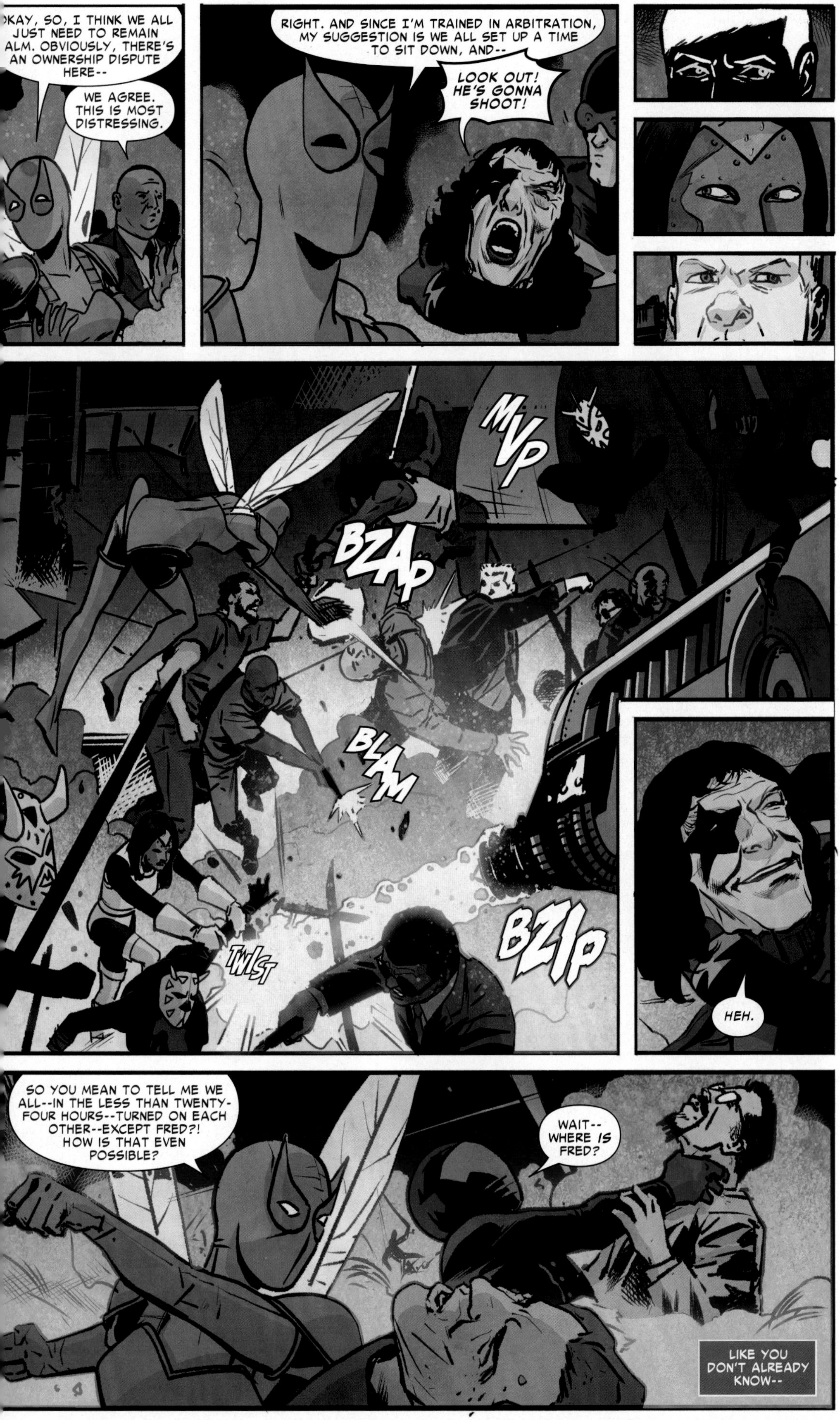
OKAY, SO, I THINK WE ALL JUST NEED TO REMAIN CALM. OBVIOUSLY, THERE'S AN OWNERSHIP DISPUTE HERE--
WE AGREE. THIS IS MOST DISTRESSING.
RIGHT. AND SINCE I'M TRAINED IN ARBITRATION, MY SUGGESTION IS WE ALL SET UP A TIME TO SIT DOWN, AND--
LOOK OUT! HE'S GONNA SHOOT!
MVP
BZAP
BLAM
TWIST
BZIP
HEH.
SO YOU MEAN TO TELL ME WE ALL--IN THE LESS THAN TWENTY-FOUR HOURS--TURNED ON EACH OTHER--EXCEPT FRED?! HOW IS THAT EVEN POSSIBLE?
WAIT-- WHERE IS FRED?
LIKE YOU DON'T ALREADY KNOW--

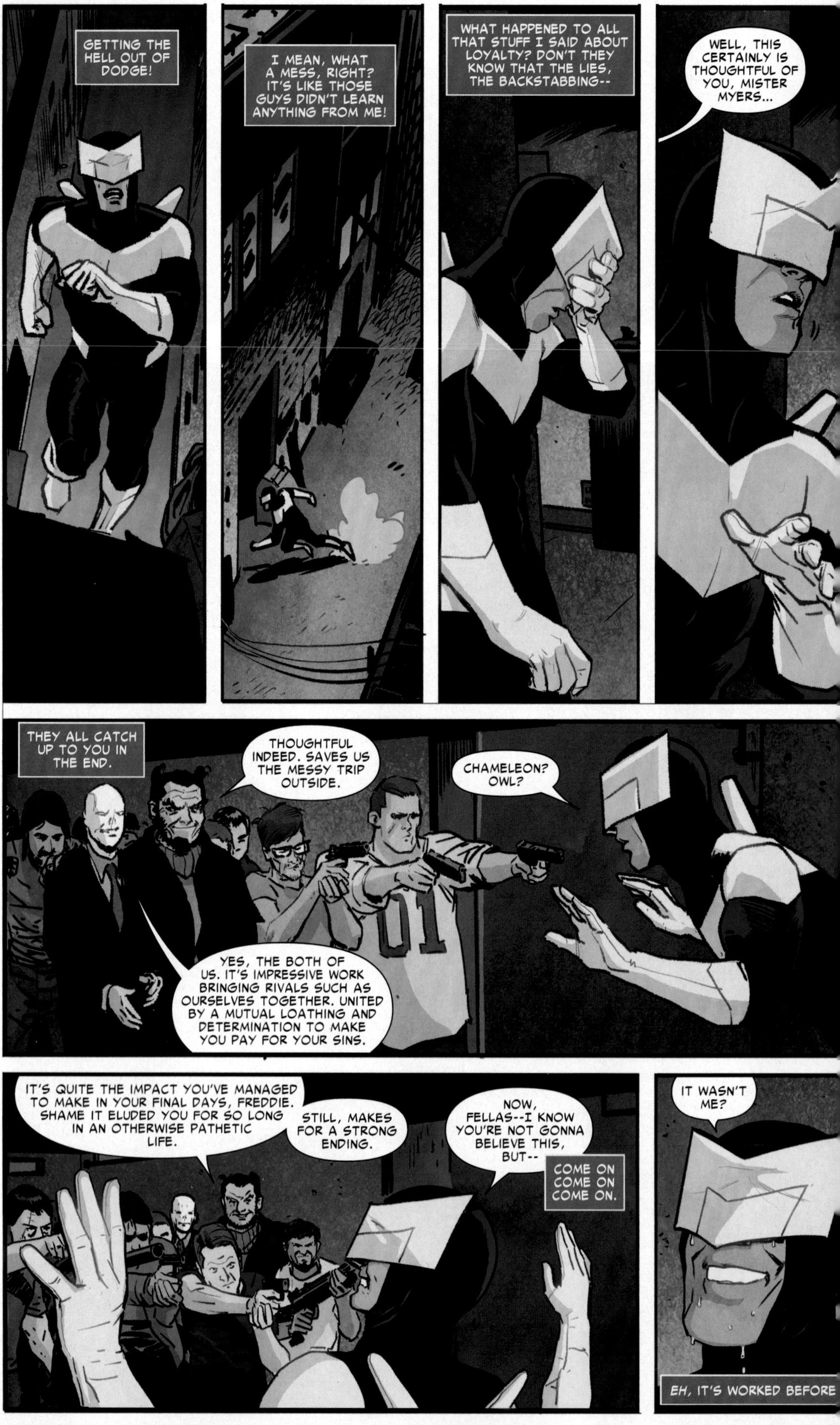
GETTING THE HELL OUT OF DODGE!
I MEAN, WHAT A MESS, RIGHT? IT'S LIKE THOSE GUYS DIDN'T LEARN ANYTHING FROM ME!
WHAT HAPPENED TO ALL THAT STUFF I SAID ABOUT LOYALTY? DON'T THEY KNOW THAT THE LIES, THE BACKSTABBING--
WELL, THIS CERTAINLY IS THOUGHTFUL OF YOU, MISTER MYERS...
THEY ALL CATCH UP TO YOU IN THE END.
THOUGHTFUL INDEED. SAVES US THE MESSY TRIP OUTSIDE.
CHAMELEON? OWL?
YES, THE BOTH OF US. IT'S IMPRESSIVE WORK BRINGING RIVALS SUCH AS OURSELVES TOGETHER. UNITED BY A MUTUAL LOATHING AND DETERMINATION TO MAKE YOU PAY FOR YOUR SINS.
IT'S QUITE THE IMPACT YOU'VE MANAGED TO MAKE IN YOUR FINAL DAYS, FREDDIE. SHAME IT ELUDED YOU FOR SO LONG IN AN OTHERWISE PATHETIC LIFE.
STILL, MAKES FOR A STRONG ENDING.
NOW, FELLAS--I KNOW YOU'RE NOT GONNA BELIEVE THIS, BUT--
COME ON COME ON COME ON.
IT WASN'T ME?
EH, IT'S WORKED BEFORE

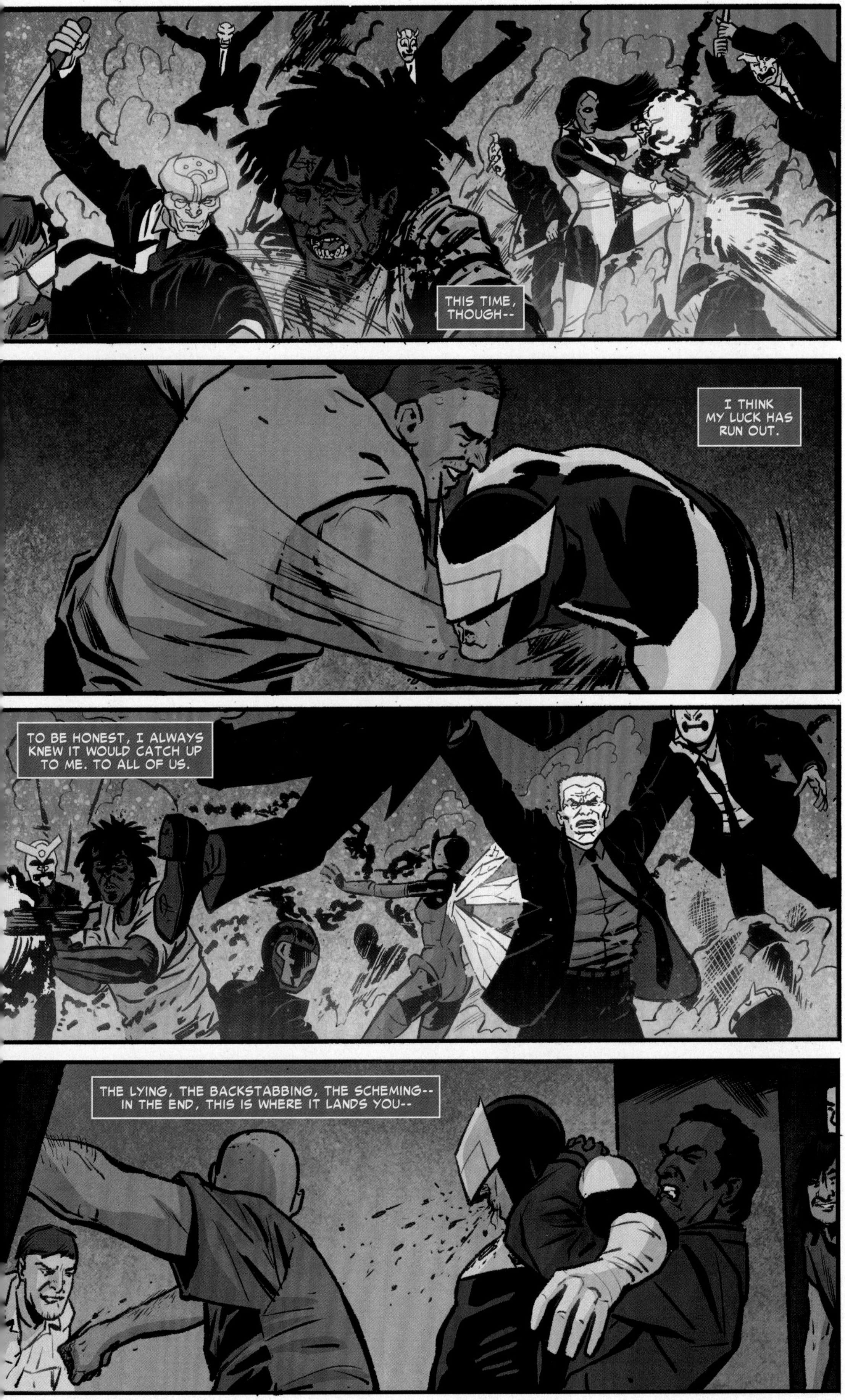
THIS TIME, THOUGH--
I THINK MY LUCK HAS RUN OUT.
TO BE HONEST, I ALWAYS KNEW IT WOULD CATCH UP TO ME. TO ALL OF US.
THE LYING, THE BACKSTABBING, THE SCHEMING-- IN THE END, THIS IS WHERE IT LANDS YOU--

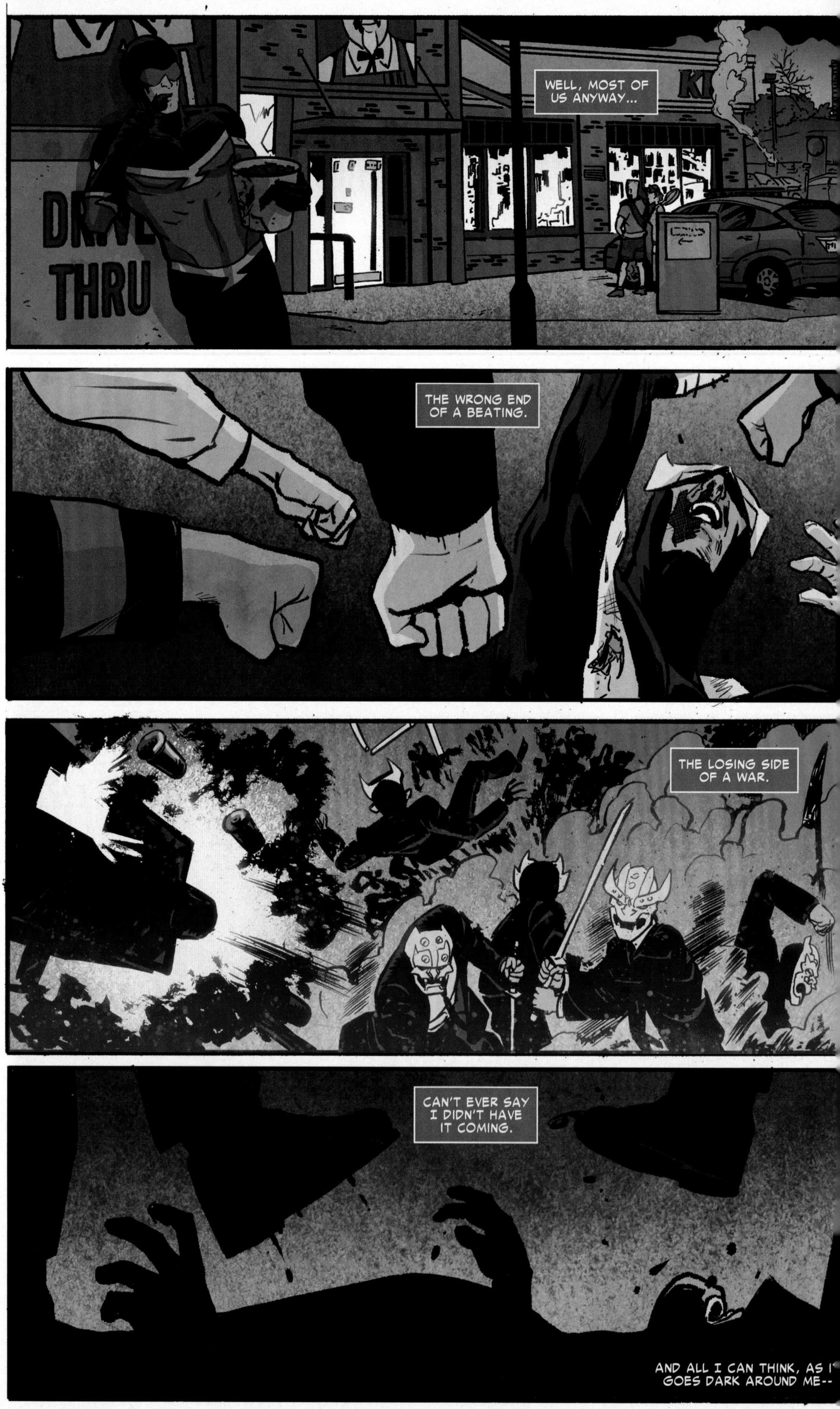
WELL, MOST OF US ANYWAY...
DRIVE THRU
THE WRONG END OF A BEATING.
THE LOSING SIDE OF A WAR.
CAN'T EVER SAY I DIDN'T HAVE IT COMING.
AND ALL I CAN THINK, AS I
GOES DARK AROUND ME--

--IS MY GOD, I CAN'T BELIEVE YOU FELL FOR IT AGAIN.

YEP. THAT IS ME.

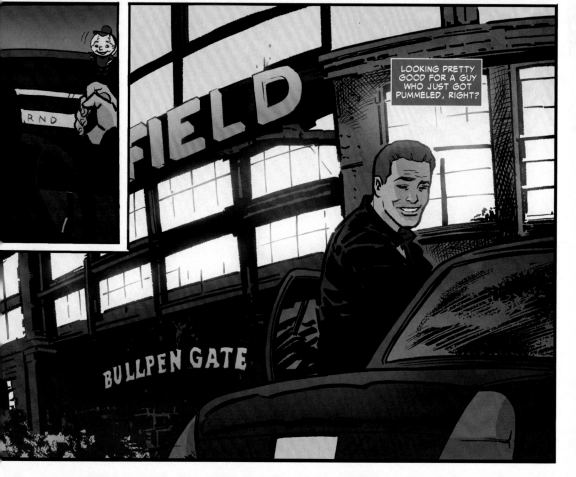

LOOKING PRETTY GOOD FOR A GUY WHO JUST GOT PUMMELED, RIGHT?

FIELD

BULLPEN GATE

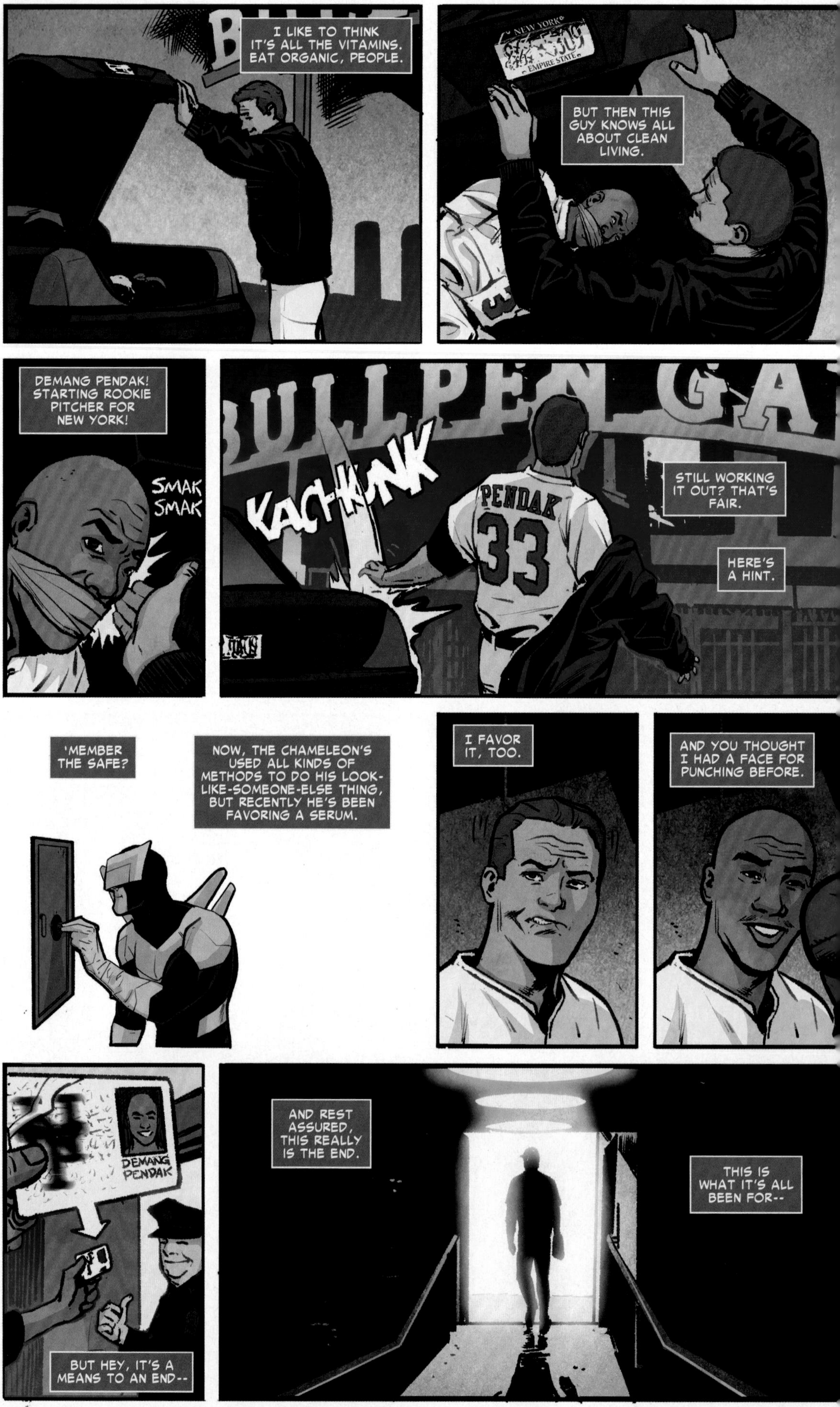
I LIKE TO THINK IT'S ALL THE VITAMINS. EAT ORGANIC, PEOPLE.
BUT THEN THIS GUY KNOWS ALL ABOUT CLEAN LIVING.
DEMANG PENDAK! STARTING ROOKIE PITCHER FOR NEW YORK!
SMAK SMAK
KACHUNK
BULLPEN GA
PENDAK
33
STILL WORKING IT OUT? THAT'S FAIR.
HERE'S A HINT.
'MEMBER THE SAFE?
NOW, THE CHAMELEON'S USED ALL KINDS OF METHODS TO DO HIS LOOK-LIKE-SOMEONE-ELSE THING, BUT RECENTLY HE'S BEEN FAVORING A SERUM.
I FAVOR IT, TOO.
AND YOU THOUGHT I HAD A FACE FOR PUNCHING BEFORE.
DEMANG PENDAK
BUT HEY, IT'S A MEANS TO AN END--
AND REST ASSURED, THIS REALLY IS THE END.
THIS IS WHAT IT'S ALL BEEN FOR--

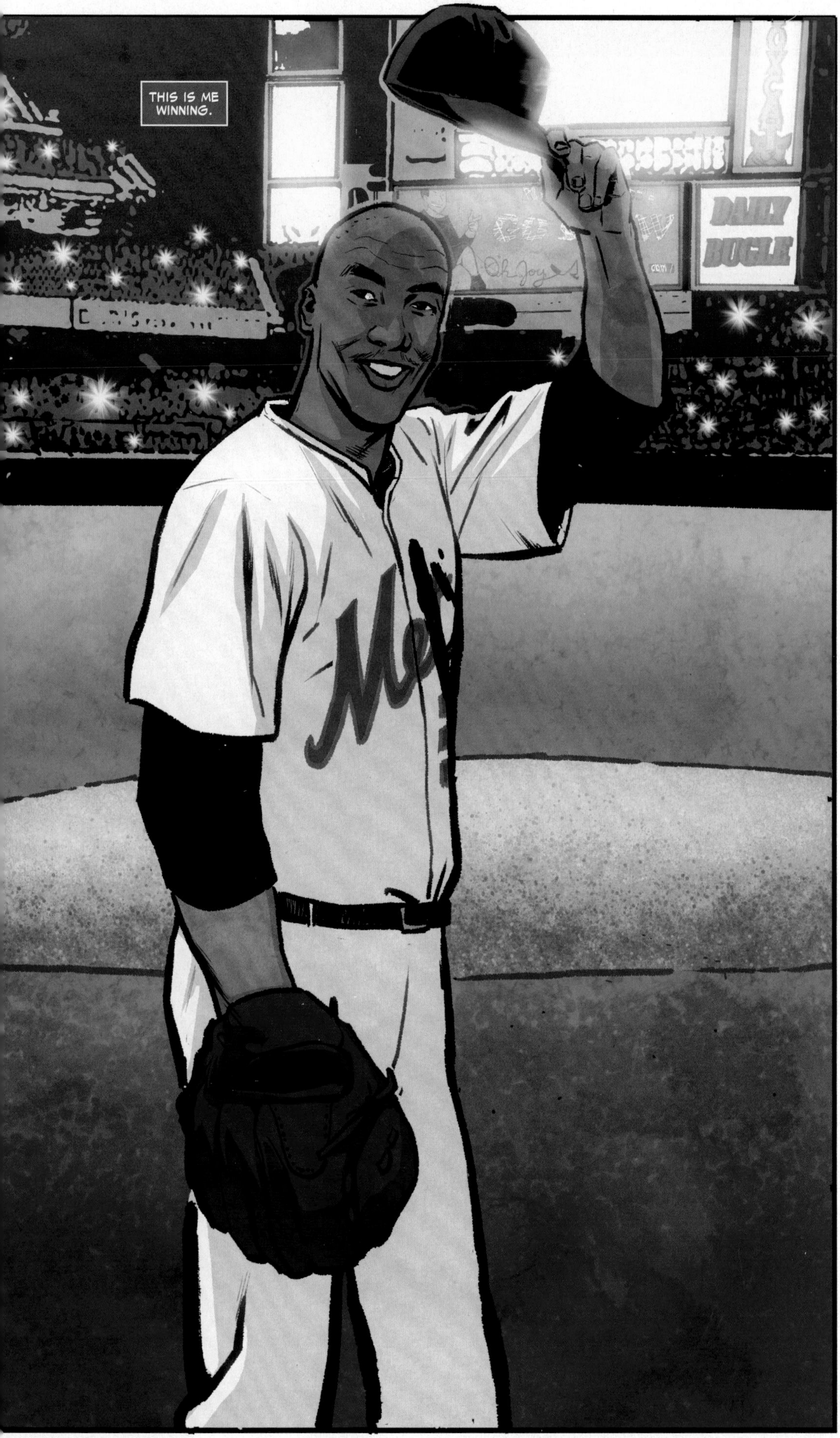
THIS IS ME WINNING.
DAILY BUGLE

17

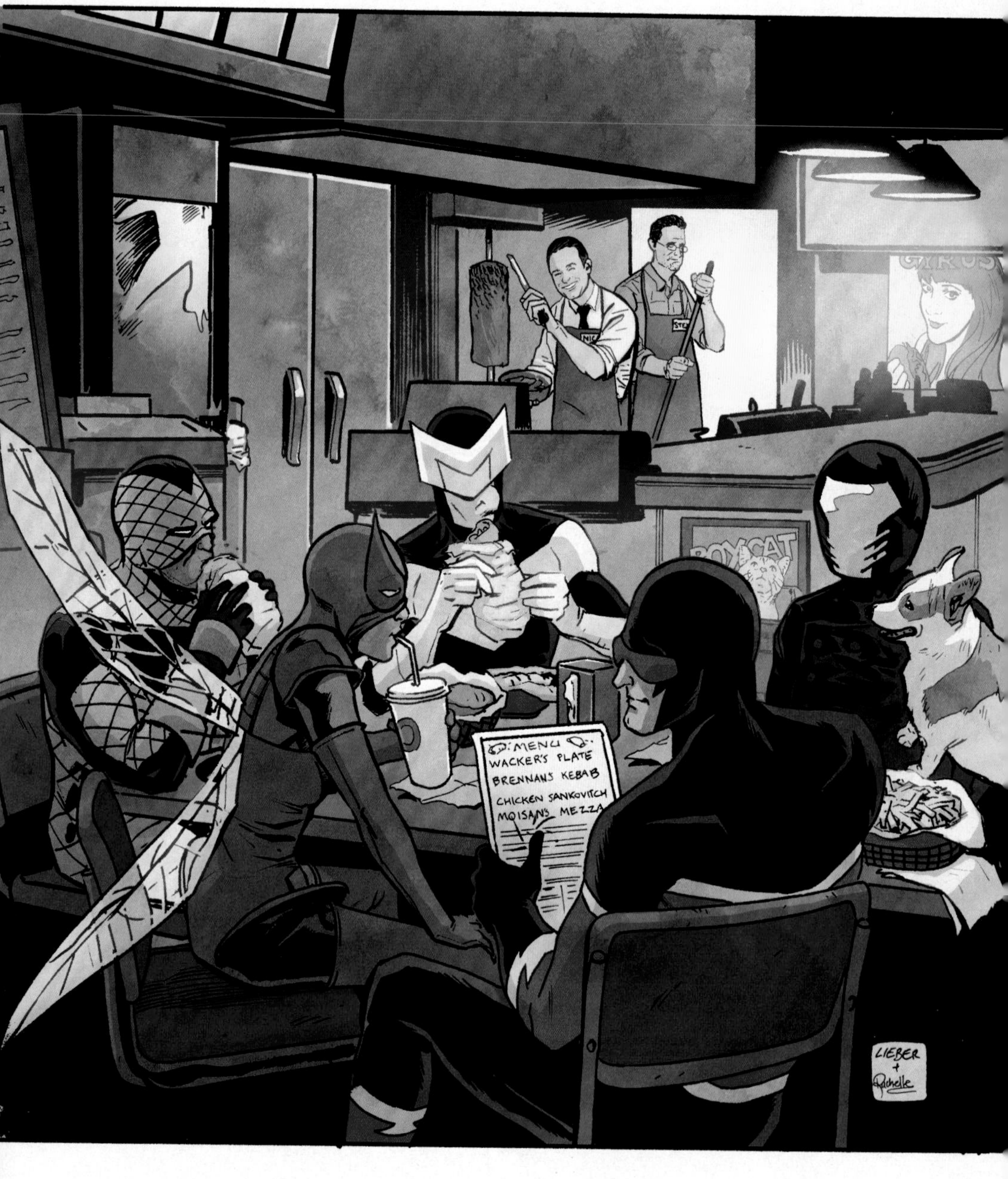
GYROS
BOYCAT
MENU
WACKER'S PLATE
BRENNAN'S KEBAB
CHICKEN SANKOVITCH
MOISAN'S MEZZA
LIEBER + Rachelle

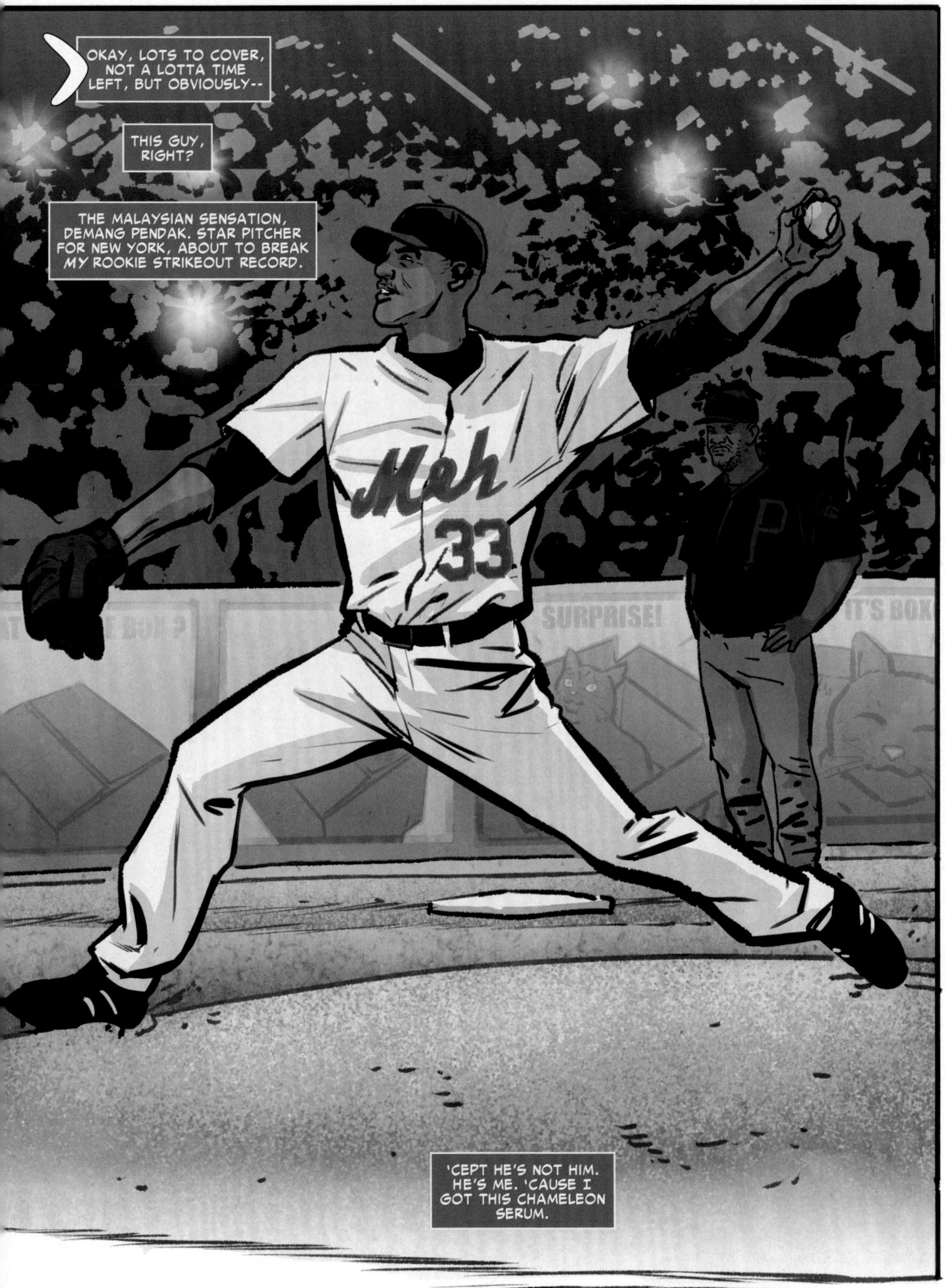
OKAY, LOTS TO COVER, NOT A LOTTA TIME LEFT, BUT OBVIOUSLY--
THIS GUY, RIGHT?
THE MALAYSIAN SENSATION, DEMANG PENDAK. STAR PITCHER FOR NEW YORK, ABOUT TO BREAK MY ROOKIE STRIKEOUT RECORD.
Meh
33
SURPRISE!
'CEPT HE'S NOT HIM. HE'S ME. 'CAUSE I GOT THIS CHAMELEON SERUM.

WHY DOES THIS STUFF ALWAYS HAVE TO BE SO CONVOLUTED?

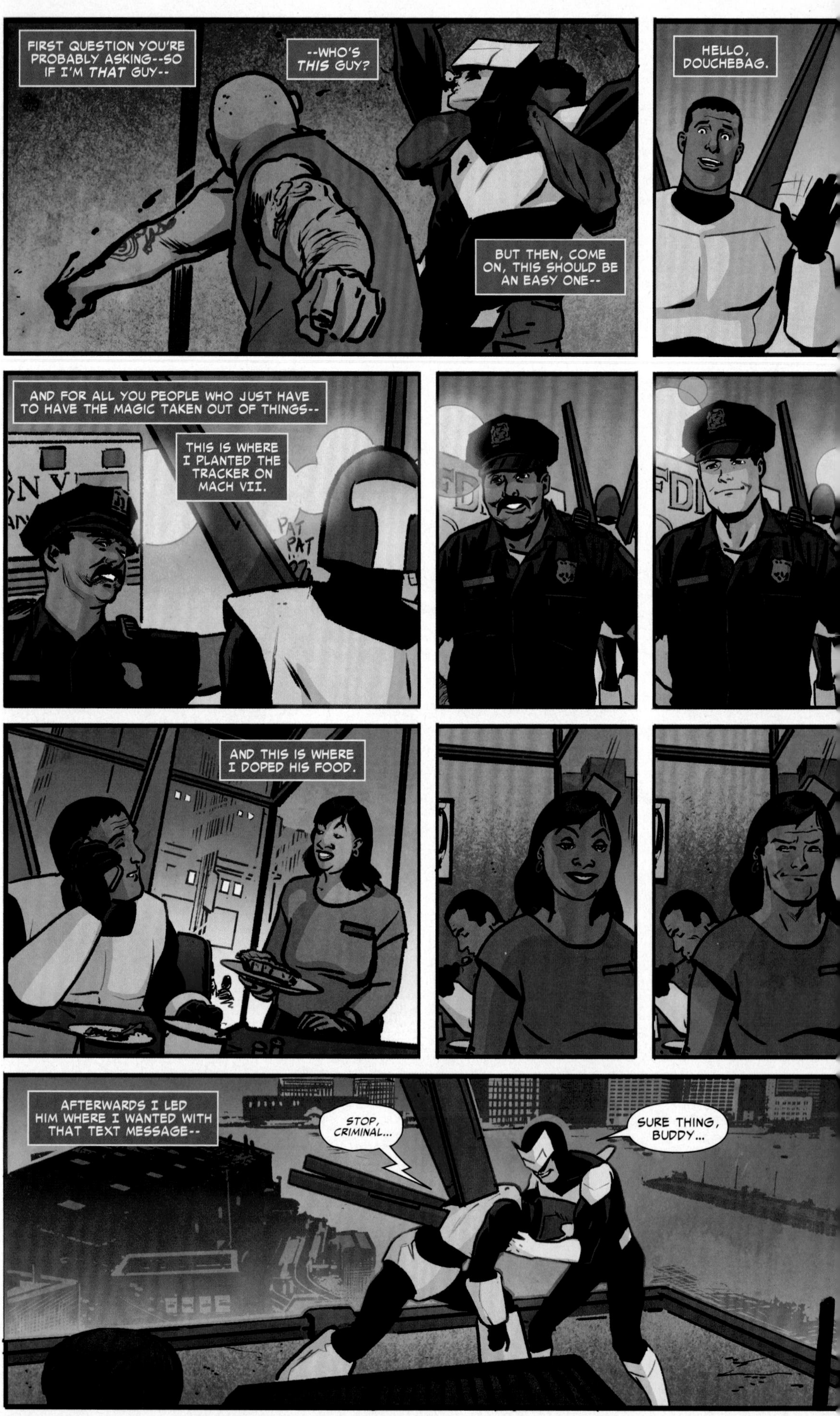
FIRST QUESTION YOU'RE PROBABLY ASKING--SO IF I'M *THAT* GUY--
--WHO'S *THIS* GUY?
BUT THEN, COME ON, THIS SHOULD BE AN EASY ONE--
HELLO, DOUCHEBAG.
AND FOR ALL YOU PEOPLE WHO JUST HAVE TO HAVE THE MAGIC TAKEN OUT OF THINGS--
THIS IS WHERE I PLANTED THE TRACKER ON MACH VII.
PAT PAT
AND THIS IS WHERE I DOPED HIS FOOD.
AFTERWARDS I LED HIM WHERE I WANTED WITH THAT TEXT MESSAGE--
STOP, CRIMINAL...
SURE THING, BUDDY...

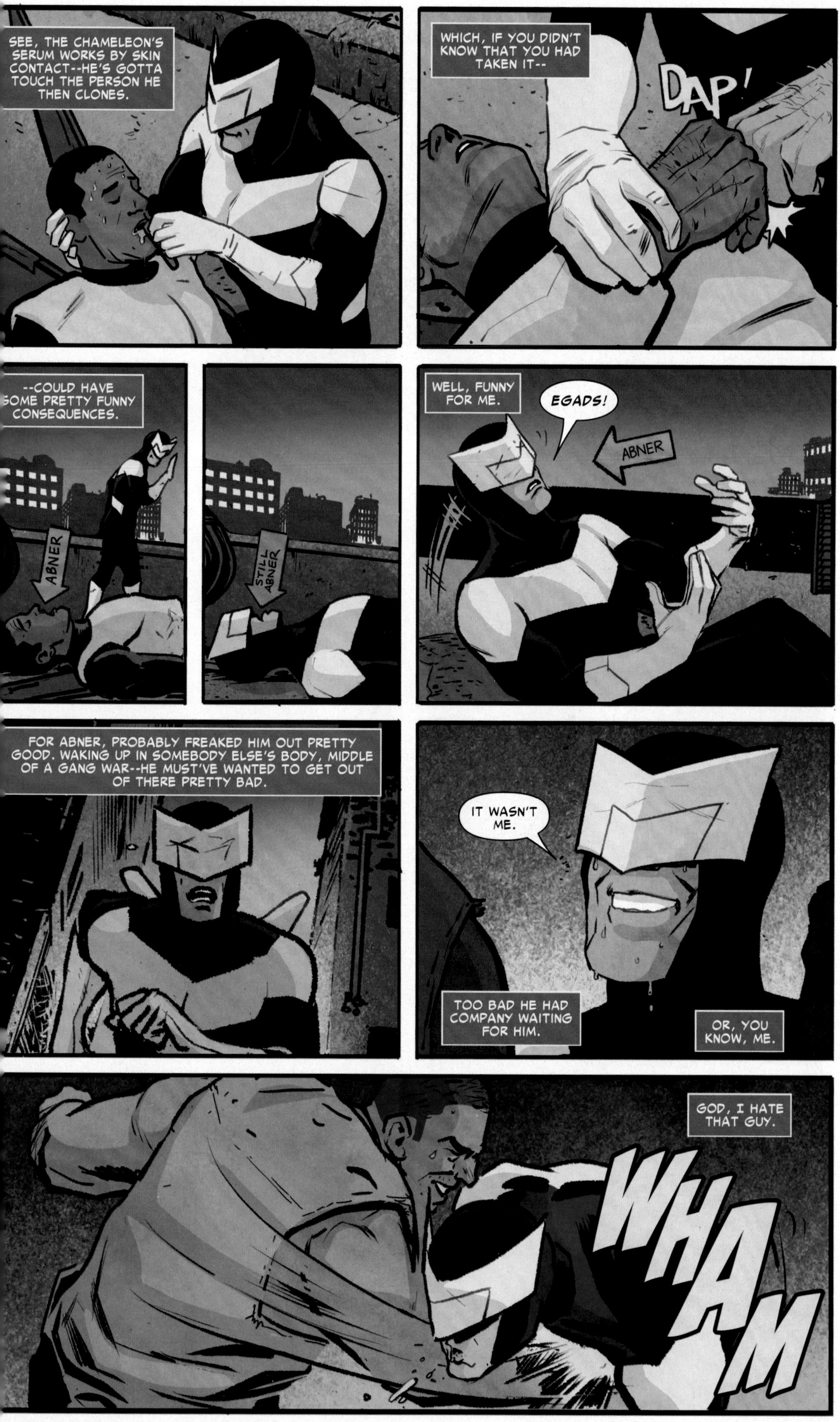

SEE, THE CHAMELEON'S SERUM WORKS BY SKIN CONTACT--HE'S GOTTA TOUCH THE PERSON HE THEN CLONES.
WHICH, IF YOU DIDN'T KNOW THAT YOU HAD TAKEN IT--
DAP!
--COULD HAVE SOME PRETTY FUNNY CONSEQUENCES.
ABNER
STILL ABNER
WELL, FUNNY FOR ME.
EGADS!
ABNER
FOR ABNER, PROBABLY FREAKED HIM OUT PRETTY GOOD. WAKING UP IN SOMEBODY ELSE'S BODY, MIDDLE OF A GANG WAR--HE MUST'VE WANTED TO GET OUT OF THERE PRETTY BAD.
IT WASN'T ME.
TOO BAD HE HAD COMPANY WAITING FOR HIM.
OR, YOU KNOW, ME.
GOD, I HATE THAT GUY.
WHAM

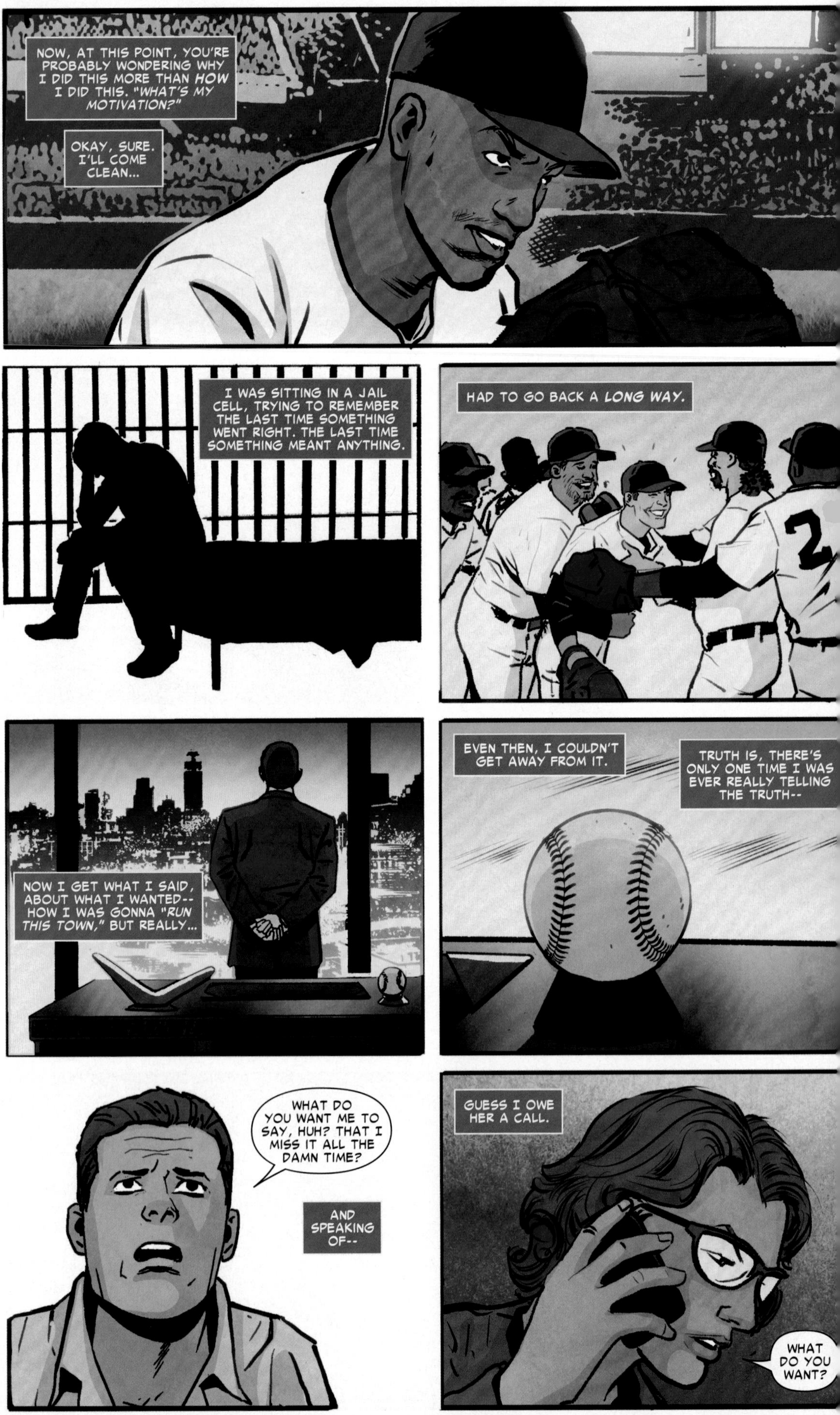
NOW, AT THIS POINT, YOU'RE PROBABLY WONDERING WHY I DID THIS MORE THAN *HOW* I DID THIS. "*WHAT'S MY MOTIVATION?*"
OKAY, SURE. I'LL COME CLEAN...
I WAS SITTING IN A JAIL CELL, TRYING TO REMEMBER THE LAST TIME SOMETHING WENT RIGHT. THE LAST TIME SOMETHING MEANT ANYTHING.
HAD TO GO BACK A *LONG WAY.*
NOW I GET WHAT I SAID, ABOUT WHAT I WANTED-- HOW I WAS GONNA "*RUN THIS TOWN,*" BUT REALLY...
EVEN THEN, I COULDN'T GET AWAY FROM IT.
TRUTH IS, THERE'S ONLY ONE TIME I WAS EVER REALLY TELLING THE TRUTH--
WHAT DO YOU WANT ME TO SAY, HUH? THAT I MISS IT ALL THE DAMN TIME?
AND SPEAKING OF--
GUESS I OWE HER A CALL.
WHAT DO YOU WANT?

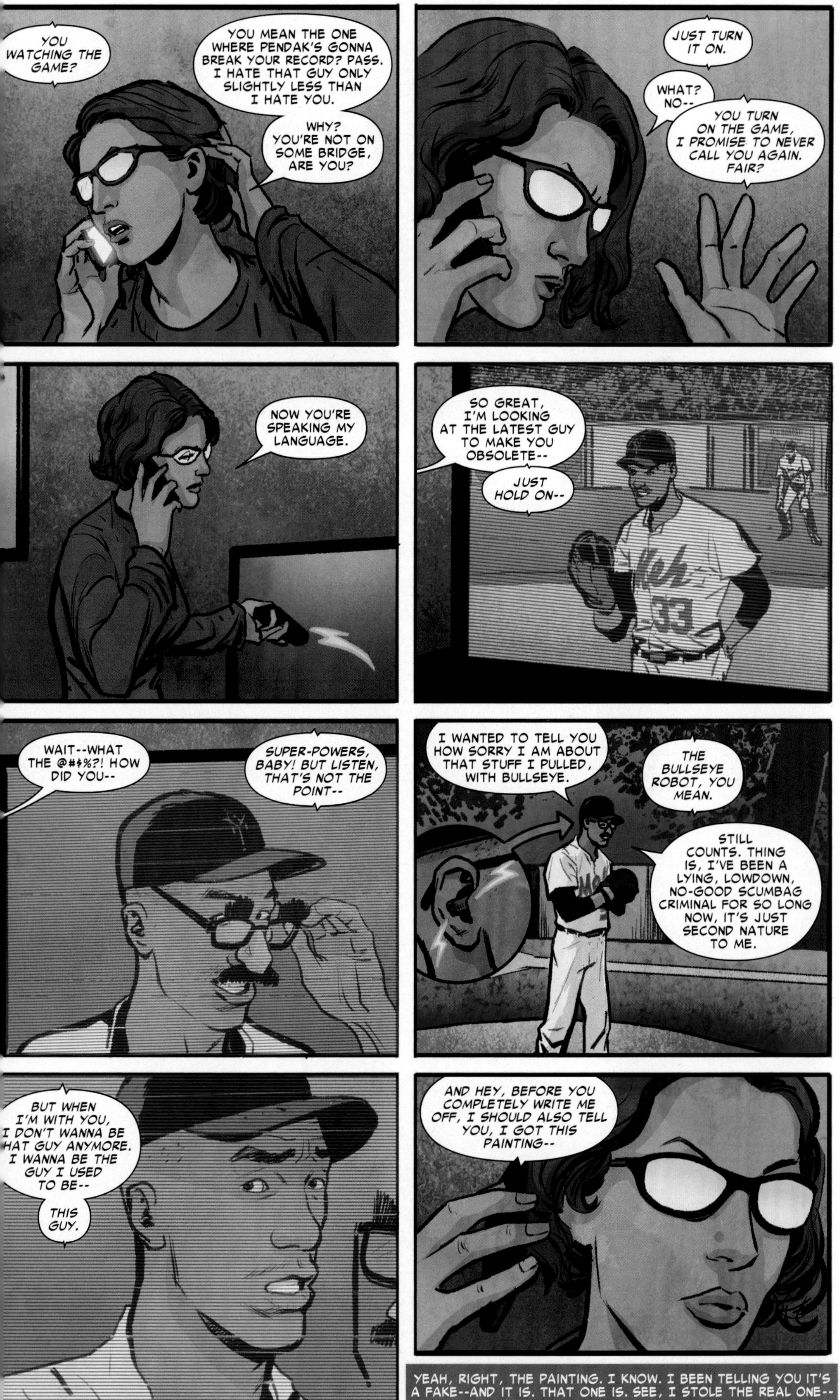

YOU WATCHING THE GAME?
YOU MEAN THE ONE WHERE PENDAK'S GONNA BREAK YOUR RECORD? PASS. I HATE THAT GUY ONLY SLIGHTLY LESS THAN I HATE YOU.
WHY? YOU'RE NOT ON SOME BRIDGE, ARE YOU?
JUST TURN IT ON.
WHAT? NO--
YOU TURN ON THE GAME, I PROMISE TO NEVER CALL YOU AGAIN. FAIR?
NOW YOU'RE SPEAKING MY LANGUAGE.
SO GREAT, I'M LOOKING AT THE LATEST GUY TO MAKE YOU OBSOLETE--
JUST HOLD ON--
WAIT--WHAT THE @#$%?! HOW DID YOU--
SUPER-POWERS, BABY! BUT LISTEN, THAT'S NOT THE POINT--
I WANTED TO TELL YOU HOW SORRY I AM ABOUT THAT STUFF I PULLED, WITH BULLSEYE.
THE BULLSEYE ROBOT, YOU MEAN.
STILL COUNTS. THING IS, I'VE BEEN A LYING, LOWDOWN, NO-GOOD SCUMBAG CRIMINAL FOR SO LONG NOW, IT'S JUST SECOND NATURE TO ME.
BUT WHEN I'M WITH YOU, I DON'T WANNA BE HAT GUY ANYMORE. I WANNA BE THE GUY I USED TO BE--
THIS GUY.
AND HEY, BEFORE YOU COMPLETELY WRITE ME OFF, I SHOULD ALSO TELL YOU, I GOT THIS PAINTING--
YEAH, RIGHT, THE PAINTING. I KNOW. I BEEN TELLING YOU IT'S A FAKE--AND IT IS. THAT ONE IS. SEE, I STOLE THE REAL ONE--

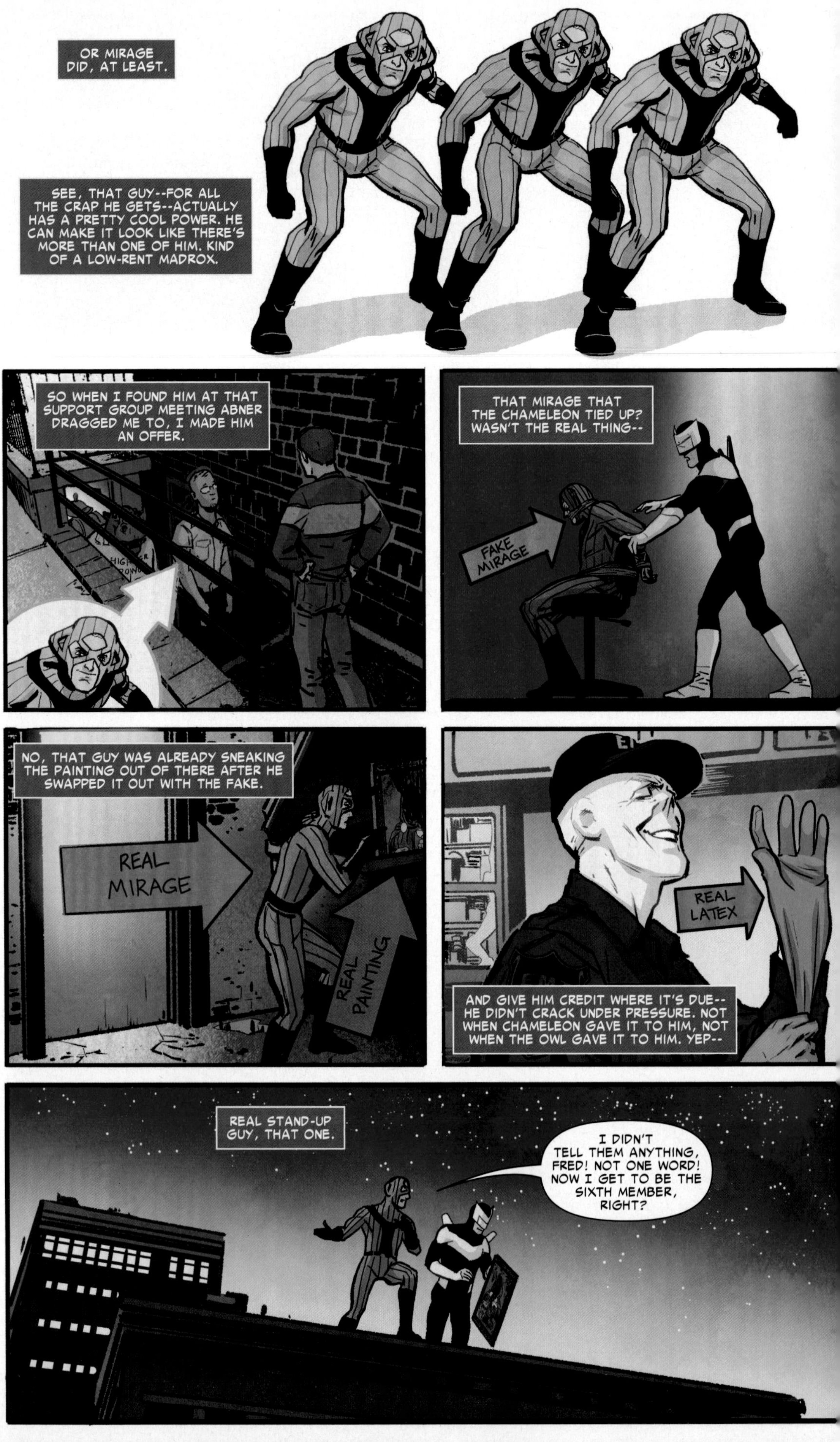
OR MIRAGE DID, AT LEAST.
SEE, THAT GUY--FOR ALL THE CRAP HE GETS--ACTUALLY HAS A PRETTY COOL POWER. HE CAN MAKE IT LOOK LIKE THERE'S MORE THAN ONE OF HIM. KIND OF A LOW-RENT MADROX.
SO WHEN I FOUND HIM AT THAT SUPPORT GROUP MEETING ABNER DRAGGED ME TO, I MADE HIM AN OFFER.
THAT MIRAGE THAT THE CHAMELEON TIED UP? WASN'T THE REAL THING--
FAKE MIRAGE
NO, THAT GUY WAS ALREADY SNEAKING THE PAINTING OUT OF THERE AFTER HE SWAPPED IT OUT WITH THE FAKE.
REAL MIRAGE
REAL PAINTING
REAL LATEX
AND GIVE HIM CREDIT WHERE IT'S DUE--HE DIDN'T CRACK UNDER PRESSURE. NOT WHEN CHAMELEON GAVE IT TO HIM, NOT WHEN THE OWL GAVE IT TO HIM. YEP--
REAL STAND-UP GUY, THAT ONE.
I DIDN'T TELL THEM ANYTHING, FRED! NOT ONE WORD! NOW I GET TO BE THE SIXTH MEMBER, RIGHT?

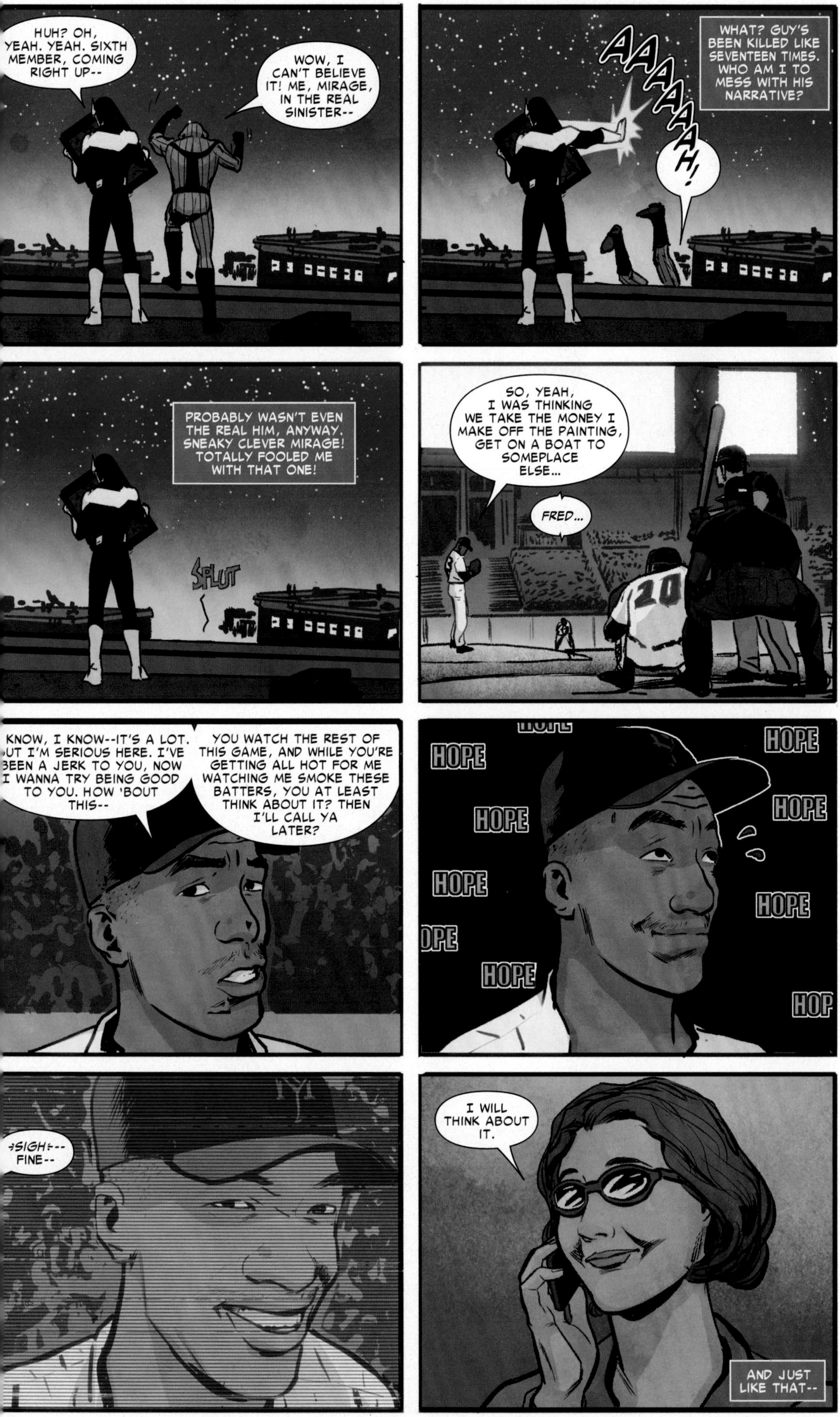
HUH? OH, YEAH. YEAH. SIXTH MEMBER, COMING RIGHT UP--
WOW, I CAN'T BELIEVE IT! ME, MIRAGE, IN THE REAL SINISTER--
AAAAAAAH!
WHAT? GUY'S BEEN KILLED LIKE SEVENTEEN TIMES. WHO AM I TO MESS WITH HIS NARRATIVE?
PROBABLY WASN'T EVEN THE REAL HIM, ANYWAY. SNEAKY CLEVER MIRAGE! TOTALLY FOOLED ME WITH THAT ONE!
SPLUT
SO, YEAH, I WAS THINKING WE TAKE THE MONEY I MAKE OFF THE PAINTING, GET ON A BOAT TO SOMEPLACE ELSE...
FRED...
KNOW, I KNOW--IT'S A LOT. UT I'M SERIOUS HERE. I'VE BEEN A JERK TO YOU, NOW I WANNA TRY BEING GOOD TO YOU. HOW 'BOUT THIS--
YOU WATCH THE REST OF THIS GAME, AND WHILE YOU'RE GETTING ALL HOT FOR ME WATCHING ME SMOKE THESE BATTERS, YOU AT LEAST THINK ABOUT IT? THEN I'LL CALL YA LATER?
HOPE HOPE HOPE HOPE HOPE HOPE HOPE HOPE HOP
SIGH--FINE--
I WILL THINK ABOUT IT.
AND JUST LIKE THAT--

--I CAN'T LOSE.

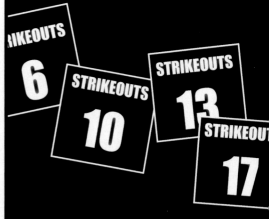

STRIKEOUTS 6

STRIKEOUTS 10

STRIKEOUTS 13

STRIKEOUTS 17

AND BOY, DOES IT FEEL GOOD TO WIN.

PENDAK

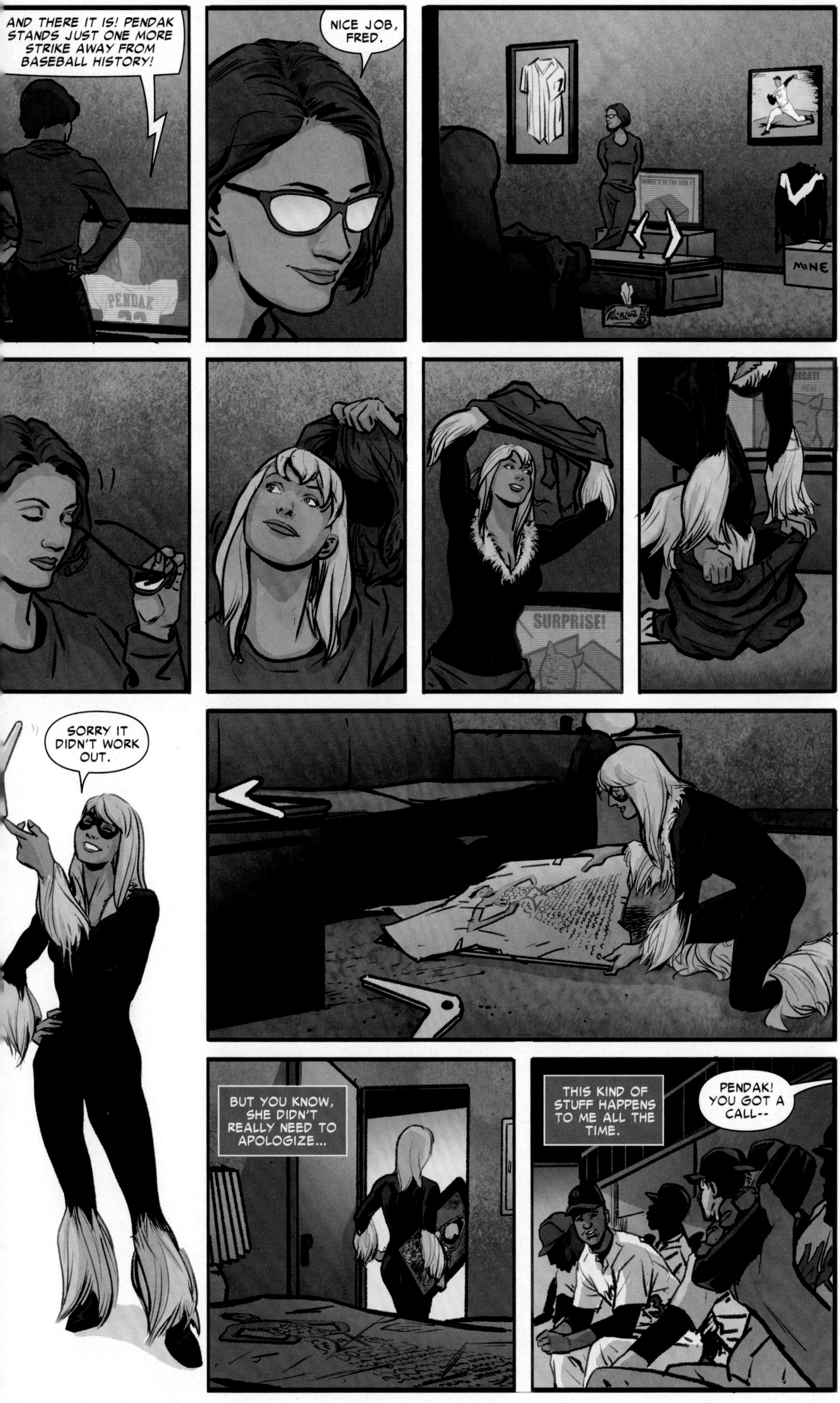
AND THERE IT IS! PENDAK STANDS JUST ONE MORE STRIKE AWAY FROM BASEBALL HISTORY!
PENDAK
NICE JOB, FRED.
MINE
SURPRISE!
SORRY IT DIDN'T WORK OUT.
BUT YOU KNOW, SHE DIDN'T REALLY NEED TO APOLOGIZE...
THIS KIND OF STUFF HAPPENS TO ME ALL THE TIME.
PENDAK! YOU GOT A CALL--

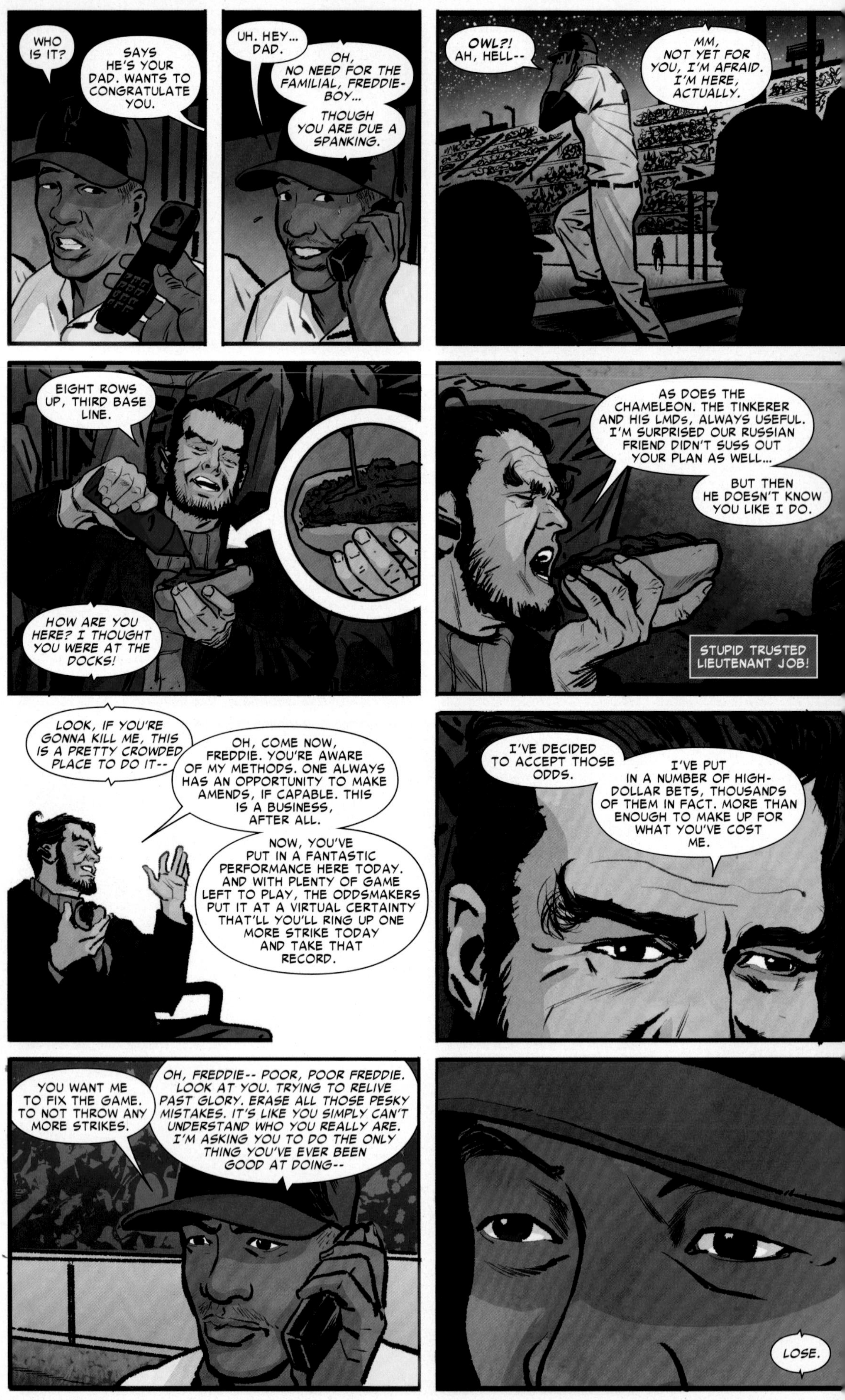
WHO IS IT?
SAYS HE'S YOUR DAD. WANTS TO CONGRATULATE YOU.
UH. HEY... DAD.
OH, NO NEED FOR THE FAMILIAL, FREDDIE-BOY...
THOUGH YOU ARE DUE A SPANKING.
OWL?! AH, HELL--
MM, NOT YET FOR YOU, I'M AFRAID. I'M HERE, ACTUALLY.
EIGHT ROWS UP, THIRD BASE LINE.
HOW ARE YOU HERE? I THOUGHT YOU WERE AT THE DOCKS!
AS DOES THE CHAMELEON. THE TINKERER AND HIS LMDs, ALWAYS USEFUL. I'M SURPRISED OUR RUSSIAN FRIEND DIDN'T SUSS OUT YOUR PLAN AS WELL...
BUT THEN HE DOESN'T KNOW YOU LIKE I DO.
STUPID TRUSTED LIEUTENANT JOB!
LOOK, IF YOU'RE GONNA KILL ME, THIS IS A PRETTY CROWDED PLACE TO DO IT--
OH, COME NOW, FREDDIE. YOU'RE AWARE OF MY METHODS. ONE ALWAYS HAS AN OPPORTUNITY TO MAKE AMENDS, IF CAPABLE. THIS IS A BUSINESS, AFTER ALL.
NOW, YOU'VE PUT IN A FANTASTIC PERFORMANCE HERE TODAY. AND WITH PLENTY OF GAME LEFT TO PLAY, THE ODDSMAKERS PUT IT AT A VIRTUAL CERTAINTY THAT'LL YOU'LL RING UP ONE MORE STRIKE TODAY AND TAKE THAT RECORD.
I'VE DECIDED TO ACCEPT THOSE ODDS.
I'VE PUT IN A NUMBER OF HIGH-DOLLAR BETS, THOUSANDS OF THEM IN FACT. MORE THAN ENOUGH TO MAKE UP FOR WHAT YOU'VE COST ME.
YOU WANT ME TO FIX THE GAME. TO NOT THROW ANY MORE STRIKES.
OH, FREDDIE-- POOR, POOR FREDDIE. LOOK AT YOU. TRYING TO RELIVE PAST GLORY. ERASE ALL THOSE PESKY MISTAKES. IT'S LIKE YOU SIMPLY CAN'T UNDERSTAND WHO YOU REALLY ARE. I'M ASKING YOU TO DO THE ONLY THING YOU'VE EVER BEEN GOOD AT DOING--
LOSE.

AND NO, IT DOES NOT ESCAPE ME THAT THIS IS HOW MY LIFE WENT DOWNHILL IN THE FIRST PLACE.

RRAYYAAYYYYWHO H!YAAAAYYYWHOC

HOW IT ALL WENT WRONG.

HE'S RIGHT--IN A WAY I'M LUCKY. WHAT WOULD NORMALLY BE A DEATH SENTENCE, I CAN FIX WITH JUST A FEW LOUSY PITCHES.

OF COURSE, IT ALSO MEANS GIVING UP WHAT'S PROBABLY MY LAST CHANCE AT A LIFE WORTH LIVING.

OR, I CAN TAKE A STAND. NOT LET THEM RUIN THIS. HOLD ON TO WHAT'S REAL, WHAT'S IMPORTANT TO ME.

OF COURSE THEN HE DOES KILL ME.

HE'S RIGHT. EITHER WAY--

I LOSE.

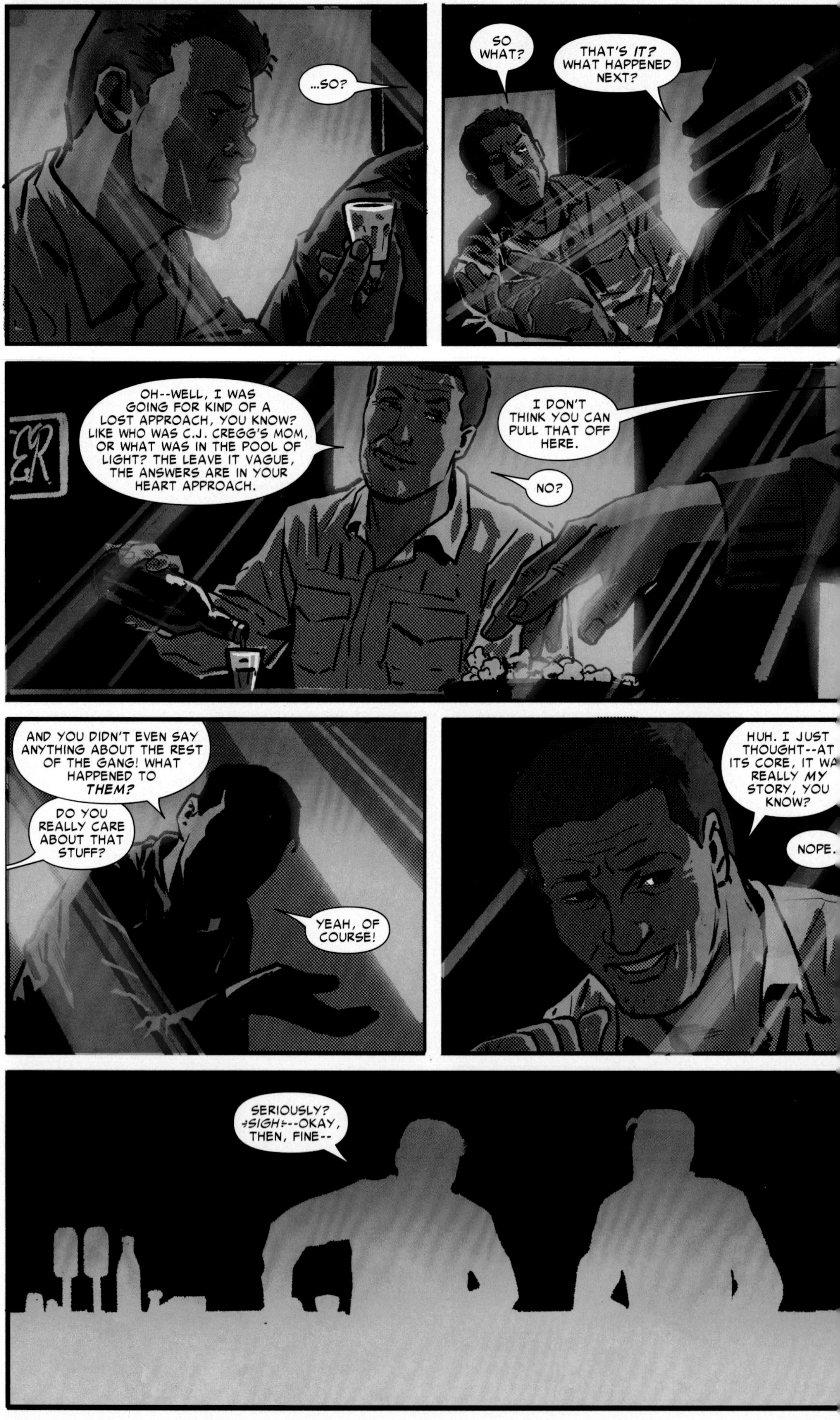
...SO?
SO WHAT?
THAT'S IT? WHAT HAPPENED NEXT?
OH--WELL, I WAS GOING FOR KIND OF A LOST APPROACH, YOU KNOW? LIKE WHO WAS C.J. CREGG'S MOM, OR WHAT WAS IN THE POOL OF LIGHT? THE LEAVE IT VAGUE, THE ANSWERS ARE IN YOUR HEART APPROACH.
I DON'T THINK YOU CAN PULL THAT OFF HERE.
NO?
AND YOU DIDN'T EVEN SAY ANYTHING ABOUT THE REST OF THE GANG! WHAT HAPPENED TO THEM?
DO YOU REALLY CARE ABOUT THAT STUFF?
YEAH, OF COURSE!
HUH. I JUST THOUGHT--AT ITS CORE, IT WA REALLY MY STORY, YOU KNOW?
NOPE.
SERIOUSLY? SIGH--OKAY, THEN, FINE--

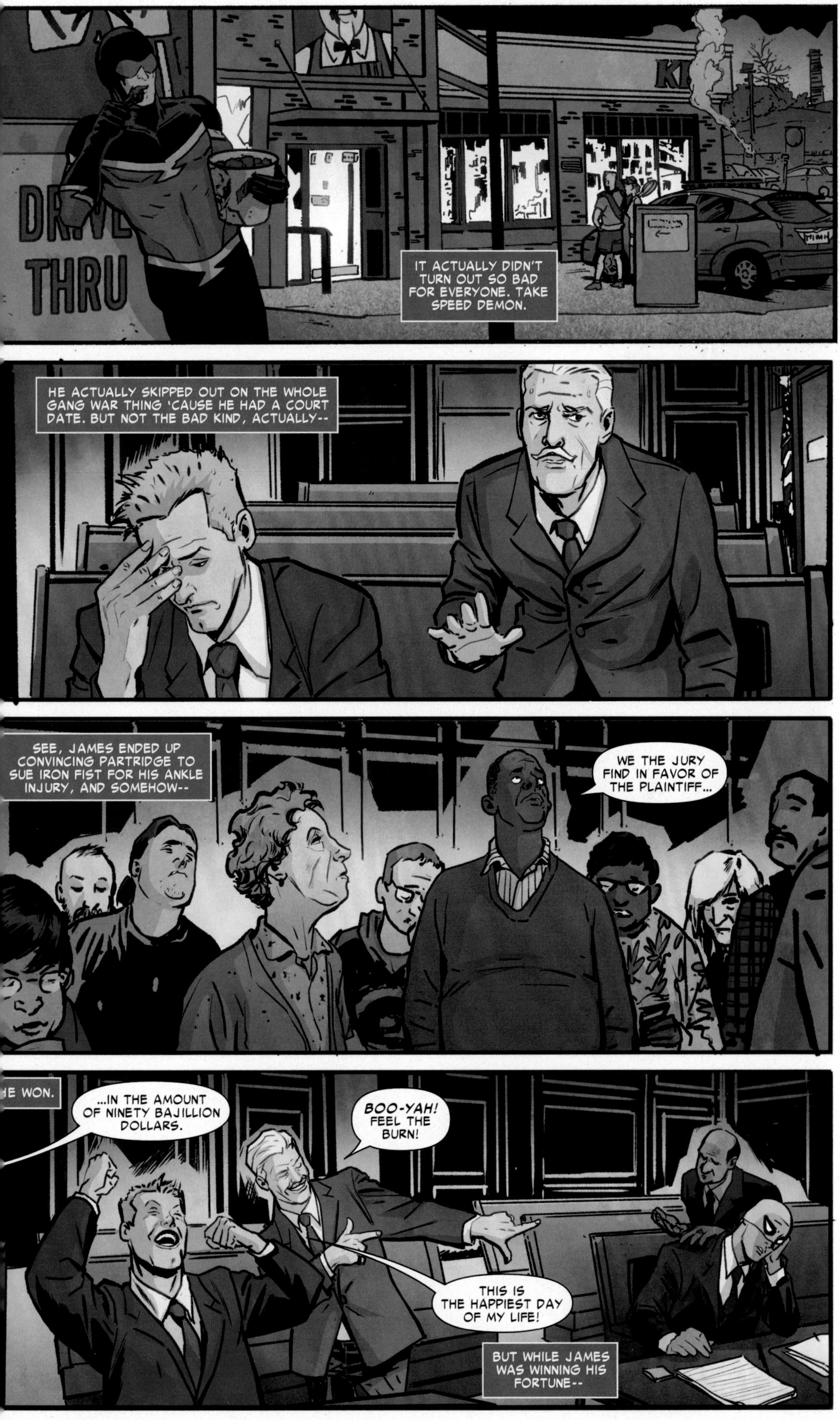
DRIVE THRU
IT ACTUALLY DIDN'T TURN OUT SO BAD FOR EVERYONE. TAKE SPEED DEMON.
HE ACTUALLY SKIPPED OUT ON THE WHOLE GANG WAR THING 'CAUSE HE HAD A COURT DATE. BUT NOT THE BAD KIND, ACTUALLY--
SEE, JAMES ENDED UP CONVINCING PARTRIDGE TO SUE IRON FIST FOR HIS ANKLE INJURY, AND SOMEHOW--
WE THE JURY FIND IN FAVOR OF THE PLAINTIFF...
HE WON.
...IN THE AMOUNT OF NINETY BAJILLION DOLLARS.
BOO-YAH! FEEL THE BURN!
THIS IS THE HAPPIEST DAY OF MY LIFE!
BUT WHILE JAMES WAS WINNING HIS FORTUNE--

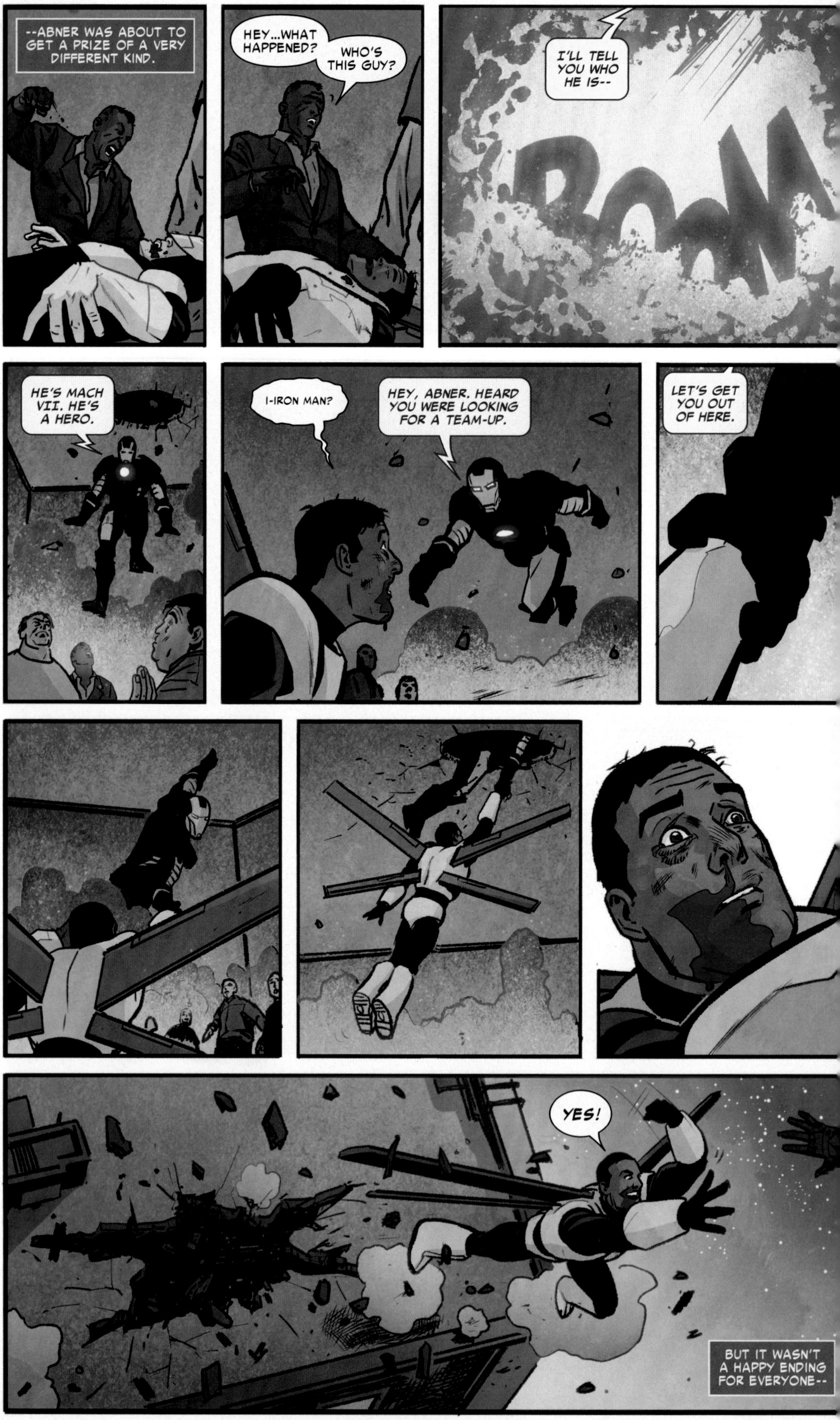
--ABNER WAS ABOUT TO GET A PRIZE OF A VERY DIFFERENT KIND.
HEY...WHAT HAPPENED?
WHO'S THIS GUY?
I'LL TELL YOU WHO HE IS--
BOOM
HE'S MACH VII. HE'S A HERO.
I-IRON MAN?
HEY, ABNER. HEARD YOU WERE LOOKING FOR A TEAM-UP.
LET'S GET YOU OUT OF HERE.
YES!
BUT IT WASN'T A HAPPY ENDING FOR EVERYONE--

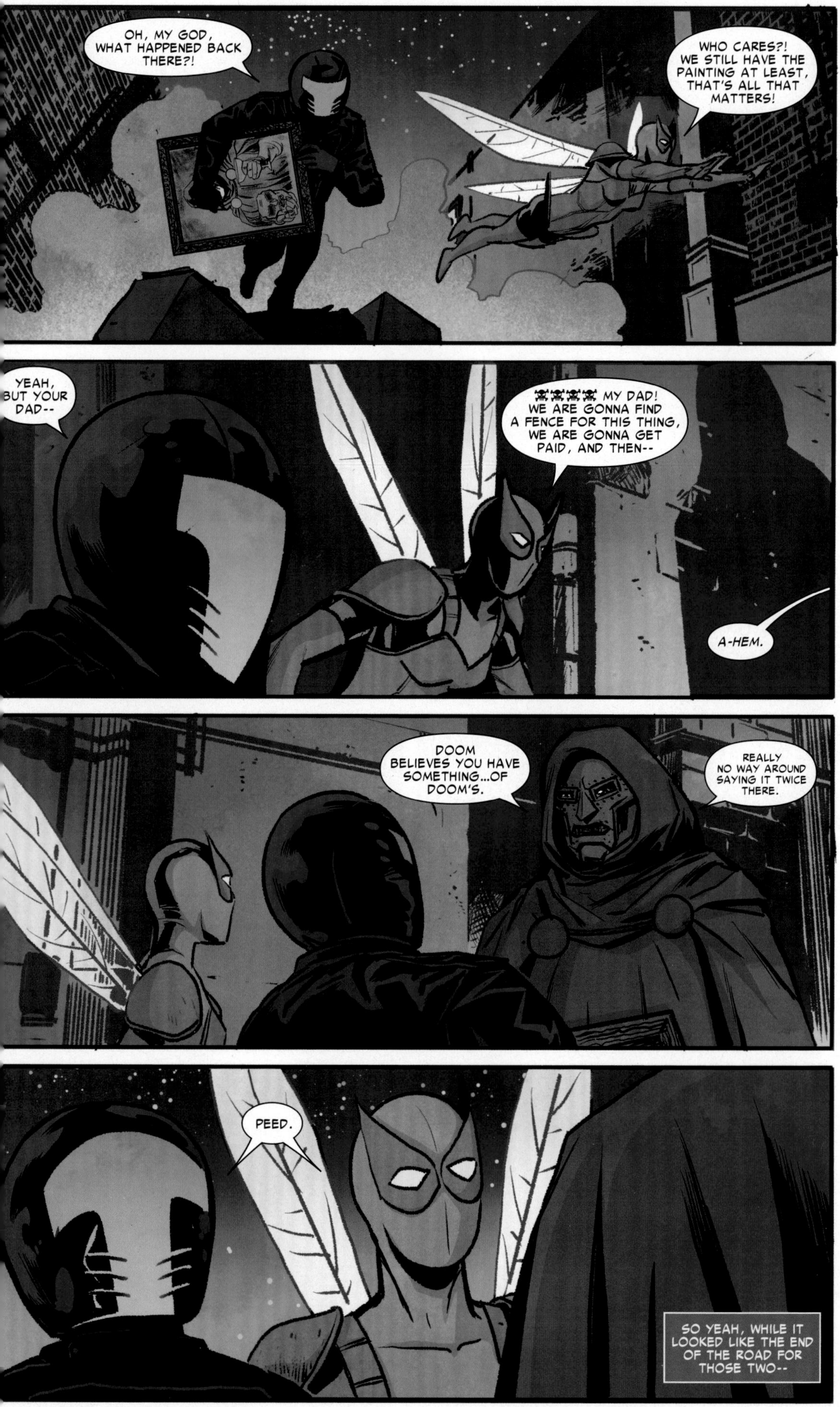
OH, MY GOD, WHAT HAPPENED BACK THERE?!
WHO CARES?! WE STILL HAVE THE PAINTING AT LEAST, THAT'S ALL THAT MATTERS!
YEAH, BUT YOUR DAD--
☠☠☠☠ MY DAD! WE ARE GONNA FIND A FENCE FOR THIS THING, WE ARE GONNA GET PAID, AND THEN--
A-HEM.
DOOM BELIEVES YOU HAVE SOMETHING...OF DOOM'S.
REALLY NO WAY AROUND SAYING IT TWICE THERE.
PEED.
SO YEAH, WHILE IT LOOKED LIKE THE END OF THE ROAD FOR THOSE TWO--

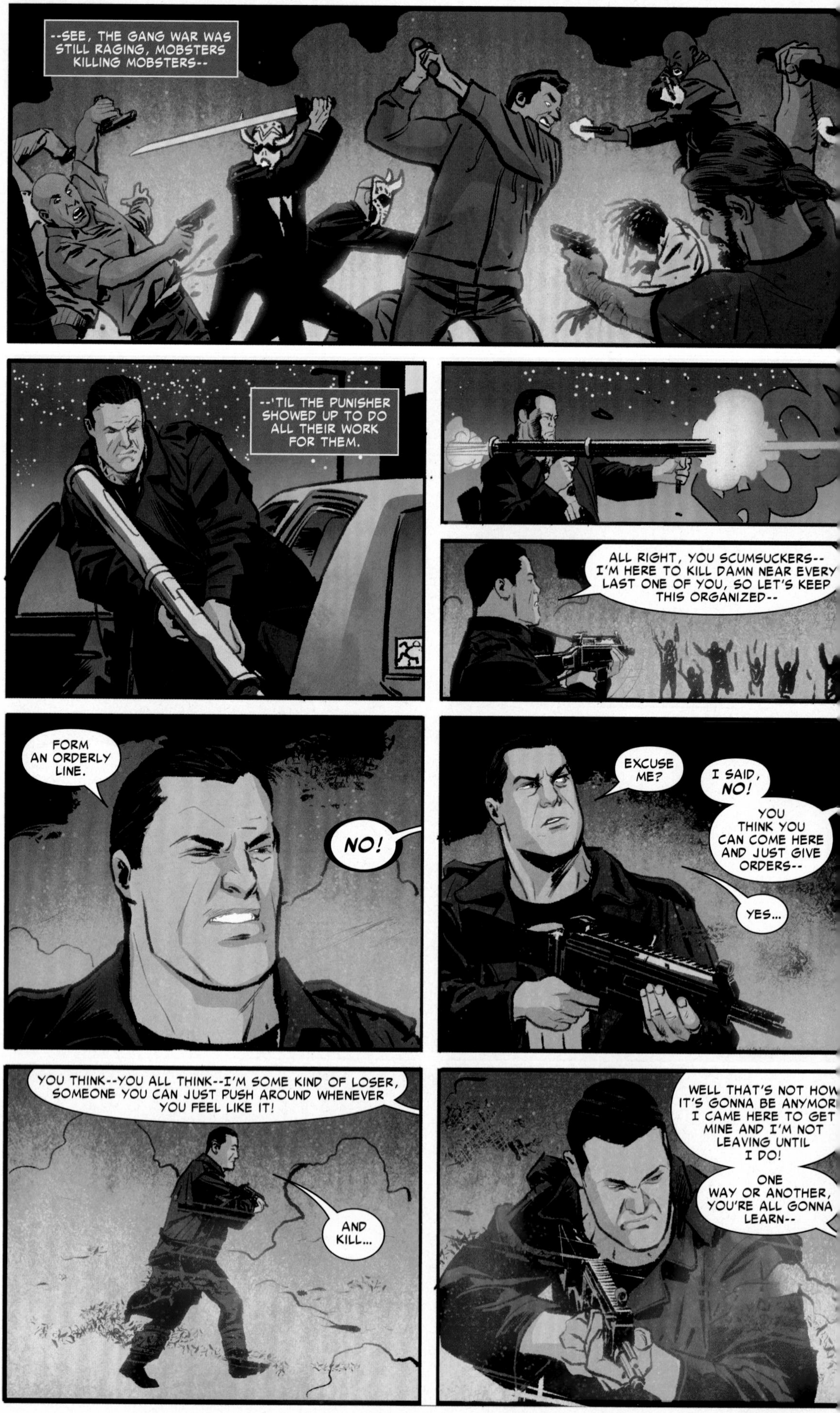
--SEE, THE GANG WAR WAS STILL RAGING, MOBSTERS KILLING MOBSTERS--
--'TIL THE PUNISHER SHOWED UP TO DO ALL THEIR WORK FOR THEM.
ALL RIGHT, YOU SCUMSUCKERS-- I'M HERE TO KILL DAMN NEAR EVERY LAST ONE OF YOU, SO LET'S KEEP THIS ORGANIZED--
FORM AN ORDERLY LINE.
NO!
EXCUSE ME?
I SAID, NO!
YOU THINK YOU CAN COME HERE AND JUST GIVE ORDERS--
YES...
YOU THINK--YOU ALL THINK--I'M SOME KIND OF LOSER, SOMEONE YOU CAN JUST PUSH AROUND WHENEVER YOU FEEL LIKE IT!
AND KILL...
WELL THAT'S NOT HOW IT'S GONNA BE ANYMOR I CAME HERE TO GET MINE AND I'M NOT LEAVING UNTIL I DO!
ONE WAY OR ANOTHER, YOU'RE ALL GONNA LEARN--

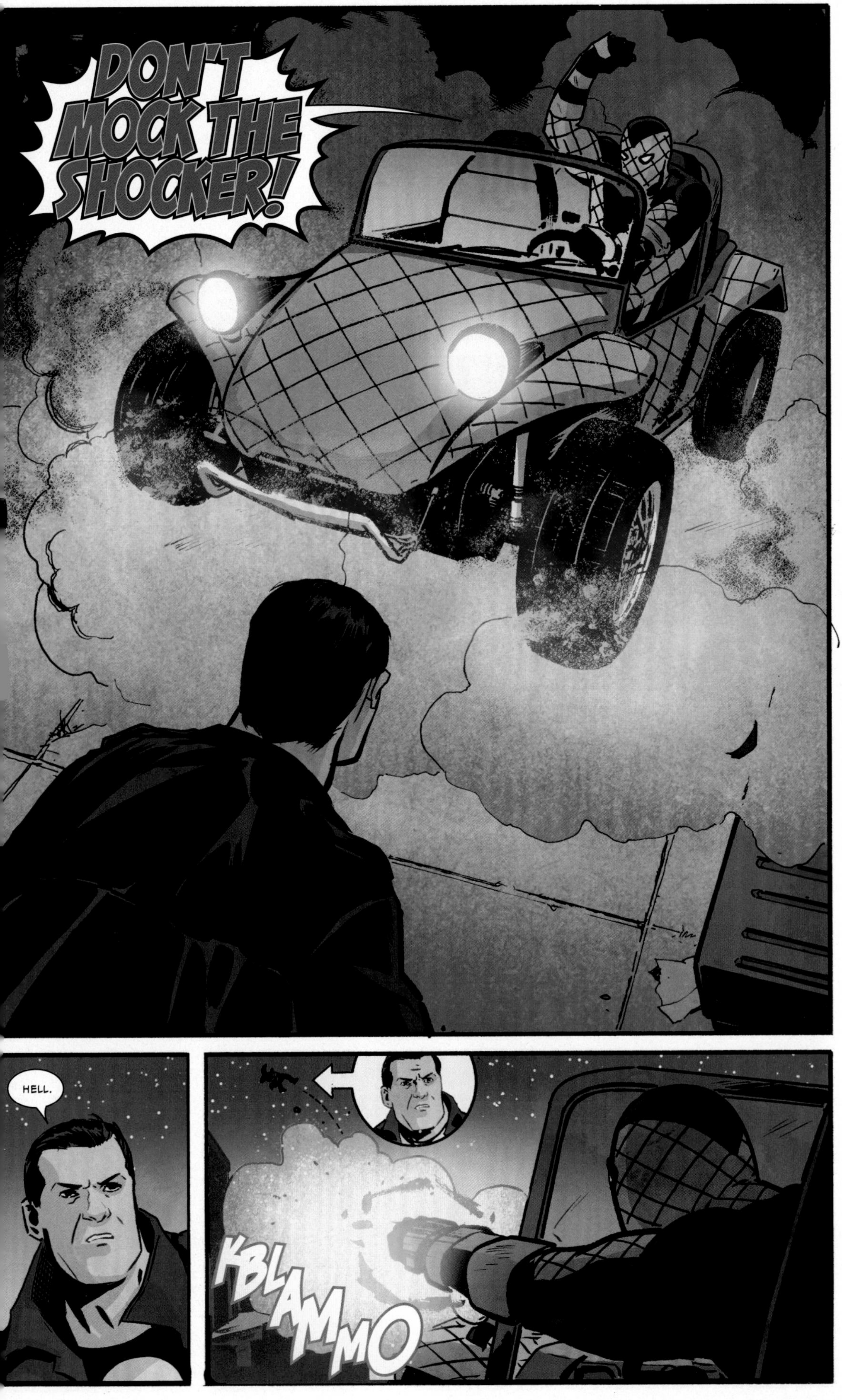
DON'T MOCK THE SHOCKER!
HELL.
KBLAMMO

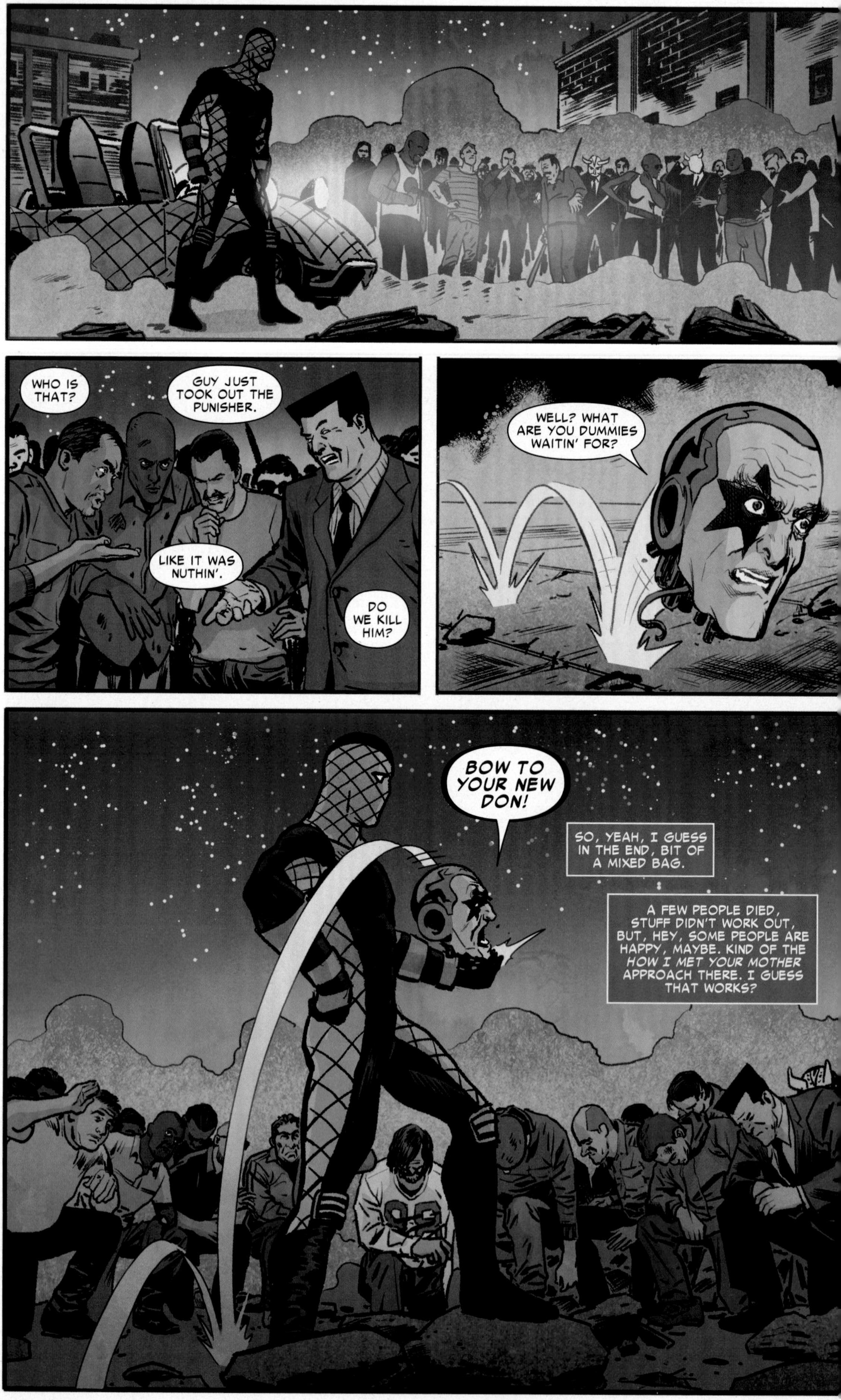
WHO IS THAT?
GUY JUST TOOK OUT THE PUNISHER.
LIKE IT WAS NUTHIN'.
DO WE KILL HIM?
WELL? WHAT ARE YOU DUMMIES WAITIN' FOR?
BOW TO YOUR NEW DON!
SO, YEAH, I GUESS IN THE END, BIT OF A MIXED BAG.
A FEW PEOPLE DIED, STUFF DIDN'T WORK OUT, BUT, HEY, SOME PEOPLE ARE HAPPY, MAYBE. KIND OF THE *HOW I MET YOUR MOTHER* APPROACH THERE. I GUESS THAT WORKS?

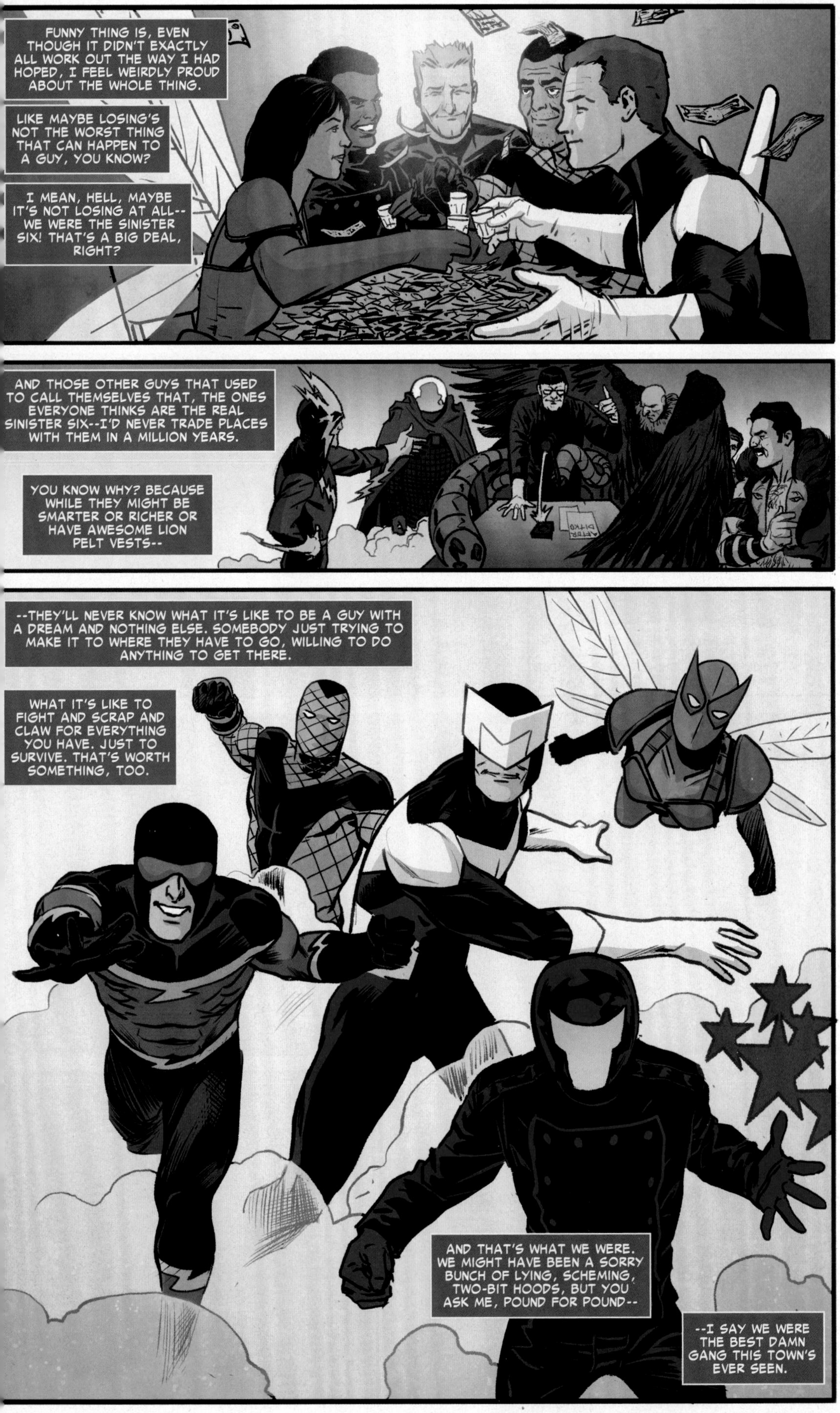
FUNNY THING IS, EVEN THOUGH IT DIDN'T EXACTLY ALL WORK OUT THE WAY I HAD HOPED, I FEEL WEIRDLY PROUD ABOUT THE WHOLE THING.
LIKE MAYBE LOSING'S NOT THE WORST THING THAT CAN HAPPEN TO A GUY, YOU KNOW?
I MEAN, HELL, MAYBE IT'S NOT LOSING AT ALL-- WE WERE THE SINISTER SIX! THAT'S A BIG DEAL, RIGHT?
AND THOSE OTHER GUYS THAT USED TO CALL THEMSELVES THAT, THE ONES EVERYONE THINKS ARE THE REAL SINISTER SIX--I'D NEVER TRADE PLACES WITH THEM IN A MILLION YEARS.
YOU KNOW WHY? BECAUSE WHILE THEY MIGHT BE SMARTER OR RICHER OR HAVE AWESOME LION PELT VESTS--
--THEY'LL NEVER KNOW WHAT IT'S LIKE TO BE A GUY WITH A DREAM AND NOTHING ELSE. SOMEBODY JUST TRYING TO MAKE IT TO WHERE THEY HAVE TO GO, WILLING TO DO ANYTHING TO GET THERE.
WHAT IT'S LIKE TO FIGHT AND SCRAP AND CLAW FOR EVERYTHING YOU HAVE. JUST TO SURVIVE. THAT'S WORTH SOMETHING, TOO.
AND THAT'S WHAT WE WERE. WE MIGHT HAVE BEEN A SORRY BUNCH OF LYING, SCHEMING, TWO-BIT HOODS, BUT YOU ASK ME, POUND FOR POUND--
--I SAY WE WERE THE BEST DAMN GANG THIS TOWN'S EVER SEEN.

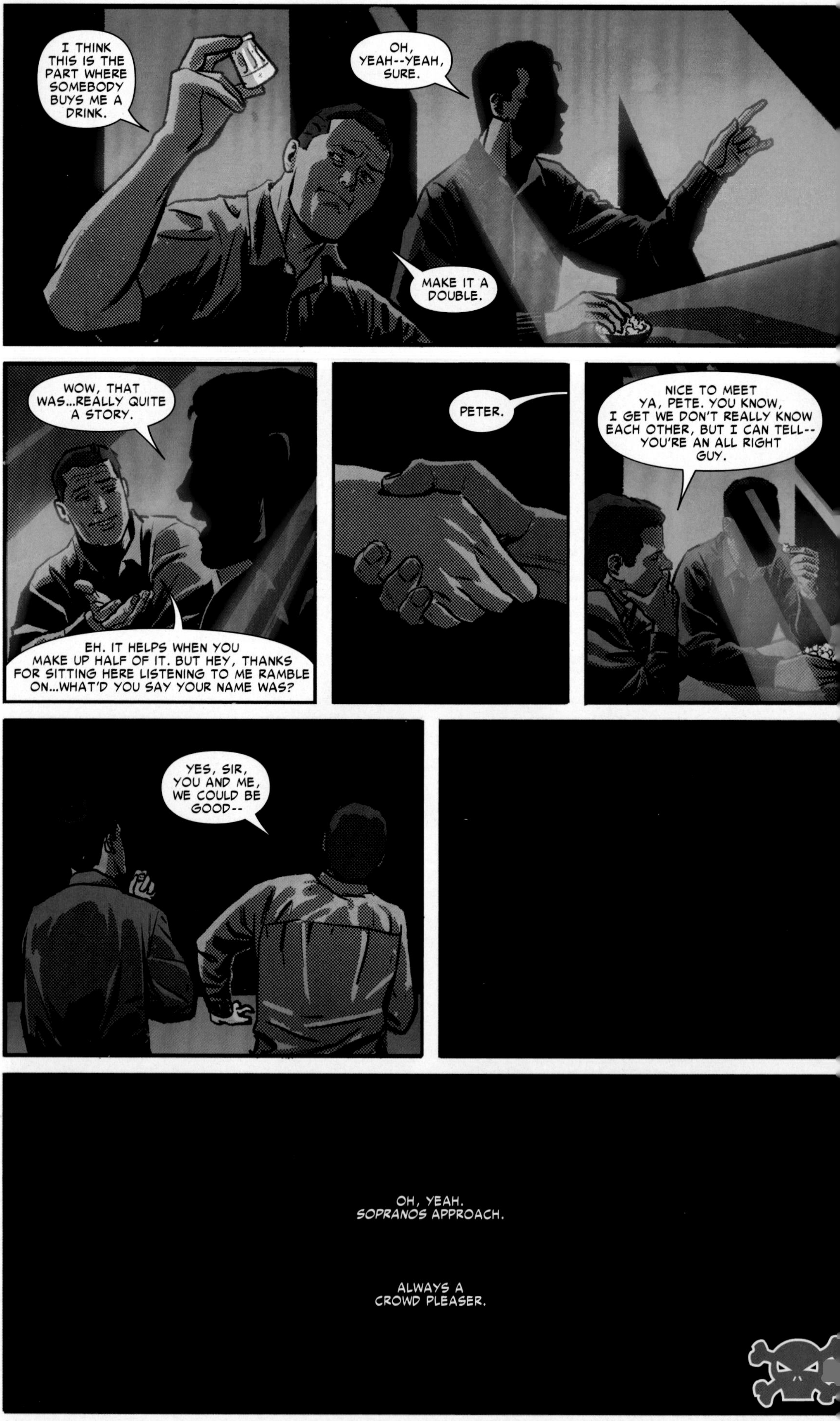
I THINK THIS IS THE PART WHERE SOMEBODY BUYS ME A DRINK.
OH, YEAH--YEAH, SURE.
MAKE IT A DOUBLE.
WOW, THAT WAS...REALLY QUITE A STORY.
EH. IT HELPS WHEN YOU MAKE UP HALF OF IT. BUT HEY, THANKS FOR SITTING HERE LISTENING TO ME RAMBLE ON...WHAT'D YOU SAY YOUR NAME WAS?
PETER.
NICE TO MEET YA, PETE. YOU KNOW, I GET WE DON'T REALLY KNOW EACH OTHER, BUT I CAN TELL--YOU'RE AN ALL RIGHT GUY.
YES, SIR, YOU AND ME, WE COULD BE GOOD--
OH, YEAH. SOPRANOS APPROACH.
ALWAYS A CROWD PLEASER.

'OE-NING IT IN...

Well, that's it. We're done. And man, what a job it's been. Like the Foes themselves, e just barely made it out alive-- but with our dreams intact. And that's really what is story's been all about. Holding on to your dreams, no matter how ridiculous. earning to love being the underdog. And understand that losing's not really the orst thing that can happen to you.

There are so many people to thank, so many people who made this book what it is. should start with

This guy, right? Nick Spencer. Who does he think he is? I guess he thinks e're all a bunch of suckers just because we were loyal to this book...we were part f a gang! I mean, I didn't read this book to be nice to him, I read it because 'm smart. Now it's over and he's all, "...was a pleasure writing for you...some f my favorite memories....", blah blah blah. (Did he say any of that? I actually idn't read his heartfelt note. I've got way better things to do.) Anyway, I ad Nick's back! He was down and out and I did him a solid by reading this book hat didn't even have Spider-Man in it. I read this book when it didn't even ave a foil embossed cover! We all know the best books have holograms on the front. Don't get me started on the characters. Nick made me care about some fourth-string losers. Gave depth to characters that seemed one-dimensional for decades, then just leaves me all high and dry! No loyalty!

All joking aside, I love this book and Nick Spencer has always been like a brother to me (never met him). I mostly have run out of negative things to say about him so I'll lie for a minute and talk about how much I actually think this is one of the most original books I've read in some time (I'm being paid to write five hundred words). Truthfully, I think we are all a little more Boomerang than Spider-Man. I certainly can relate to the Punisher using Uber more than I can being bit by a radioactive spider. In the end that's the brilliance of "Superior Foes of Spider-Man". We are all a rag-tag gang of procrastinating underachievers (Yes, I'm late. Deadlines are stupid). We all need to stick together because none of us on our own is anything. You know it's true! The only way books like this get made is if we stick together! Watch each other's backs!

At the end of the day, I laughed out loud more than once. Nick couldn't have done it without Steve Lieber (or us fans who bought the book). I'm a better person for having this title on my shelf. It's funny, it's smart, it's got a heart of gold underneath all that screwed up super villain bluster (I'm not sure why that sounds super familiar to me but it's a great quote, maybe for the cover of the next trade paperback). I'm not sure why great reads like this sometimes don't last, but I'm happy they see the light of day. Maybe if Nick worked harder, or perhaps if I didn't just have Marvel sending me PDFs of the issues instead of buying copies like a real true believer we would've got that chromium, die-cut, polybagged issue one hundred! Next month, I will miss this book very, very, very, very, very, very much! (Five hundred on the nose! Suck it, Nick Spencer!)

—CM Punk
Fighter guy. Professional
procrastinator.

-Nick Spencer

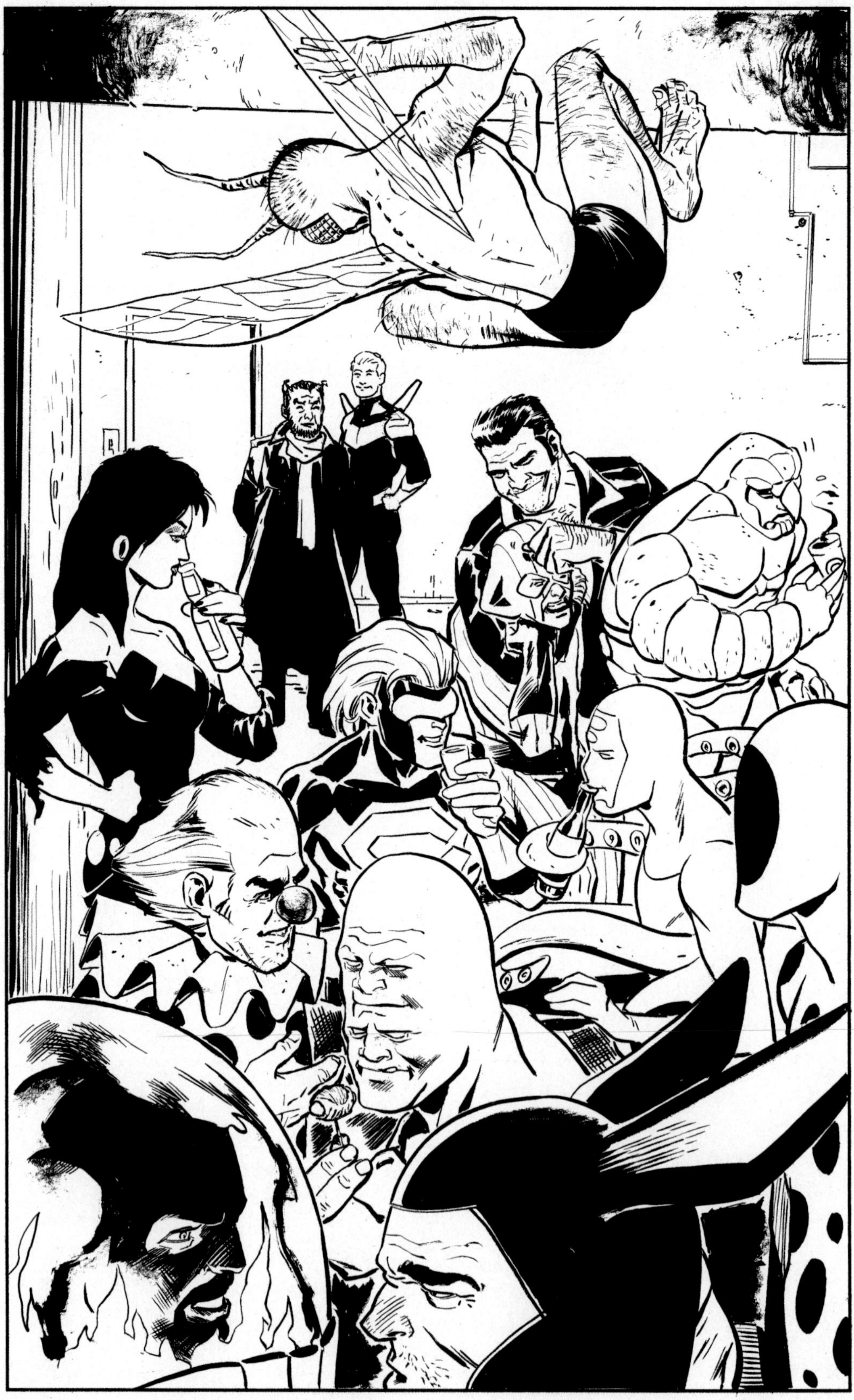

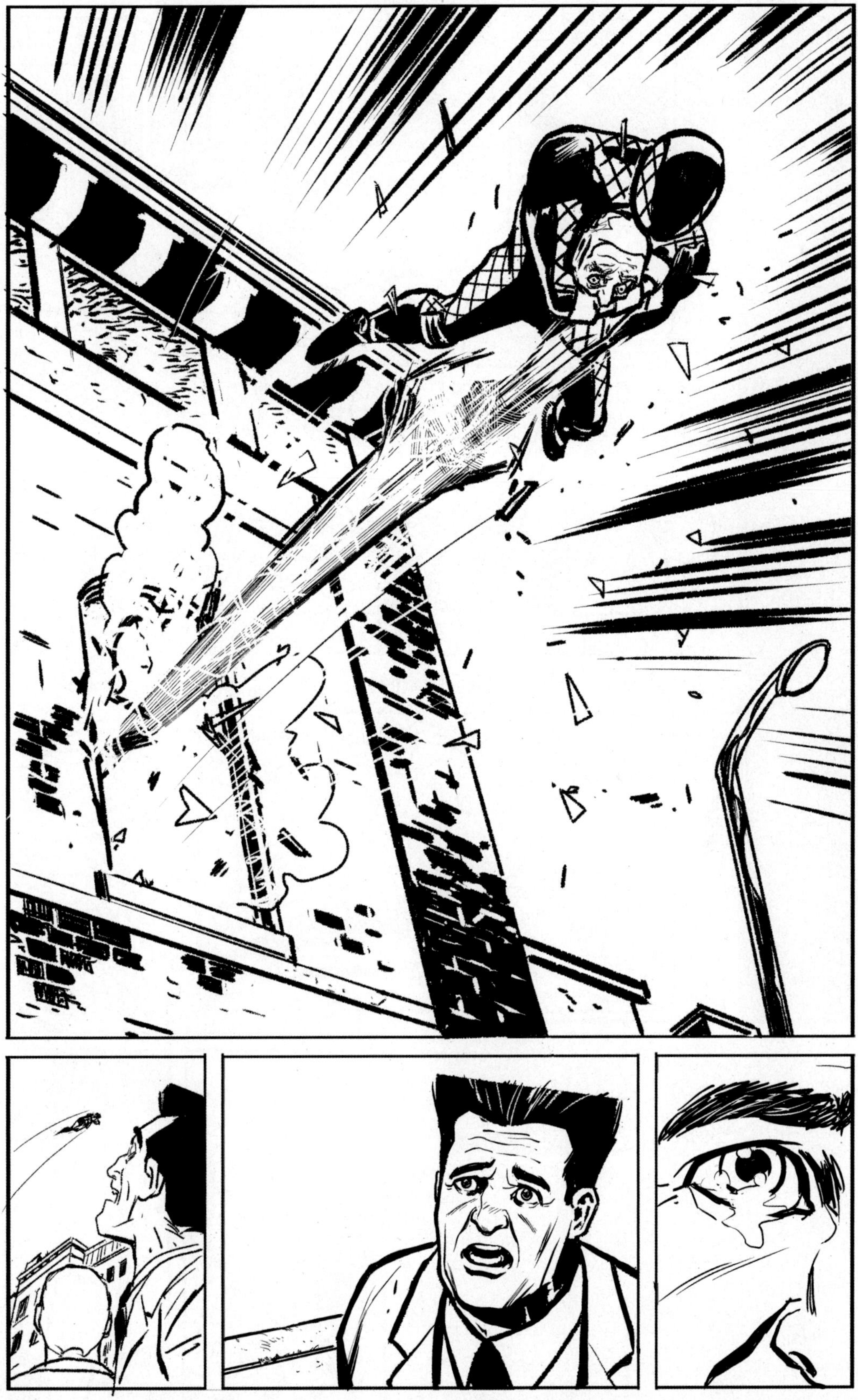

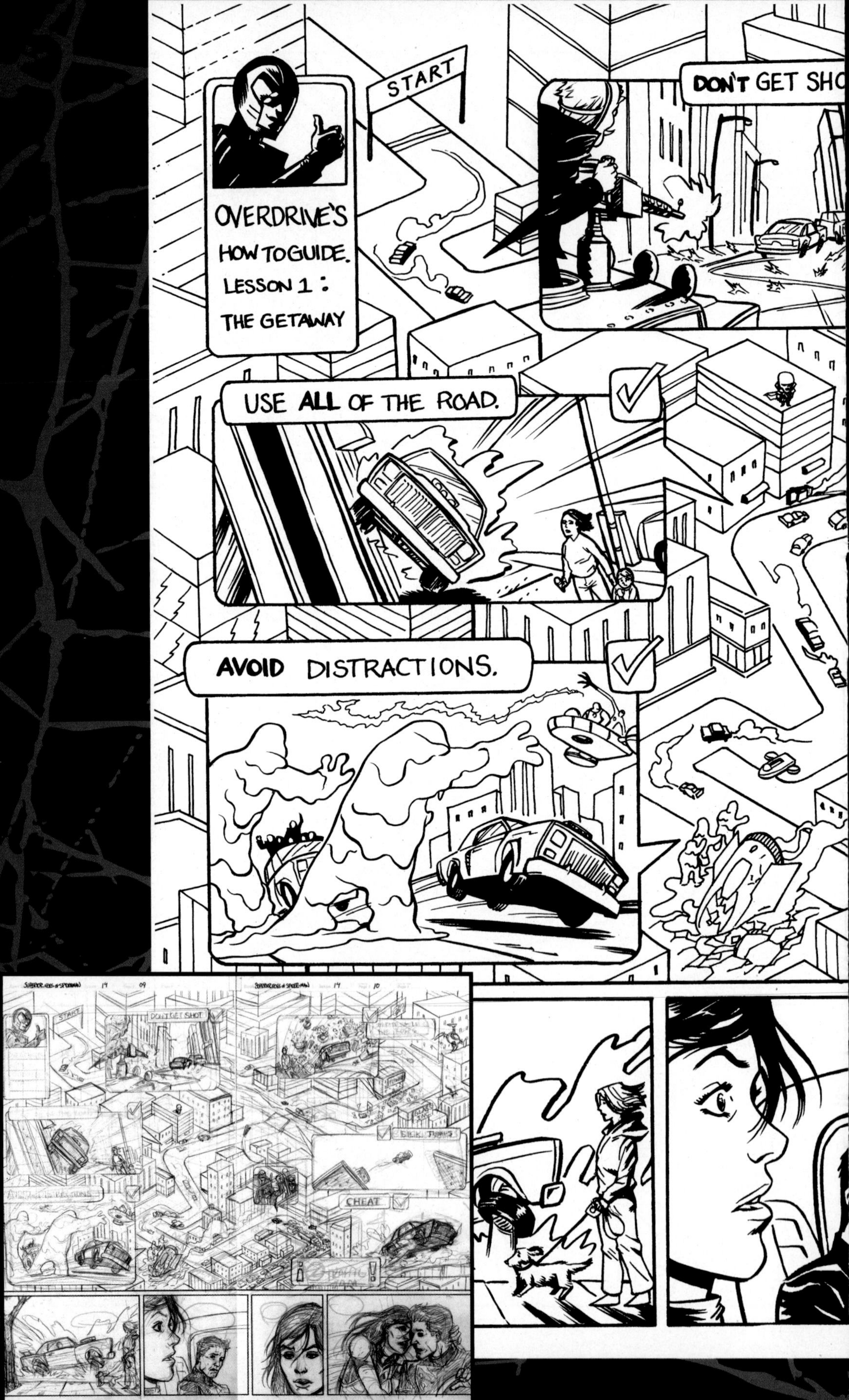
OVERDRIVE'S HOW TO GUIDE.
LESSON 1:
THE GETAWAY
START
DON'T GET SHO
USE ALL OF THE ROAD.
AVOID DISTRACTIONS.
START
DON'T GET SHOT
CHEAT

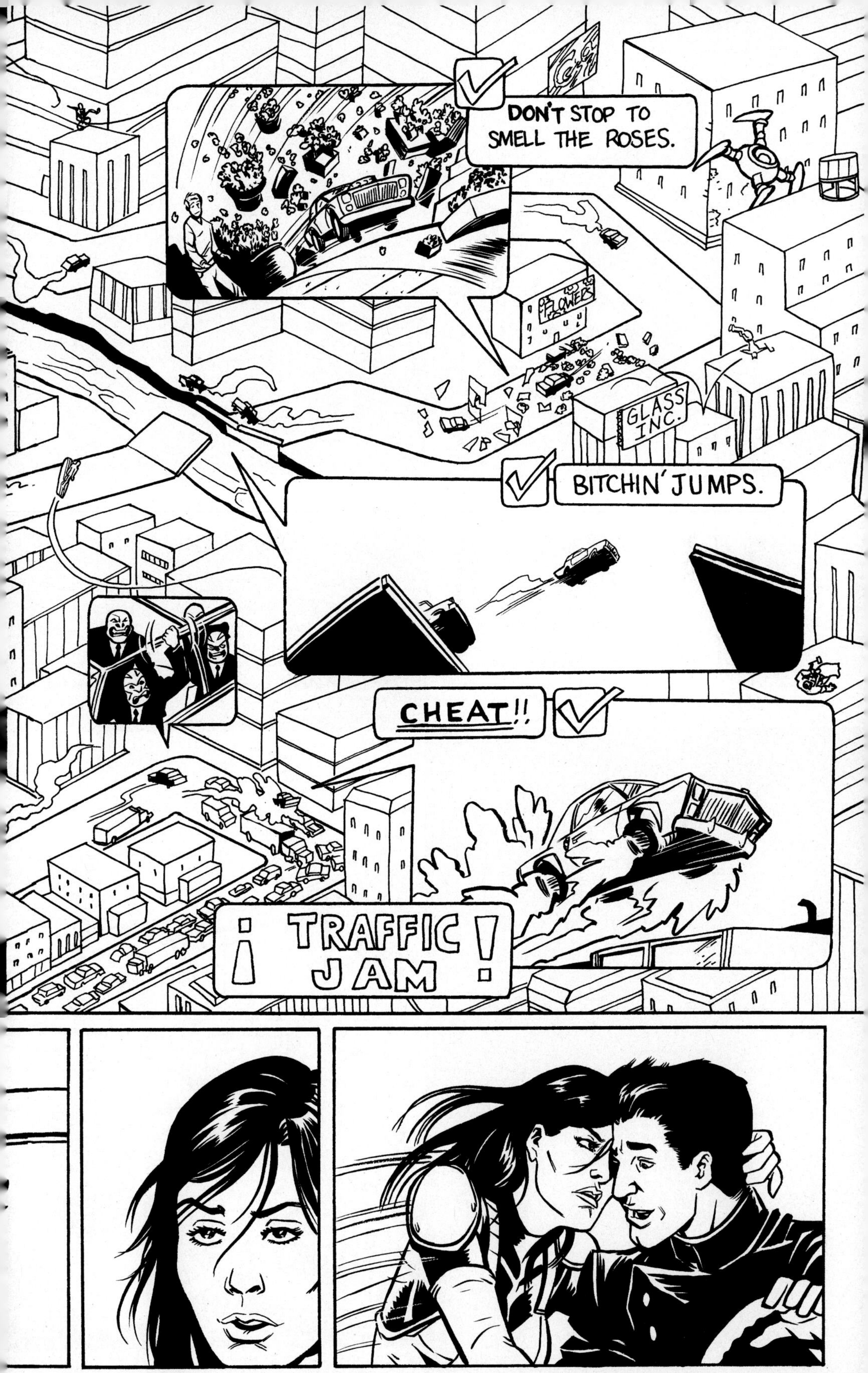
DON'T STOP TO SMELL THE ROSES.
FLOWERS
GLASS INC.
BITCHIN' JUMPS.
CHEAT!!
¡ TRAFFIC JAM !

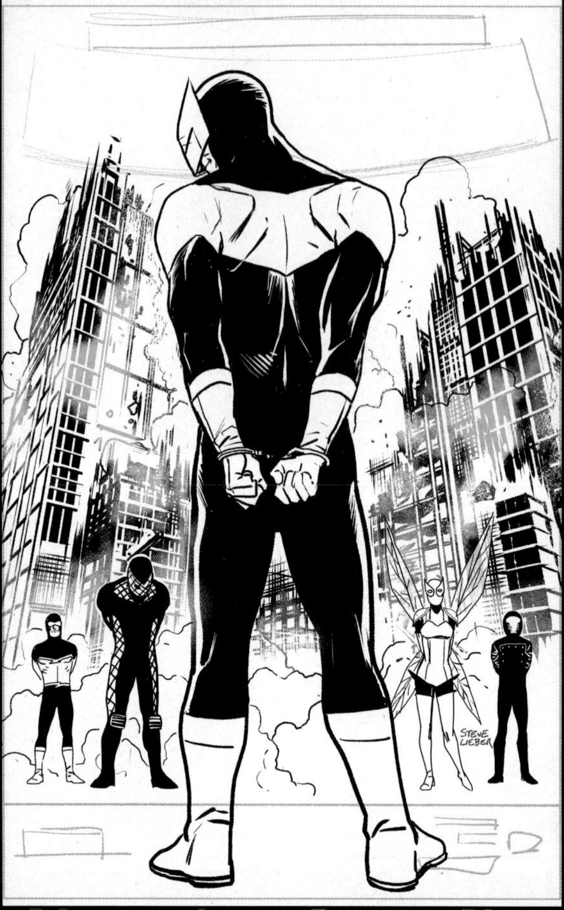
STEVE LIEBER

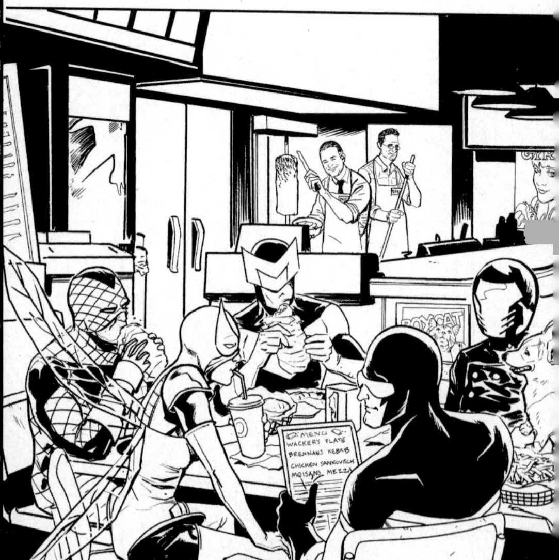
MENU
LIEBER

ISSUE #16-17
COVER ART BY STEVE LIEBER